AN AMERICAN ARTIST
IN AFRICA, 1937

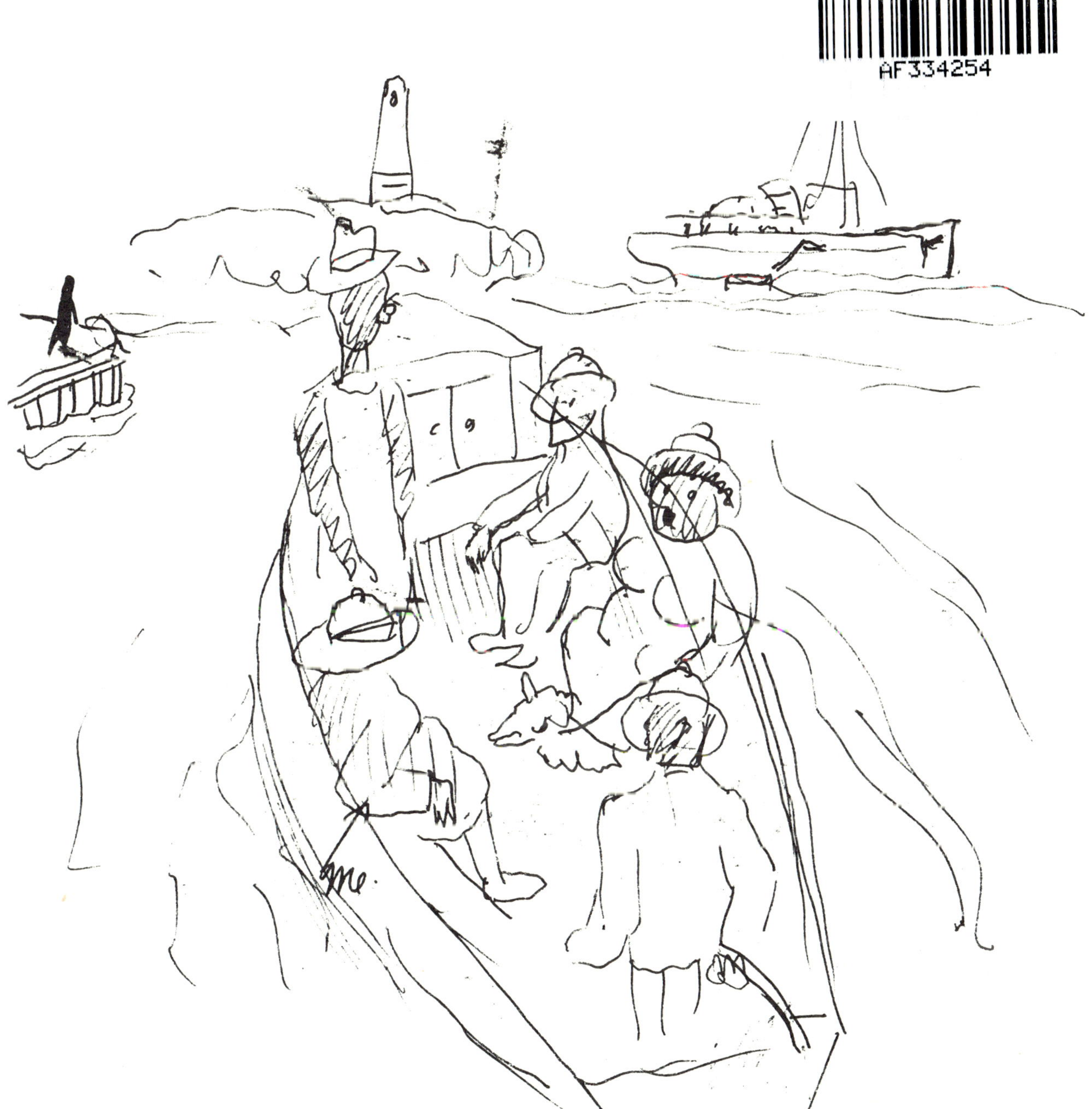

foreword

When Wanda Norstrom was eleven, she suffered scarlet fever. The doctor told her mother she was dying. The mother kneeled at the bedside, prayed, promised Wanda anything she wanted if she lived. Wanda's eyes awakened from delirium at sound of a promise, and a soft voice spoke, "I want to be an artist."

Promise fulfilled with struggle by Wanda; working from twelve, chief of soda bar at Brin's Drug Store, earning way through high school and The Art Institute of Chicago, the latter with help of scholarships. Winning the John Quincy Adams Travelling Fellowship at graduation, she continued art studies in Paris, left midcourse, sailed to Africa, painted, at times the sole white person in the bush. The contents of this book were taken from her diary, letters, and sketches in graphite, ink, and water color.

Wanda, endowed so fully with the inspirit of cheer, lived a life completing her dreams as well as giving an abundant infusion of the creative spirit to others. Born in Chicago, November 21, 1912, she died at Cape May, New Jersey, October 24, 1972. The years after her African experience were spent as an architectural designer with little time for painting; first as Art Director of the Eastern Division of Container Corporation of America in Philadelphia, Pennsylvania, later with her own company where colors, calliopes of colors, became her signature. In spite of overfilled schedules, she painted in transparent water color that effused an aura of oil on canvas, but with touch of a brush made of dew drop bristles, and exhibited at The Pennsylvania Academy of Fine Arts, the American Swedish Museum and other museums around the country, as well as teaching courses at The University of the Arts and Temple University. Finally she resigned to paint at the seashore as Artist-Director of Cape May Country Art League. It lasted a summer and an autumn, months of souls flocking from beaches and cities to paint and sculpt and print in classes at the League. A rebirth blossomed in Wanda's painting, a wholly new stream of exquisite joy. But something mysterious had transpired in Africa that shed a radiance to Wanda's life and cast a strange shadow around her death.

georgiana peacher

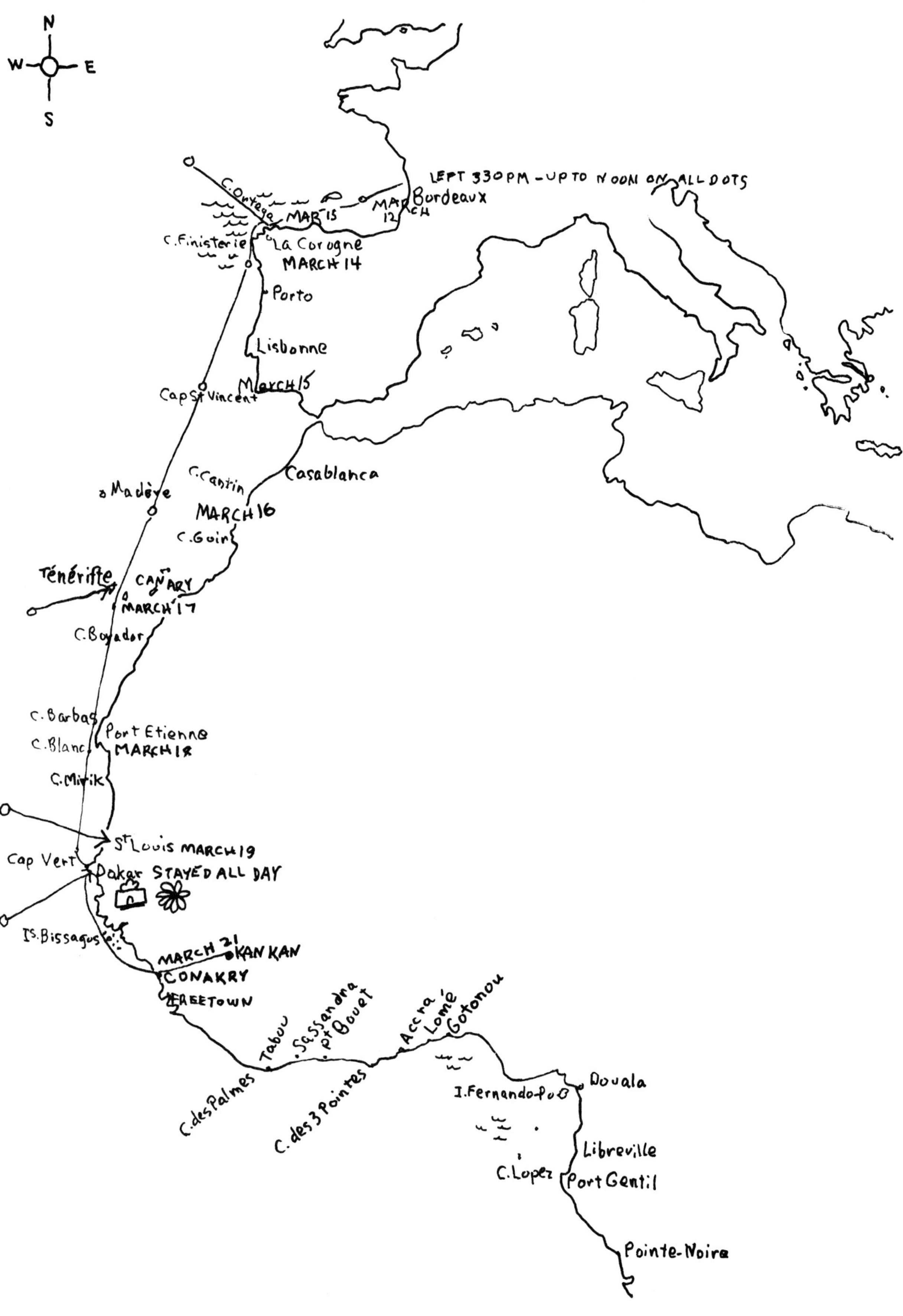

N
W E
S
LEFT 330 PM - UP TO NOON ON ALL DOTS
C. Ortega
MAR 15
MARCH 12
Bordeaux
C. Finisterie
La Corogne
MARCH 14
Porto
Lisbonne
MARCH 15
Cap St Vincent
C. Cantin
Casablanca
Madère
MARCH 16
C. Guir
Ténérifte
CANARY
MARCH 17
C. Bojador
C. Barbas
Port Etienne
C. Blanc
MARCH 18
C. Mirik
St Louis MARCH 19
Cap Vert
Dakar STAYED ALL DAY
I's. Bissagos
MARCH 21
KANKAN
CONAKRY
FREETOWN
Tabou
Sassandra
pt Bouet
Accra
Lomé
Cotonou
C. des Palmes
C. des 3 Pointes
I. Fernando-Po
Douala
Libreville
C. Lopez
Port Gentil
Pointe-Noire

MARCH 12, 1937

THIRD CLASS ACCOMMODATIONS NOT SO GOOD. THE

SEA QUITE ROUGH. EVERYBODY SICK. I FELL AND LEG

ALL SWOLLEN. TWO NEGRO SOLDIERS HAVE BEEN

VERY KIND TO ME.

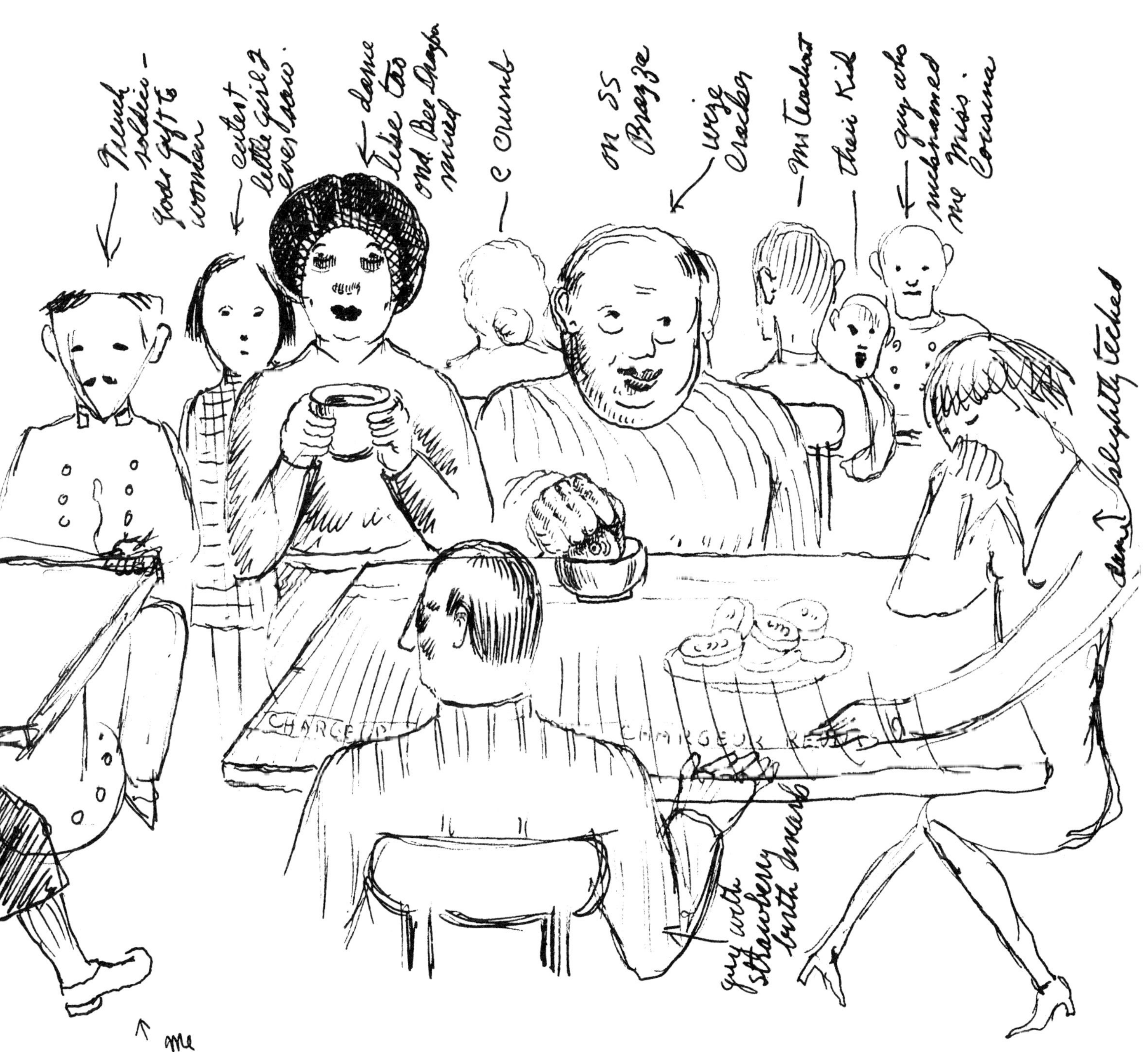

MARCH 13

GAVE A BABY A BATH. ALMOST KILLED THE KID AS THE SEA WAS GETTING ROUGHER. DID IT BECAUSE EVERY-ONE WAS STILL SEA SICK AND I THOUGHT I COULD HELP. I WAS NOT SEA SICK. I HEATED THE WATER OVER A STERNO STOVE. MY ROOMMATE, A MISSIONARY, CLARA CRUMB. EMPTIED HER VOMIT FOR HER. HER NERVES ARE GETTING ON MY NERVES.

MARCH 17

SAW THE CANARY ISLANDS AT 5:30 THIS MORNING. AT FIRST JUST A VIOLET MIST. THE SUN CAME UP AND I SAW SNOW ON TOP. BEGAN TAKING QUININE. IN TROPICS NOW, EVEN WITH THE SAHARA. HUGH LINES CATCH FISH FOR OUR MEALS.

MARCH 19

DAKAR TODAY. NEGROES SWAM TO THE BOAT TO GREET US. GOT OFF BOAT. EVERYTHING WAS LIKE A DREAM. WALKED ALONG THE STREETS AND THROUGH THE MARKETS. MEN WERE EMBROIDERING WHILE WALK-ING DOWN THE STREET. BUSES WERE LOADED WITH COLORFUL PEOPLE. HAD COFFEE IN A CAFE. NEGROS LIVED IN ANY OLD KIND OF LEAN-TO. AN OLD MAN MADE PASSES AT GIRLS ABOUT 10 OR 12 YEARS. SEVERAL NEGROES GOT ON THE BOAT AT DAKAR, BUT WERE PLACED AT A TABLE BY THEMSELVES.

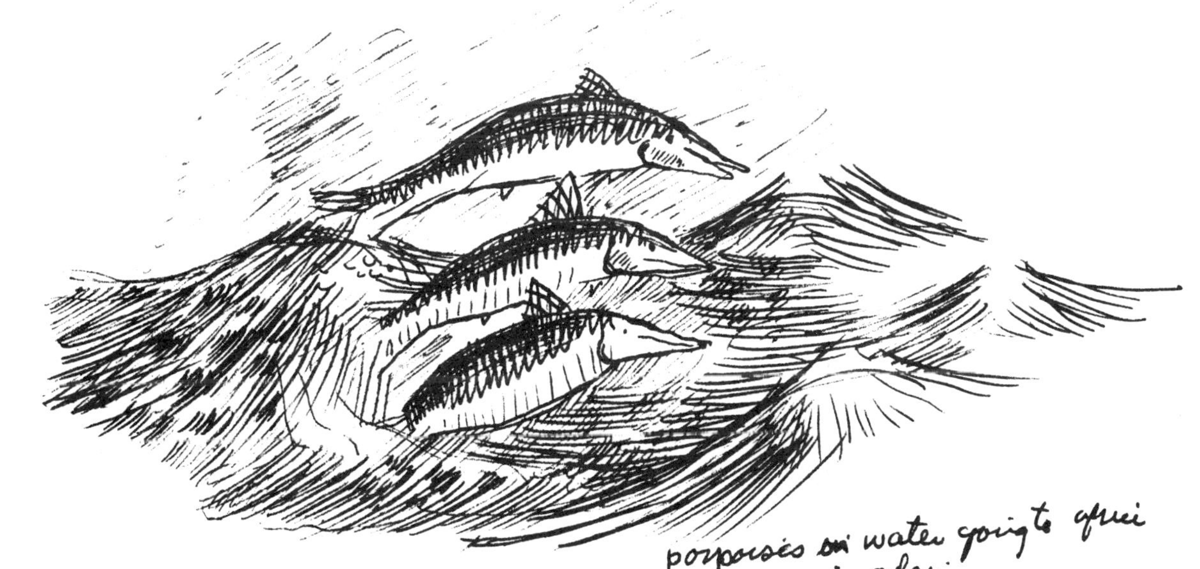

porpoises on water going to afrii
they jump up in order.
Negroe walking 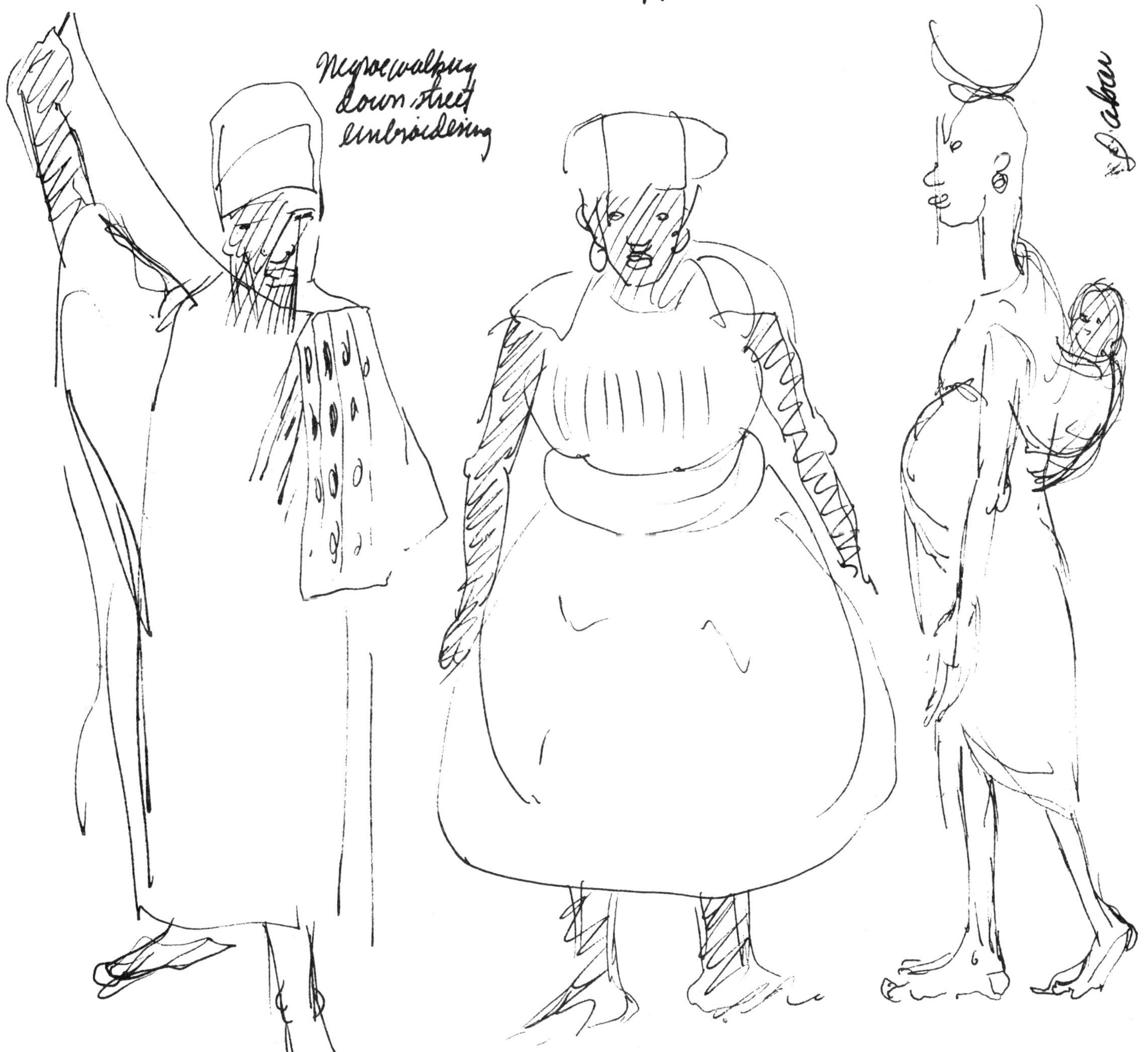
down street
embroidering

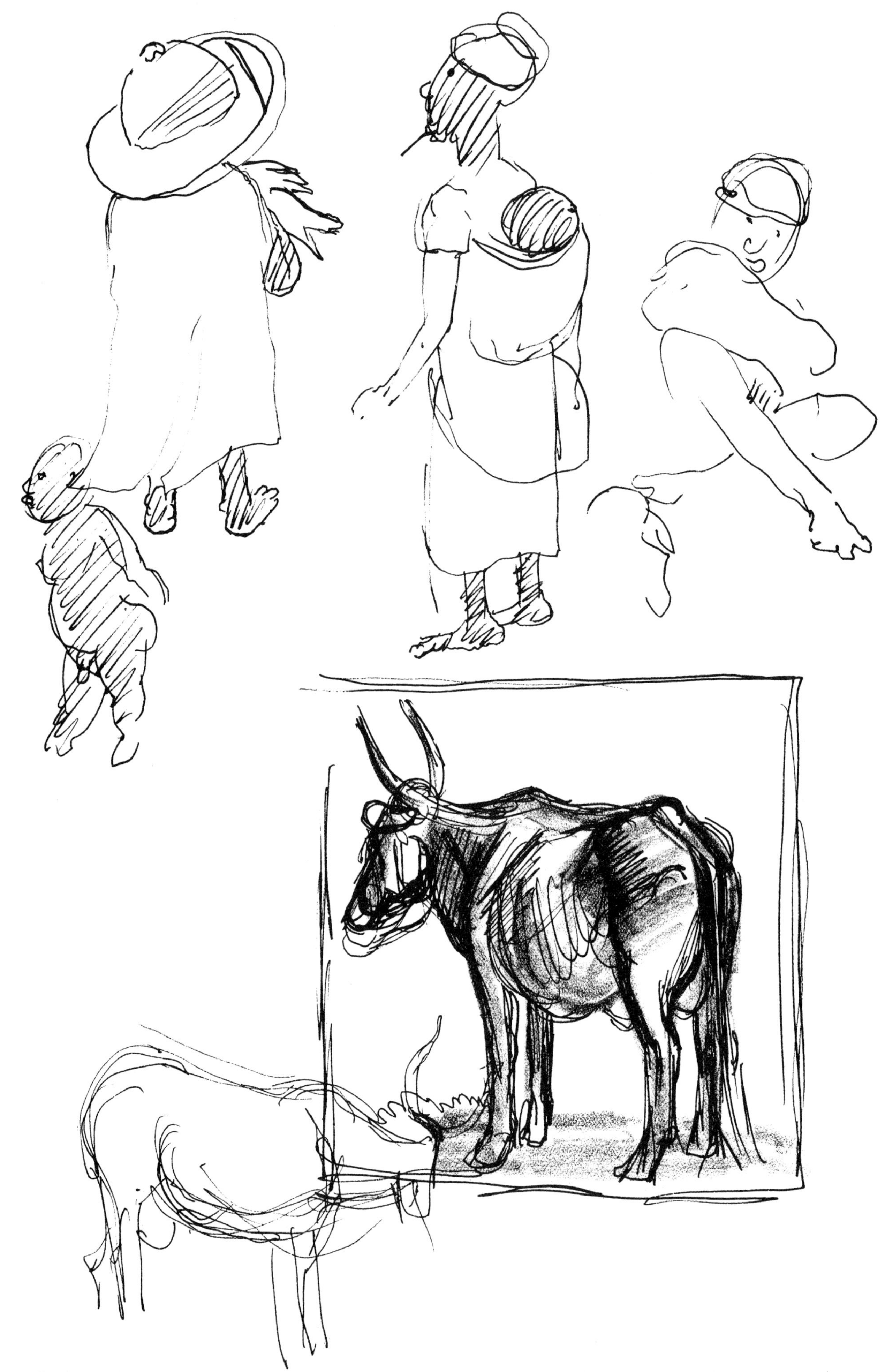

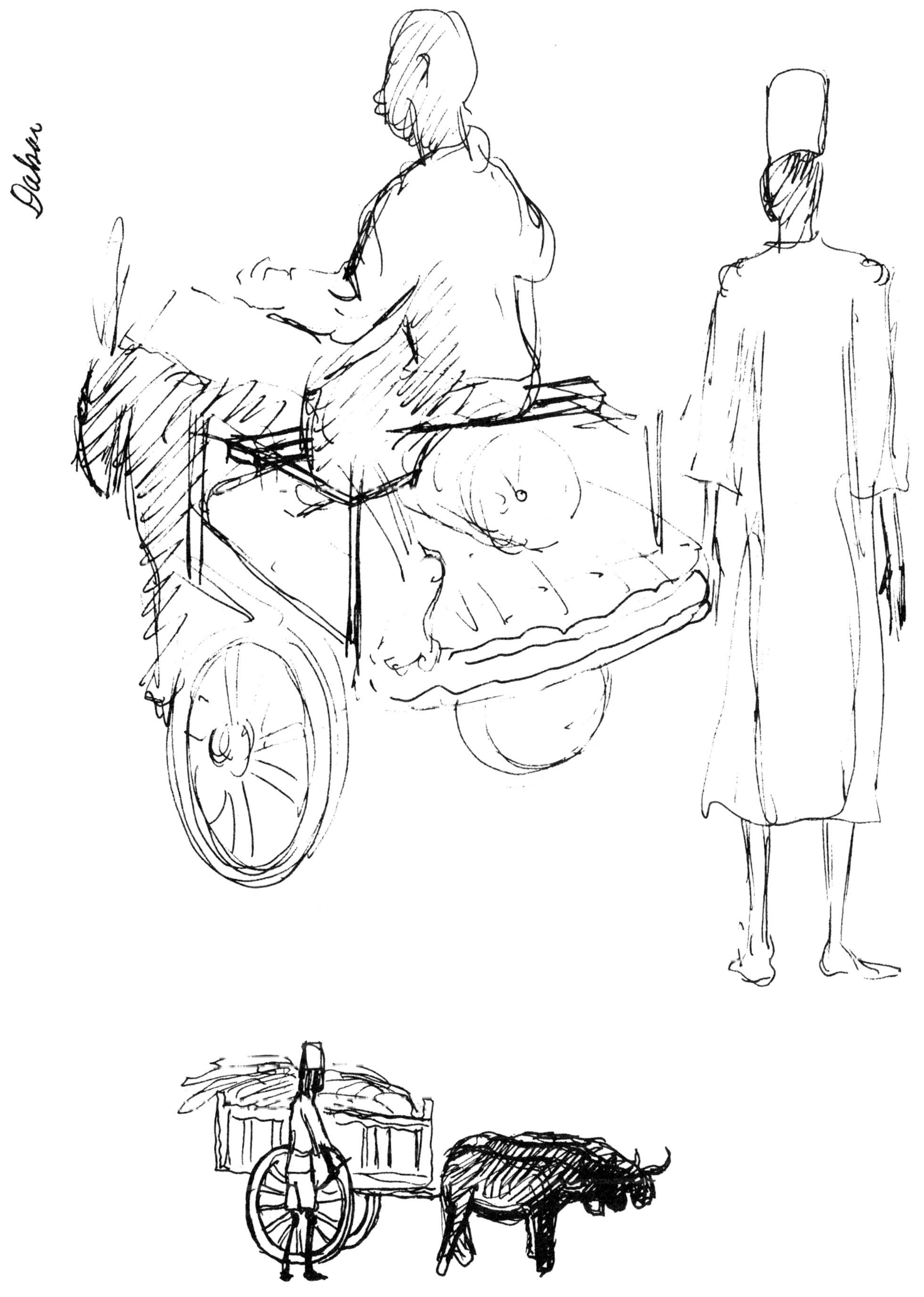

Dahn

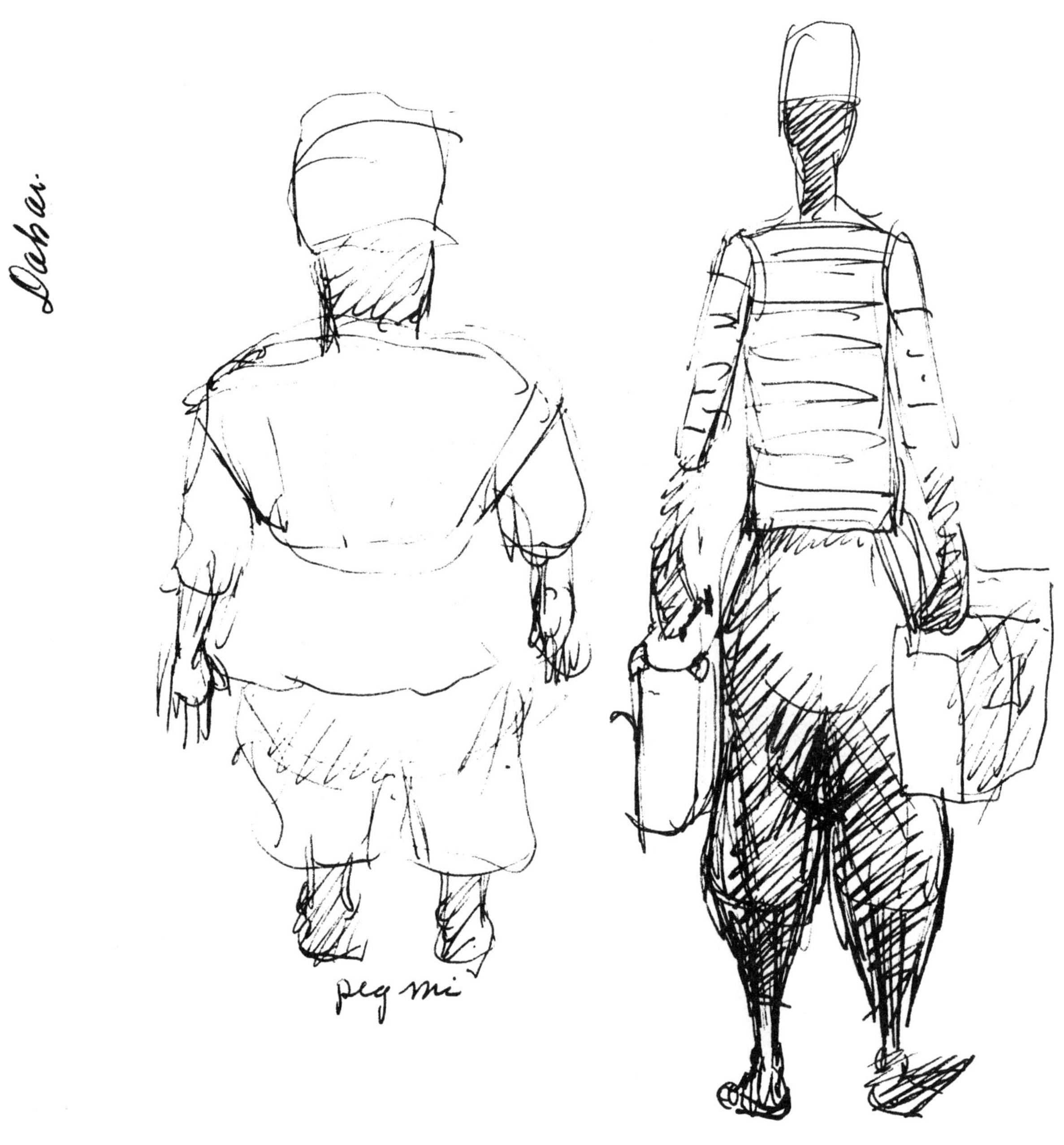

MEN CARRIED HEAVY LOADS SLOWLY.

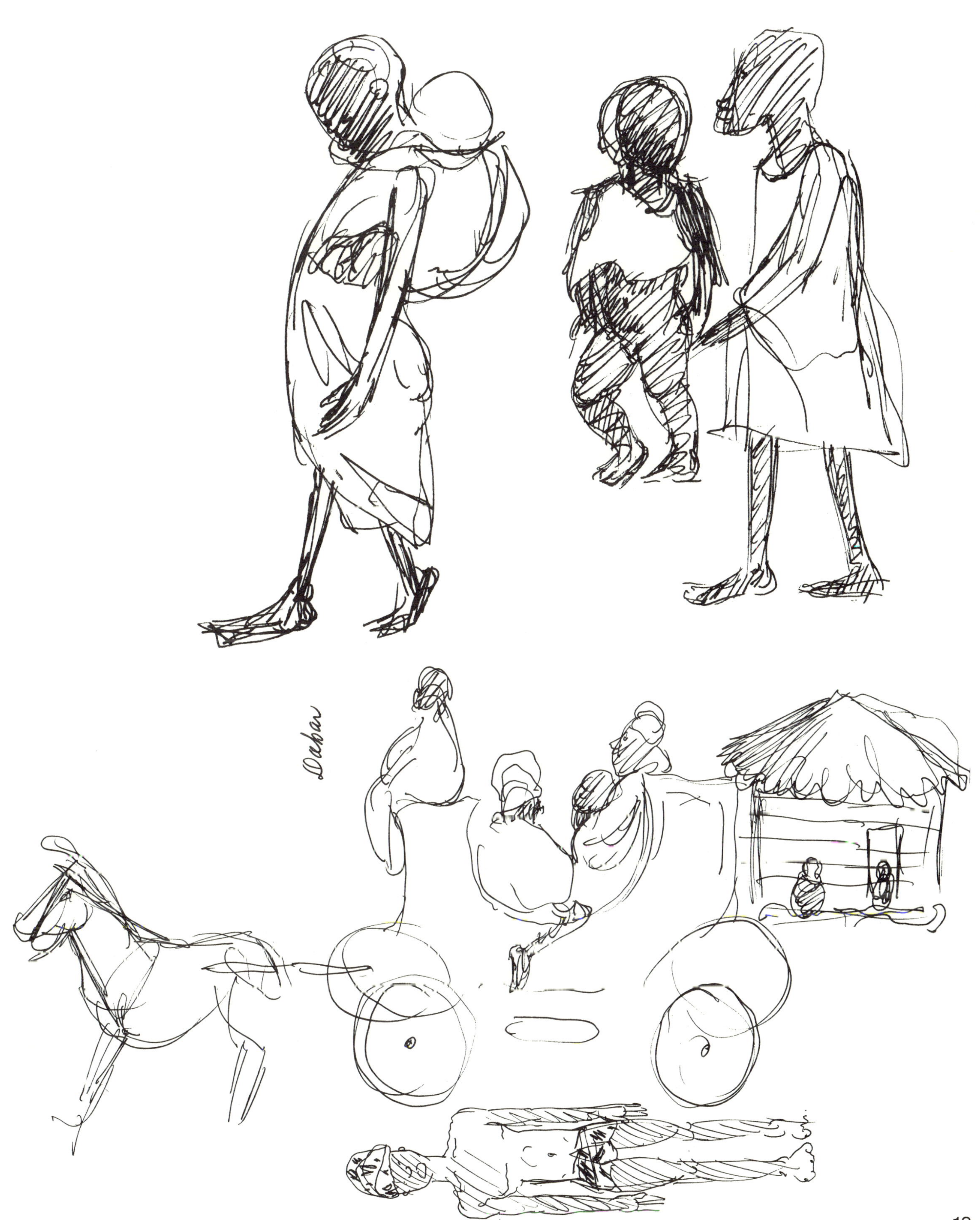
Daba

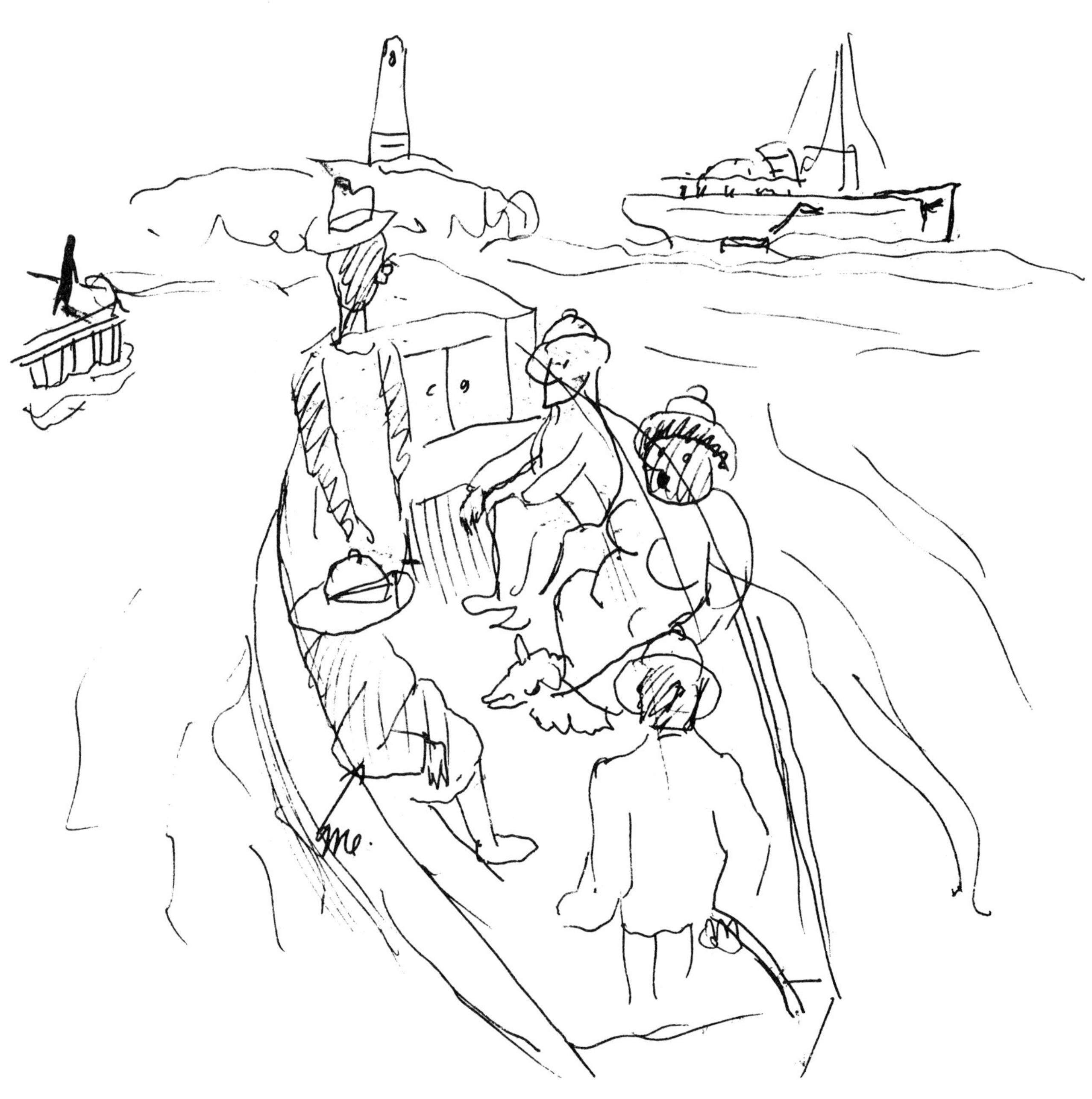

Coming off ship Brazza
March 21st.

PALM SUNDAY

ARRIVED CONAKRY 6 AM. THE BRAZZA ANCHORED
AWAY IN THE OCEAN. A NATIVE PADDLED A BOAT OUT
TO TAKE FOUR OF US TO SHORE. AT THE DOCK MEN
FOUGHT OVER MY SUITCASES. NAKED LITTLE BOYS ON
THE STREETS WERE CARRYING PALMS. THEY RAN
AFTER ME ASKING IF I NEEDED A BOY.

II IS SO BEAUTIFUL HERE: BUTTERFLIES, BIRDS,
FLOWERS AND TREES IN BLOOM. TROPICAI .

GOT A ROOM AT THE GRAND HOTEL.
SOMETHING ATE A HOLE IN MY ROBE.
SAW A TARANTULA UNDER THE SINK.
I LET IT RUN AROUND ME.
IT LOOKED LIKE A RAT
WHEN IT RAN.

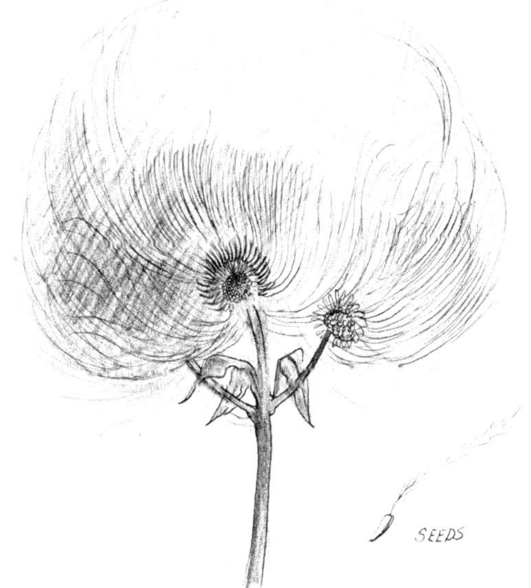

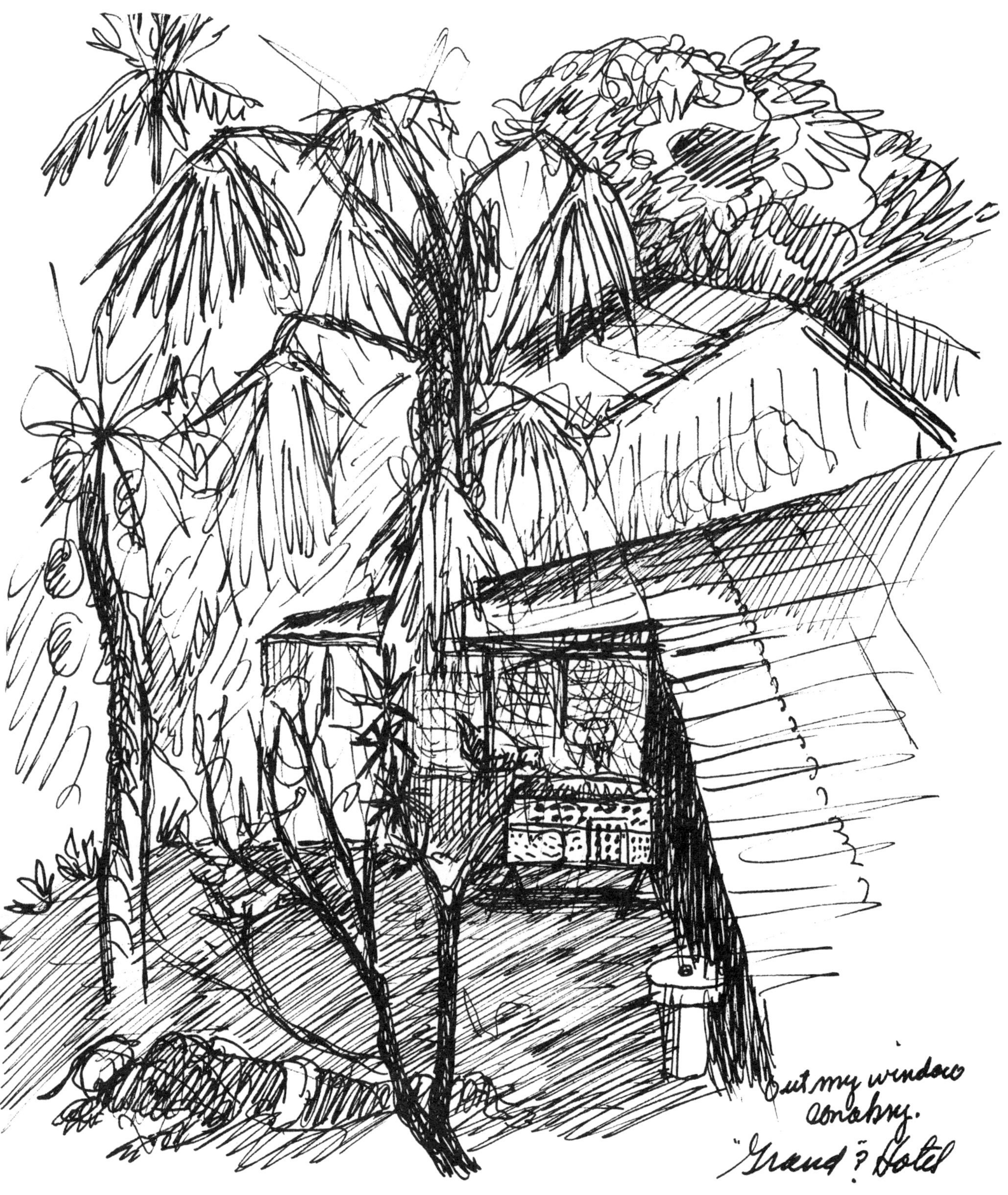

Out my window
Conakry.
"Grand?" Hotel

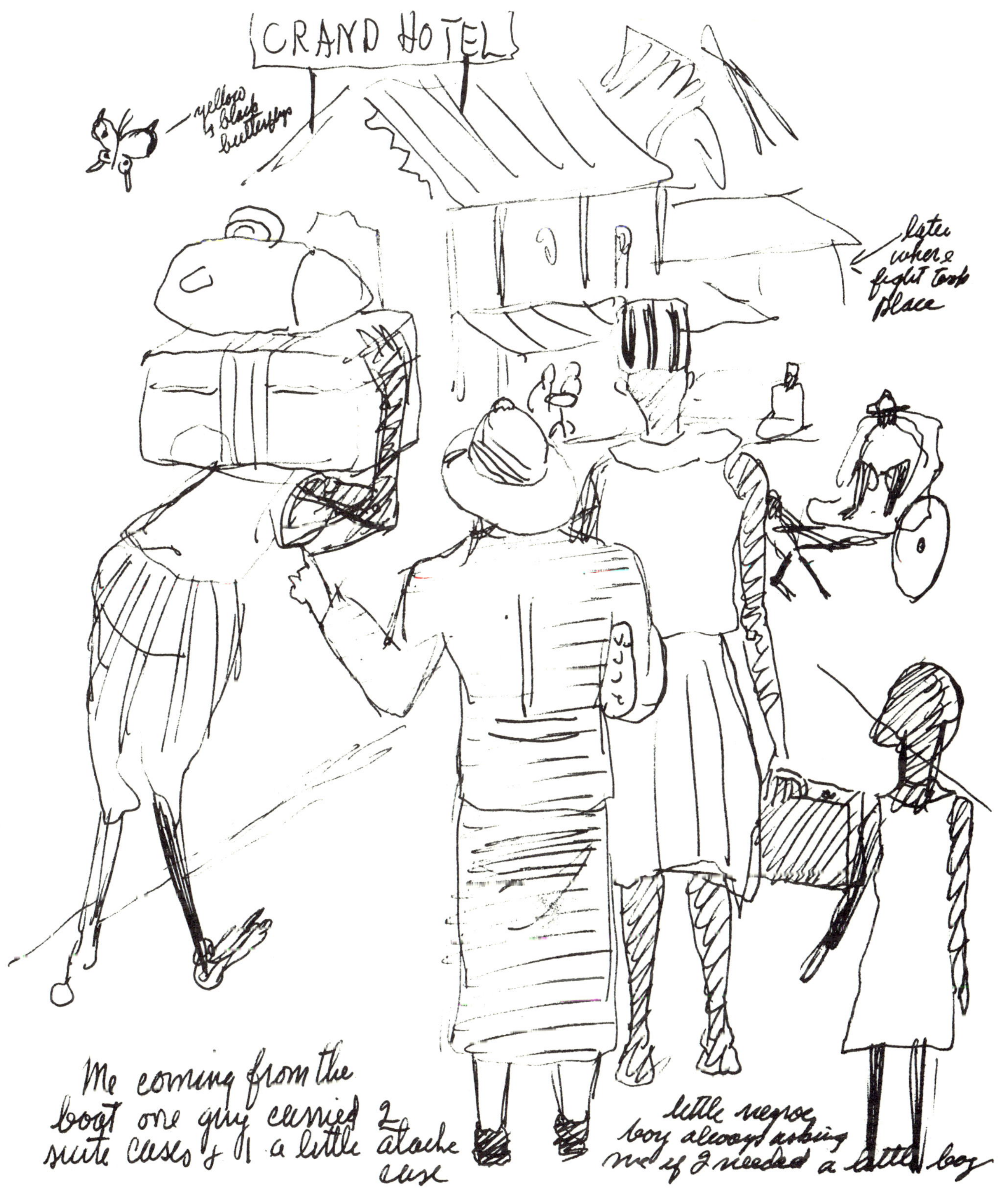
GRAND HOTEL
yellow & black butterflys
later where fight took place
Me coming from the boat one guy carried 2 suit cases & 1 a little atache case
little negro boy always asking me if I needed a little boy

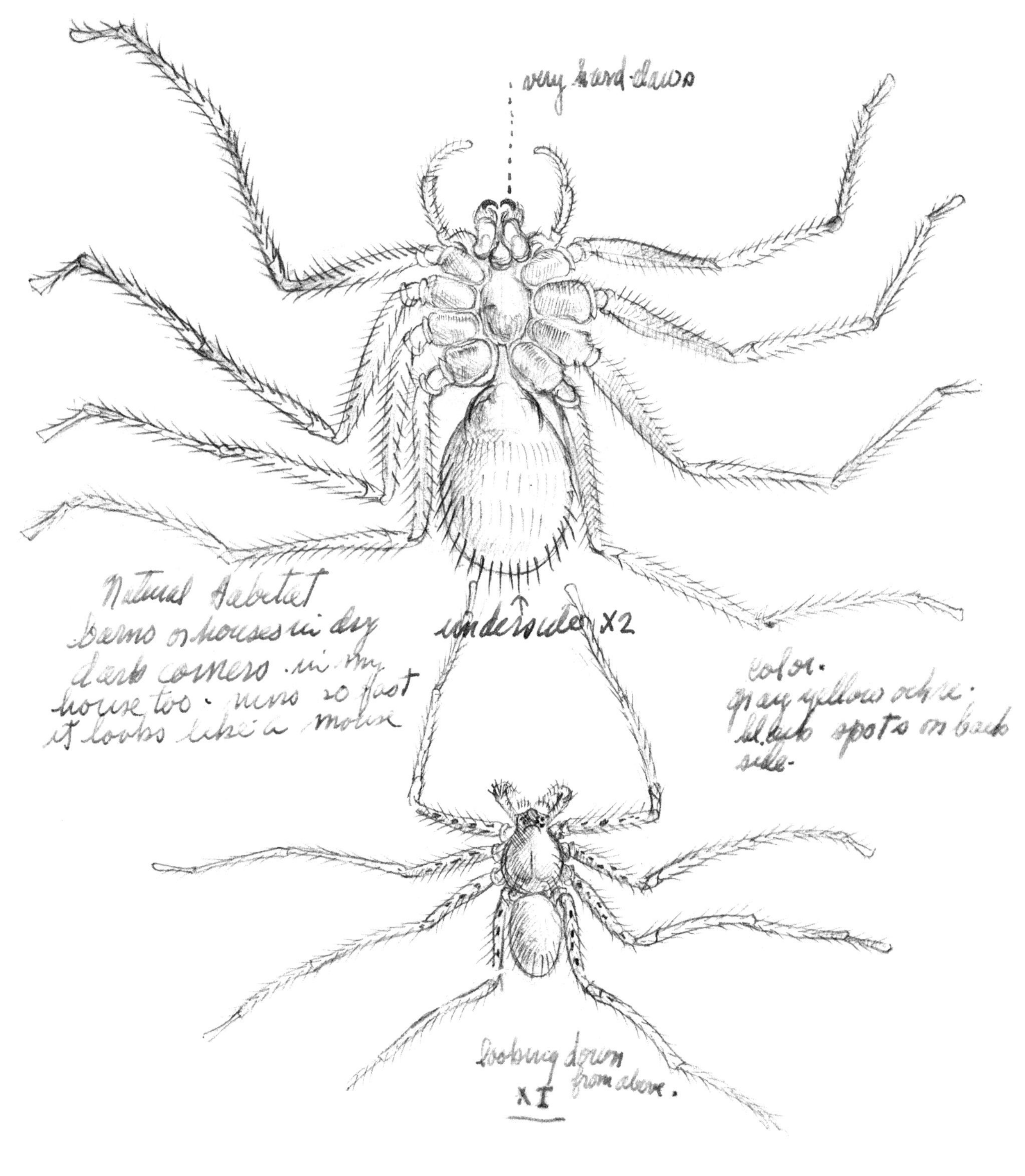

A TARANTULA RAN

ON THE WALL WHILE I WAS TAKING

A BATH AT THE SINK

THE BED'S NOT SO HOT. TRIED TO FIND A SPOT

WITHOUT LUMPS.

AND IT'S BEDBUGGY.

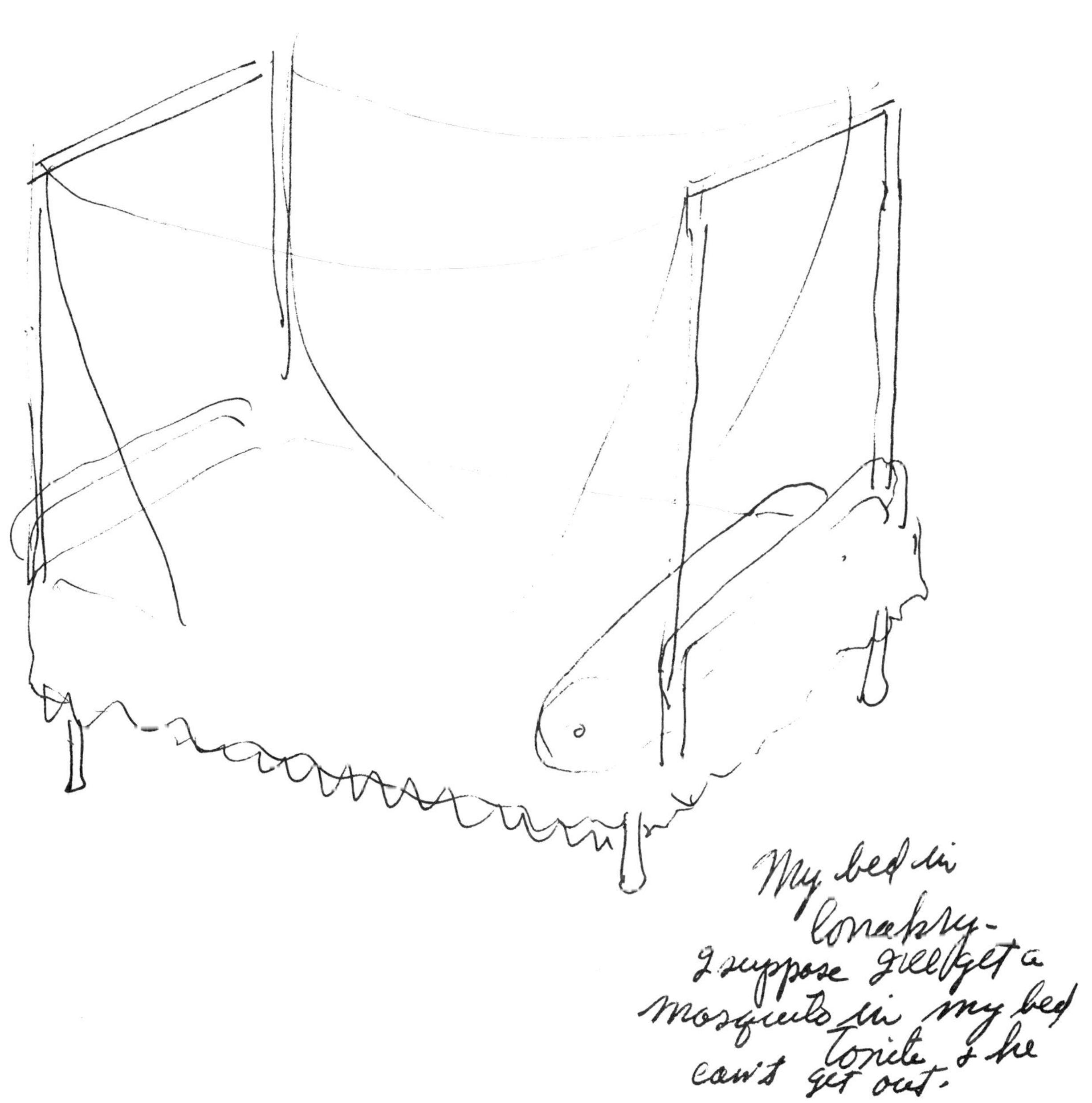

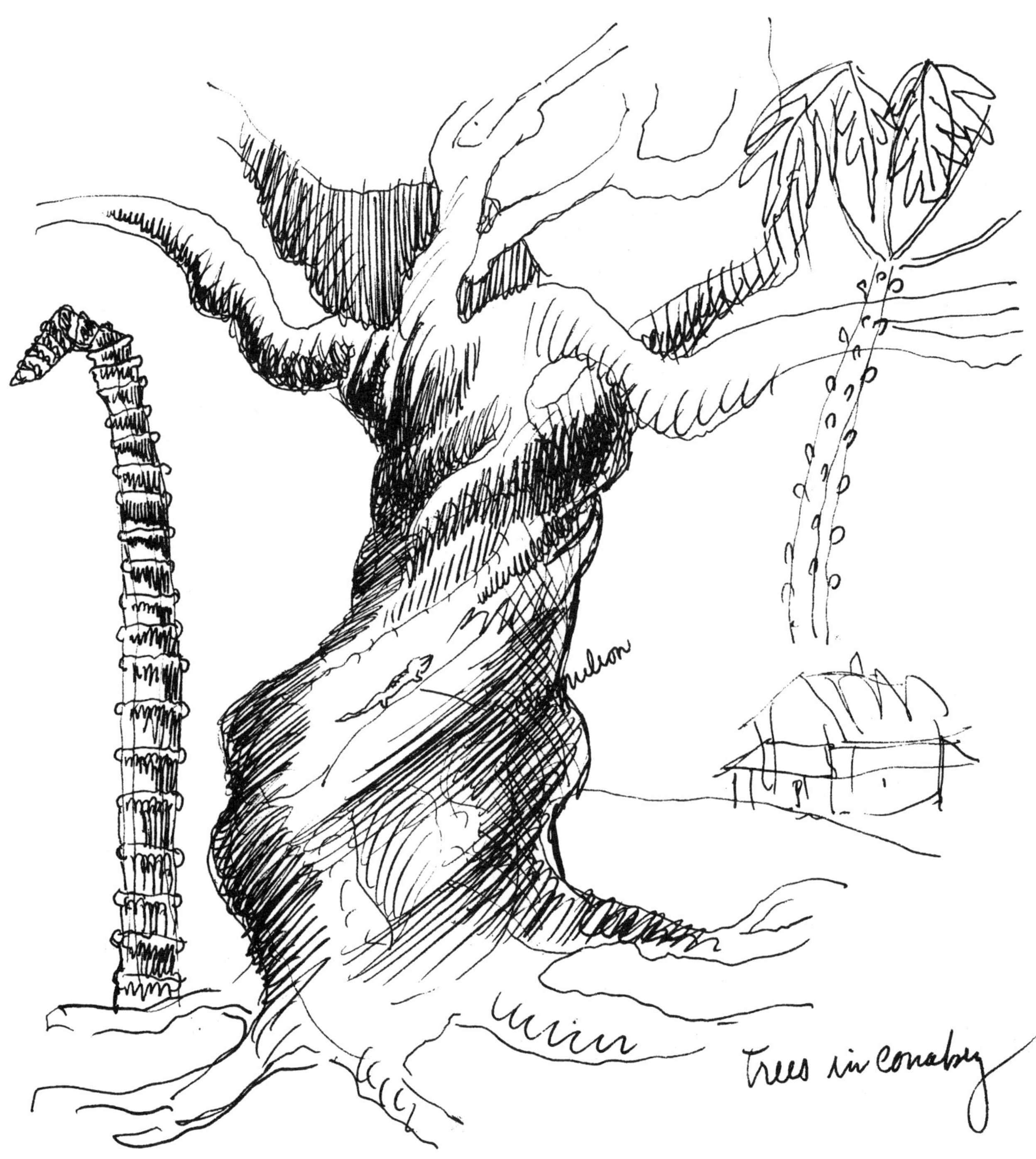

Trees in Conakry

MARCH 22

MY TRAIN LEAVES CONAKRY FOR KANKAN AT 6:00 AM. FIRST OF ALL I HAD TO WAKE UP MY LANDLORD. ALMOST GOT MOBBED WHEN I TRIED TO PURCHASE MY TICKET. GOT ON TRAIN. AT ALL STATIONS NEGROES GOT ON AND TRIED TO SELL YOU STUFF. A NEGRESS GOT ON AND COULDN'T GET OFF. SHE SCREECHED AND YELLED FOR 25 MILES TO THE NEXT STOP. A NEGRO TRIED TO SELL FLOWERS TO SOME PEOPLE. THEY TOOK THEM AND THREW THEM OUT THE WINDOW. HAD LUNCH AT A STOP. MOBS OF COLORFUL NEGROES AROUND. A MAN GOT OFF THE TRAIN TO URINATE. SCENERY OF MOUNTAINS AND WATERFALLS. A MAN CLEANED HIS TEETH WITH A BUTCHER KNIFE.

IT TAKES TWO DAYS TO GET INTO THE INTERIOR AT KANKAN WHERE I WANT TO PAINT IN THE BUSH.

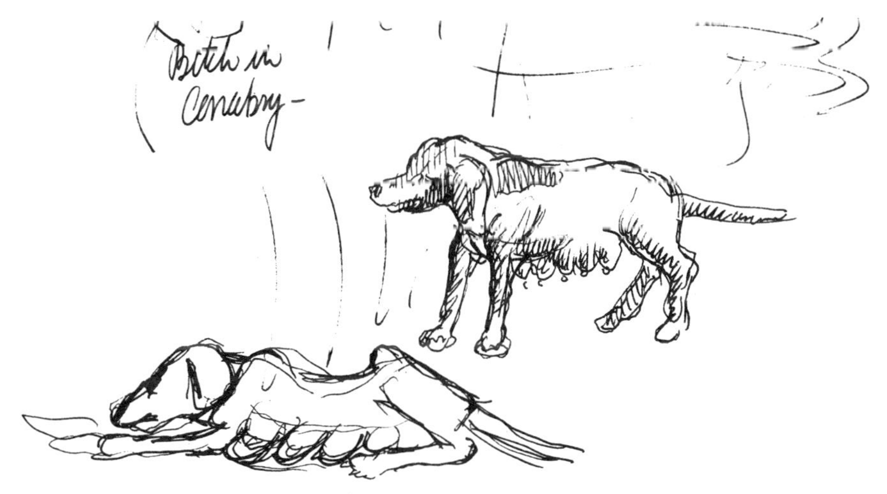

THE AFRICAN TRAINS ARE LIKE BOXCARS. I COULDN'T GET ANYTHING TO EAT, BUT PURCHASED THINGS ALONG THE ROAD. BANANAS, ORANGES AND PINE-APPLES ARE HANDED TO YOU RIGHT OFF THE TREES! ONE IS ABLE TO GET A GOOD IDEA OF NATIVE LIFE FROM AFRICAN TRAINS. AT 4 O'CLOCK THE TRAIN STOPS SO THAT THE MOHAMMEDANS CAN GET OFF AND PRAY: YOU'D THINK THEY'D NEVER FINISH.

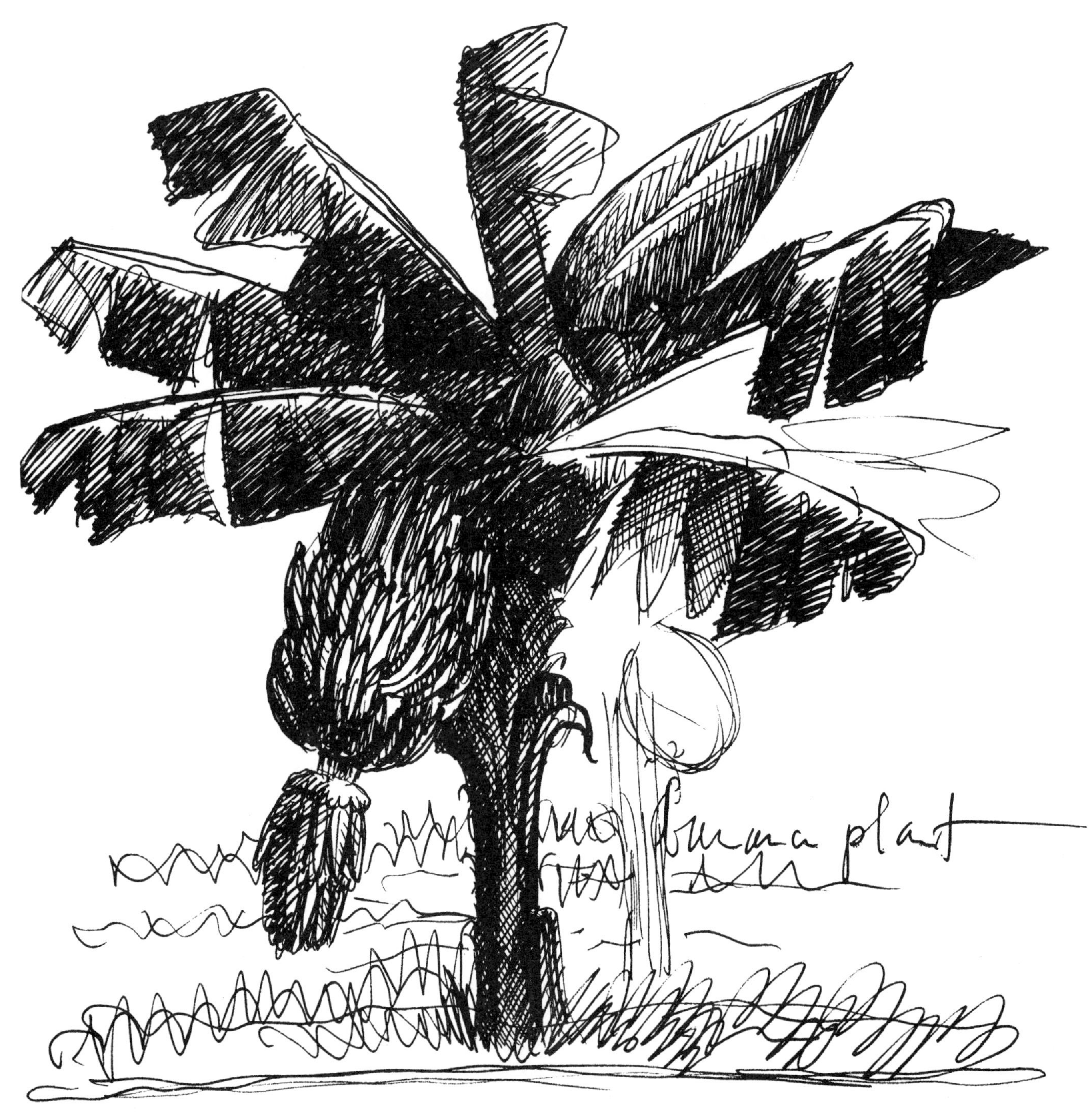

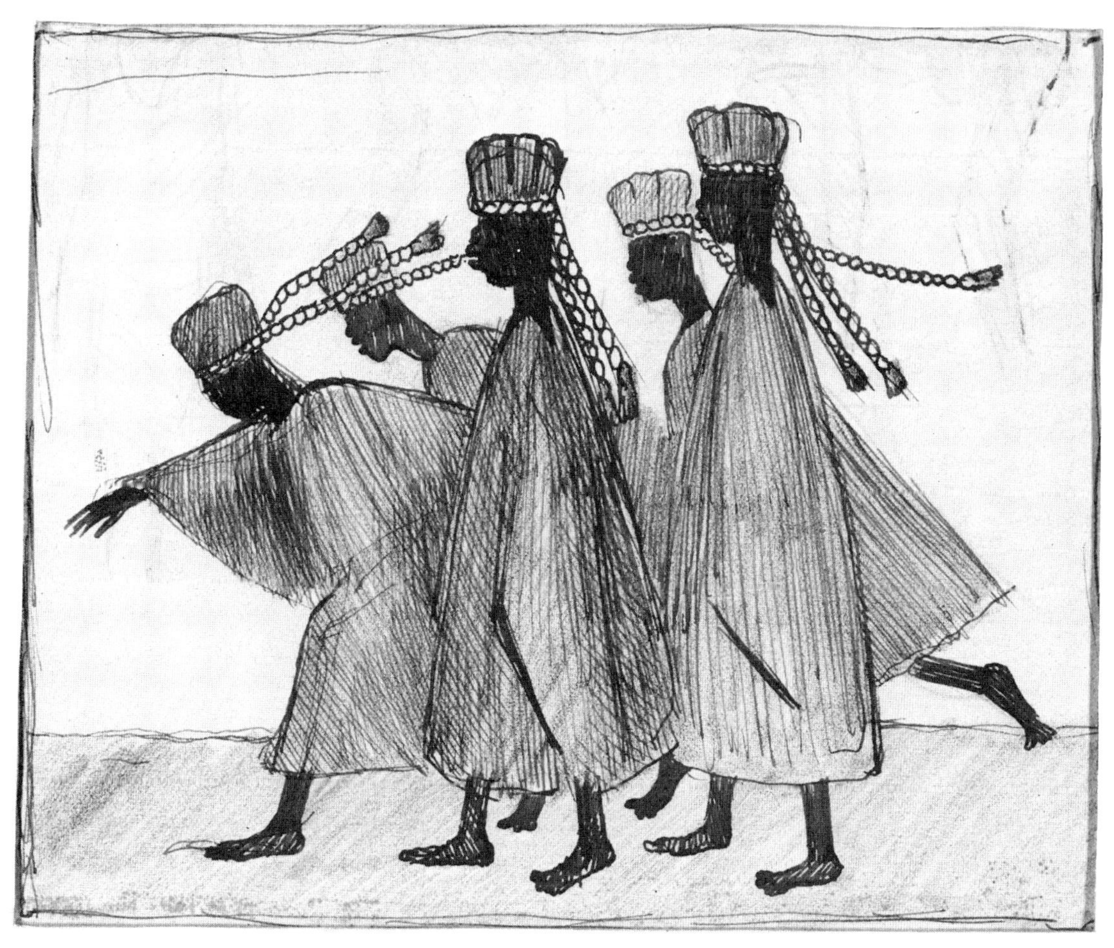

MARCH 25   **KANKAN**

HAD MY FIRST TASTE OF NATIVE MUSIC. AN INSTRU-

MENT OF RATTLES AND GOD FEARING YELLS.

GOT A HOUSE TO LIVE IN. RIGHT OUTSIDE MY WINDOW

IS A TYPICAL NATIVE VILLAGE. I GOT A MONKEY.

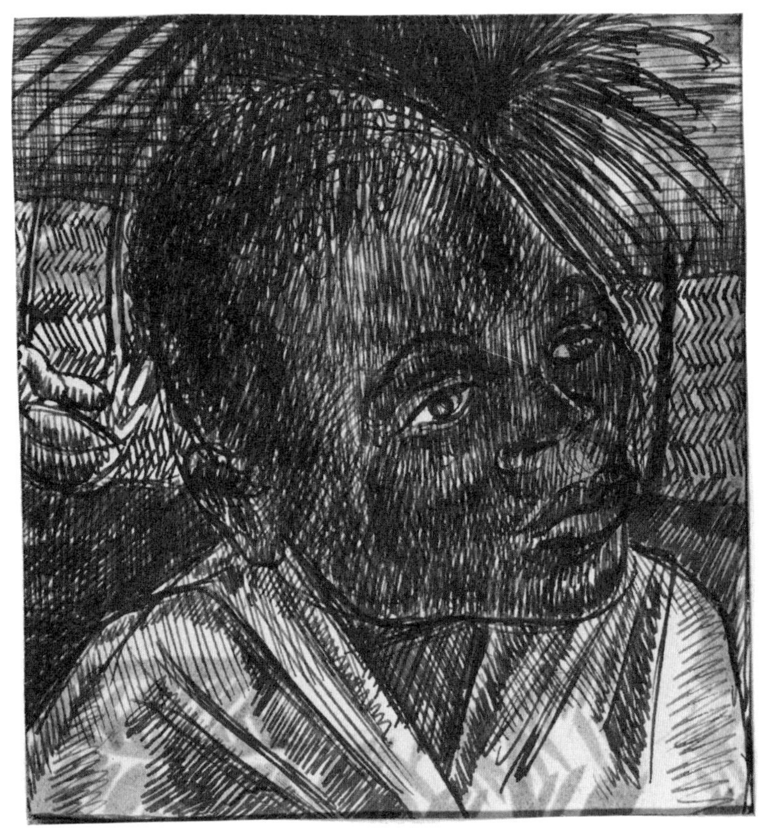

I SKETCHED A LITTLE BOY. THE PEOPLE SORT OF LIKE TO POSE. A BOY ASKED ME TO SKETCH HIM. I DID AND HAD A WHOLE MOB ON MY TAIL. I TOOK THEM ALL HOME WITH ME AND DID ONE AT A TIME AND GAVE EACH ONE 25 CENTS. THEY WERE SUCH SWELL MODELS BUT MOBBED ME FOR THEIR PAY.

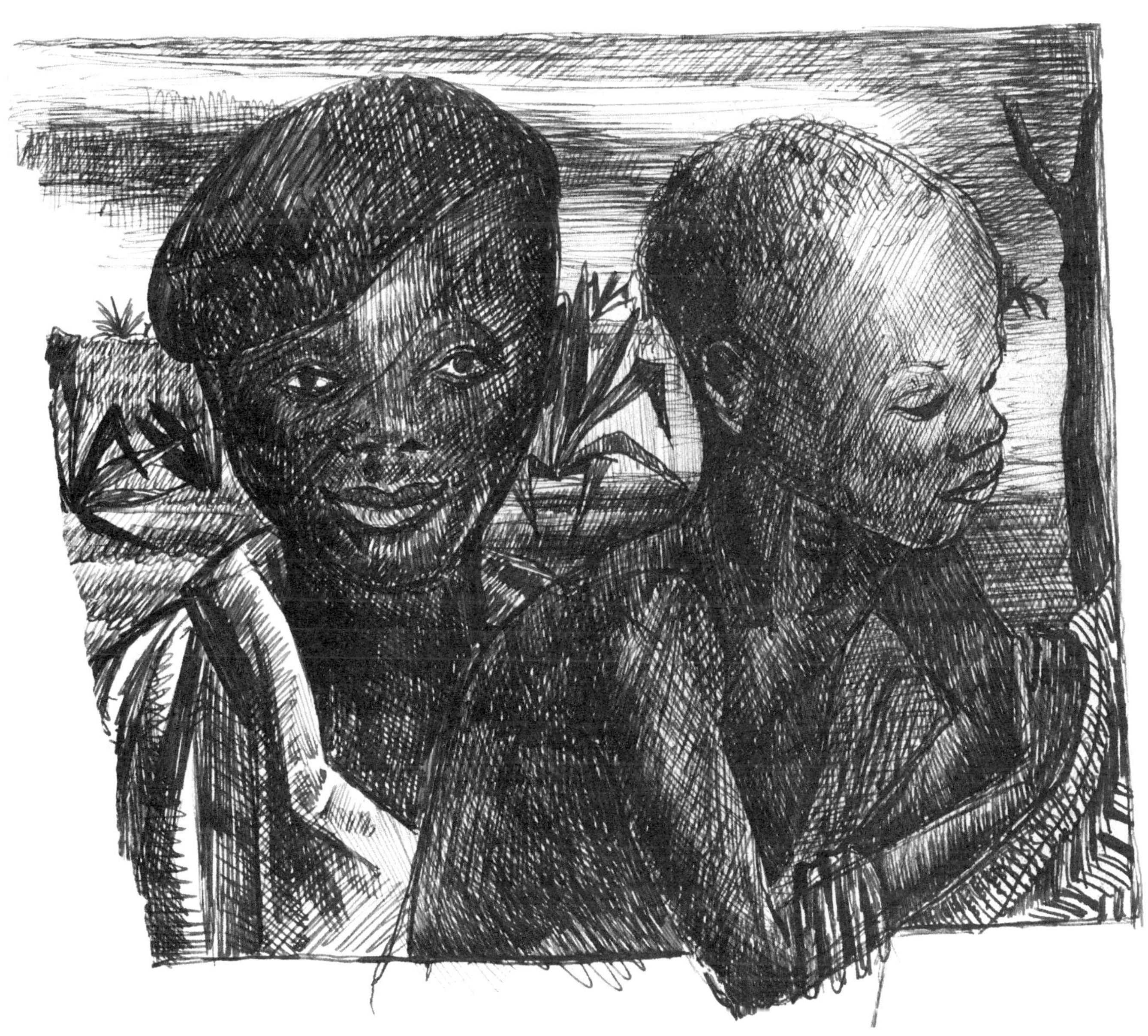

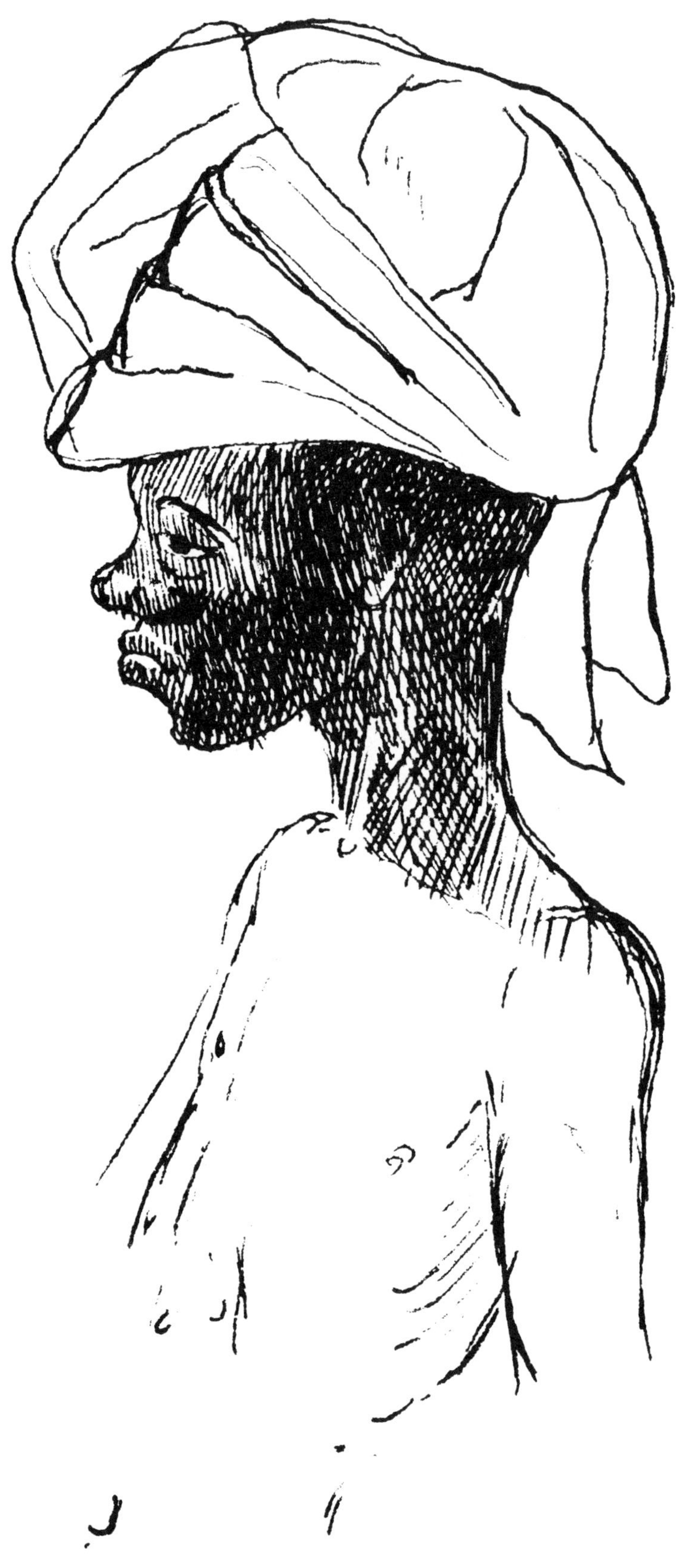

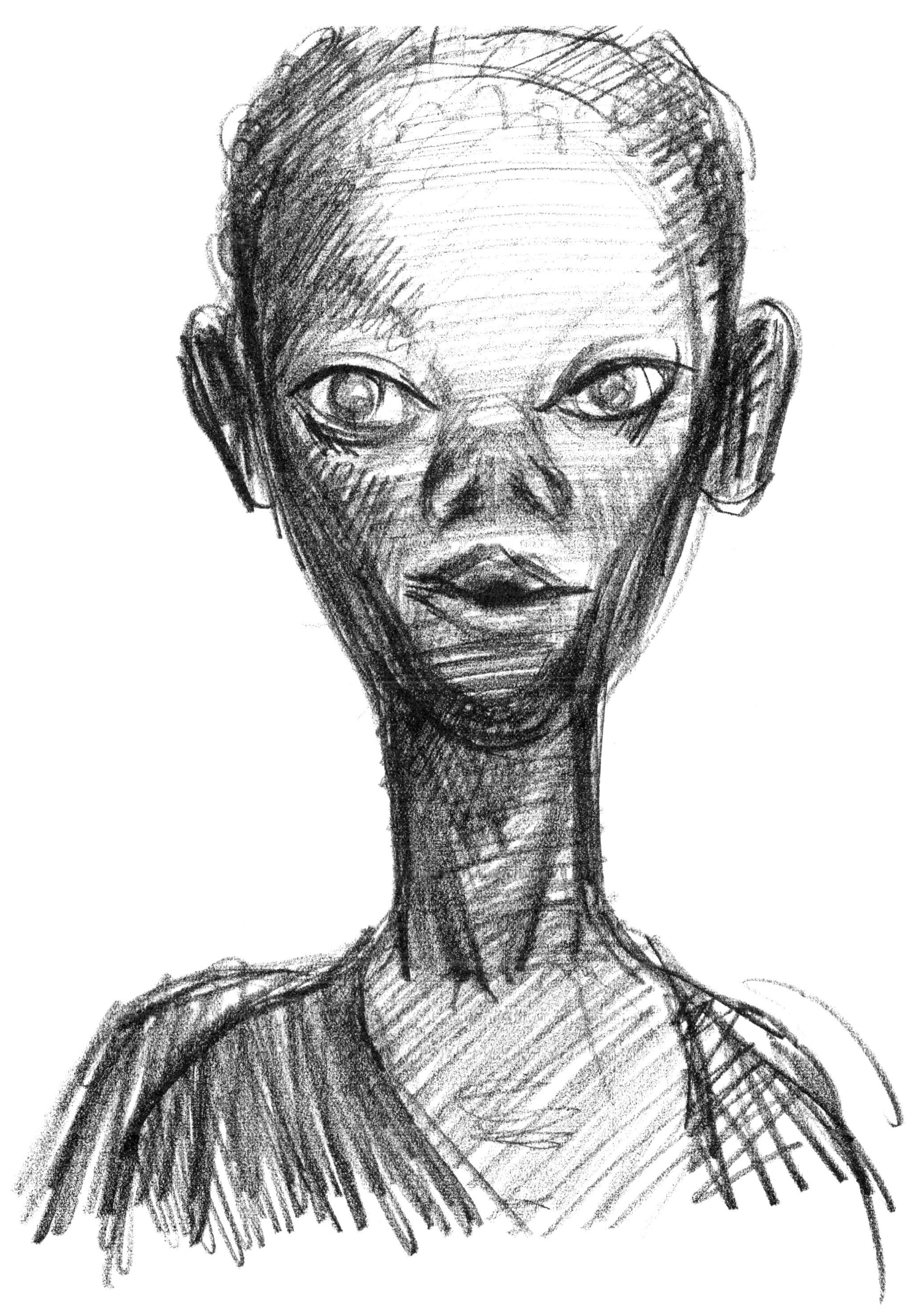

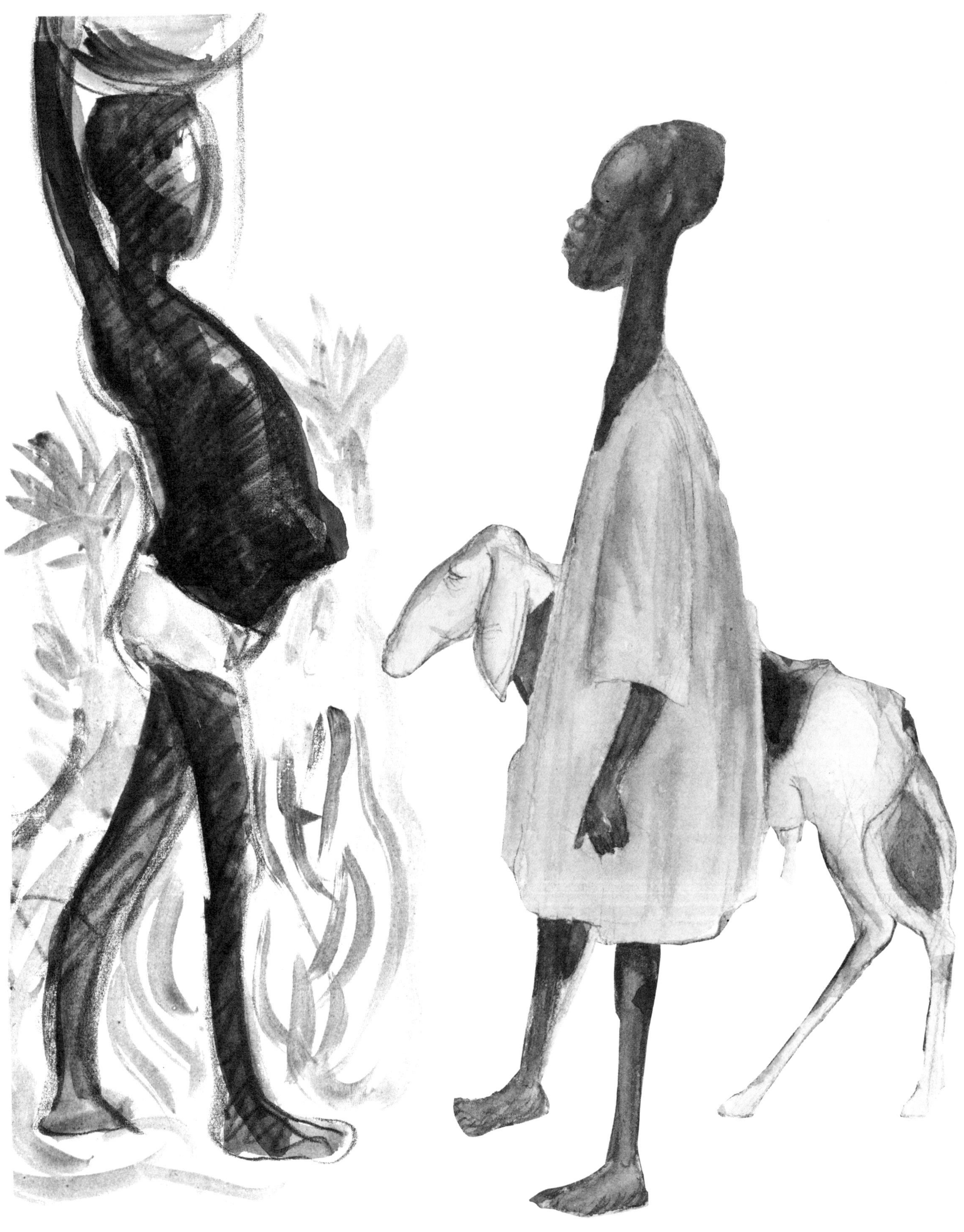

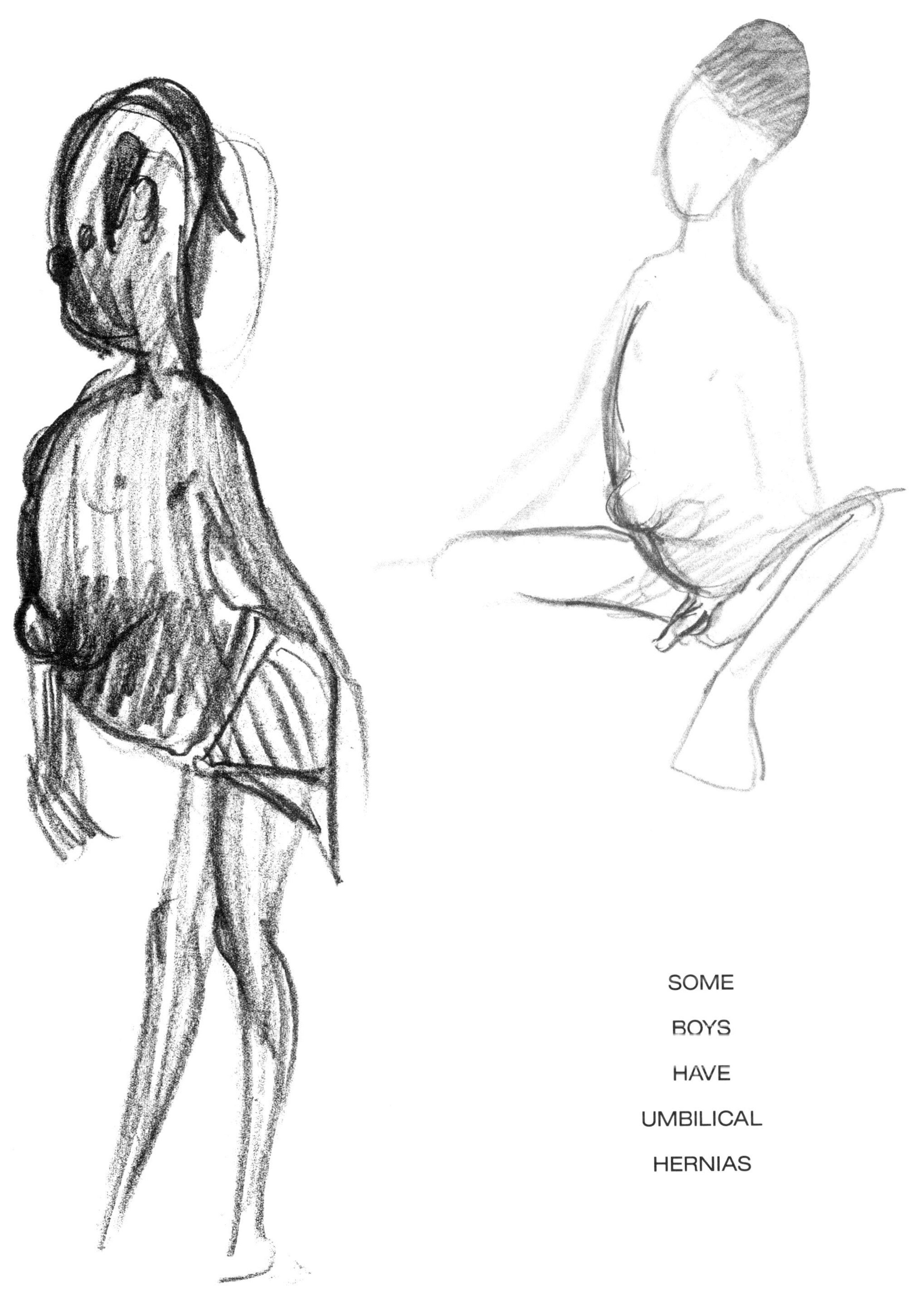

SOME
BOYS
HAVE
UMBILICAL
HERNIAS

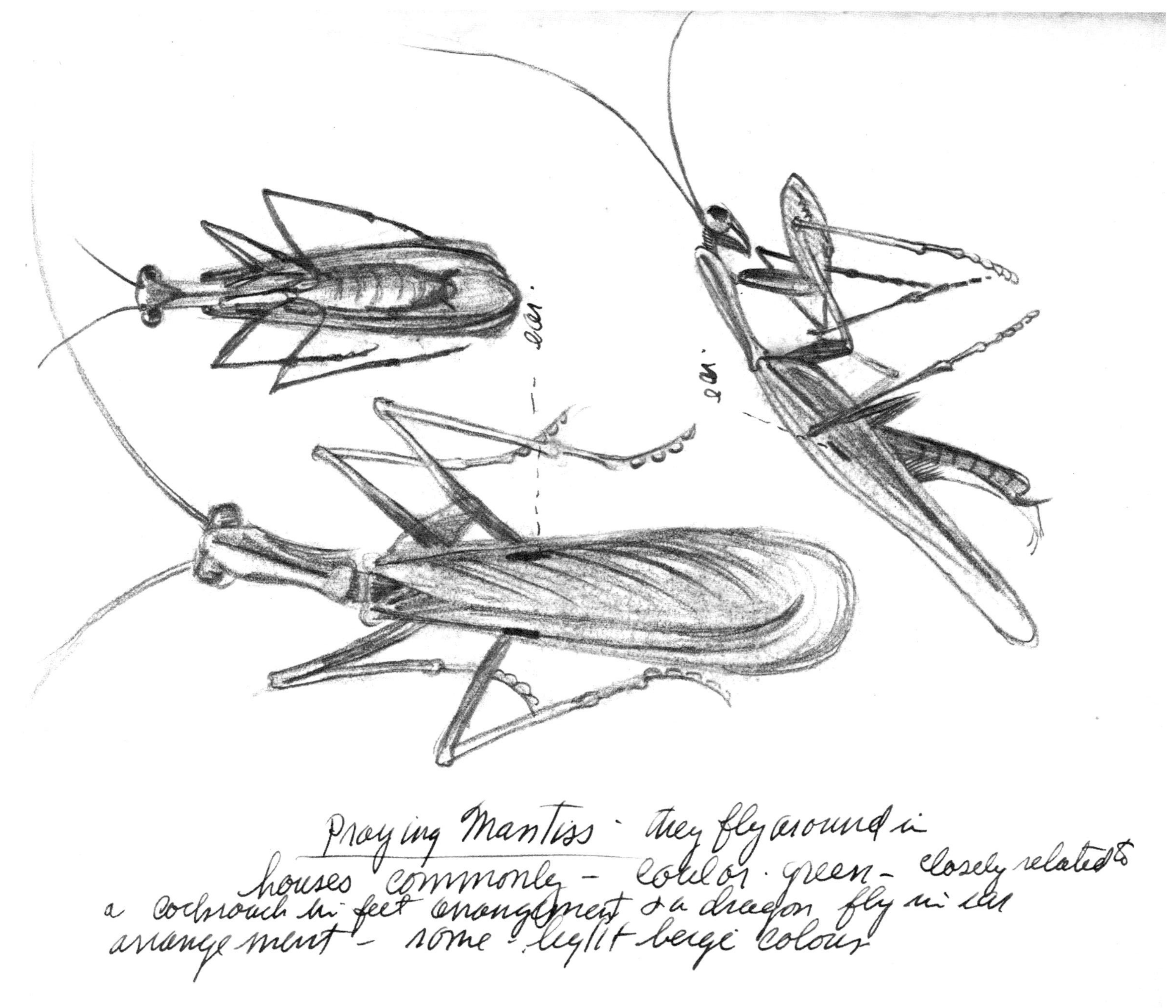

Praying Mantiss · they fly around in
houses commonly — color · green — closely related to
a cockroach in feet arrangement & a dragon fly in its
arrangement — some · light beige colour

PRAYING MANTISES ARE FLYING AROUND

LIKE MOSQUITOES

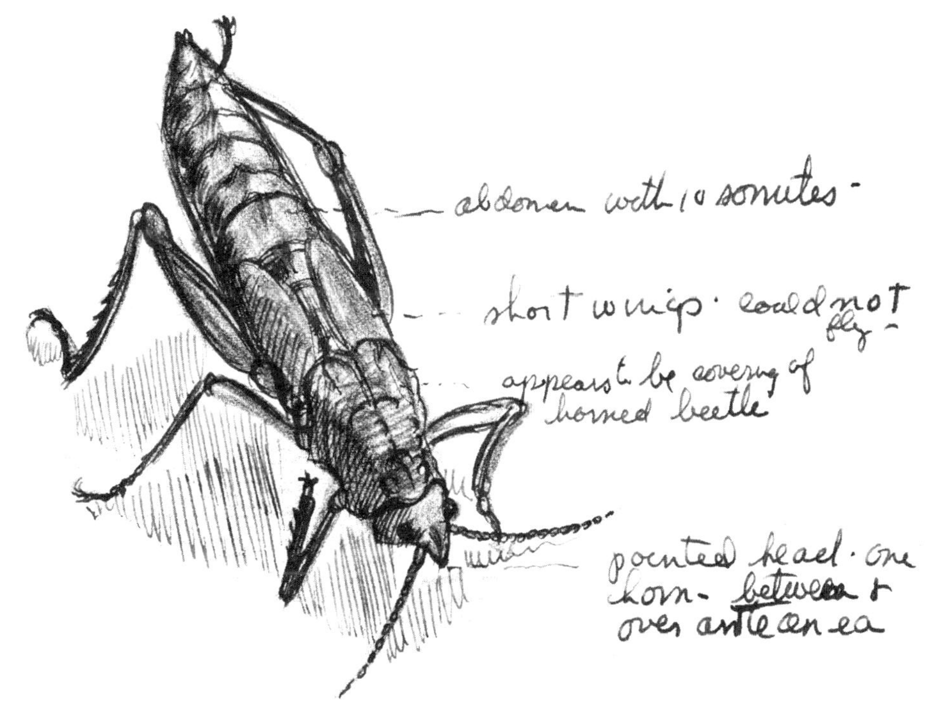

cricket Natural size ·
do not fly —

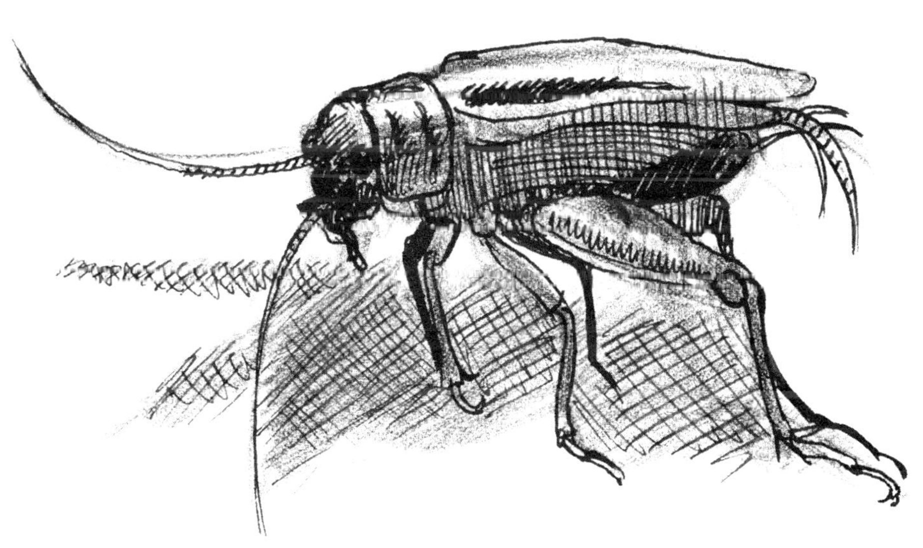

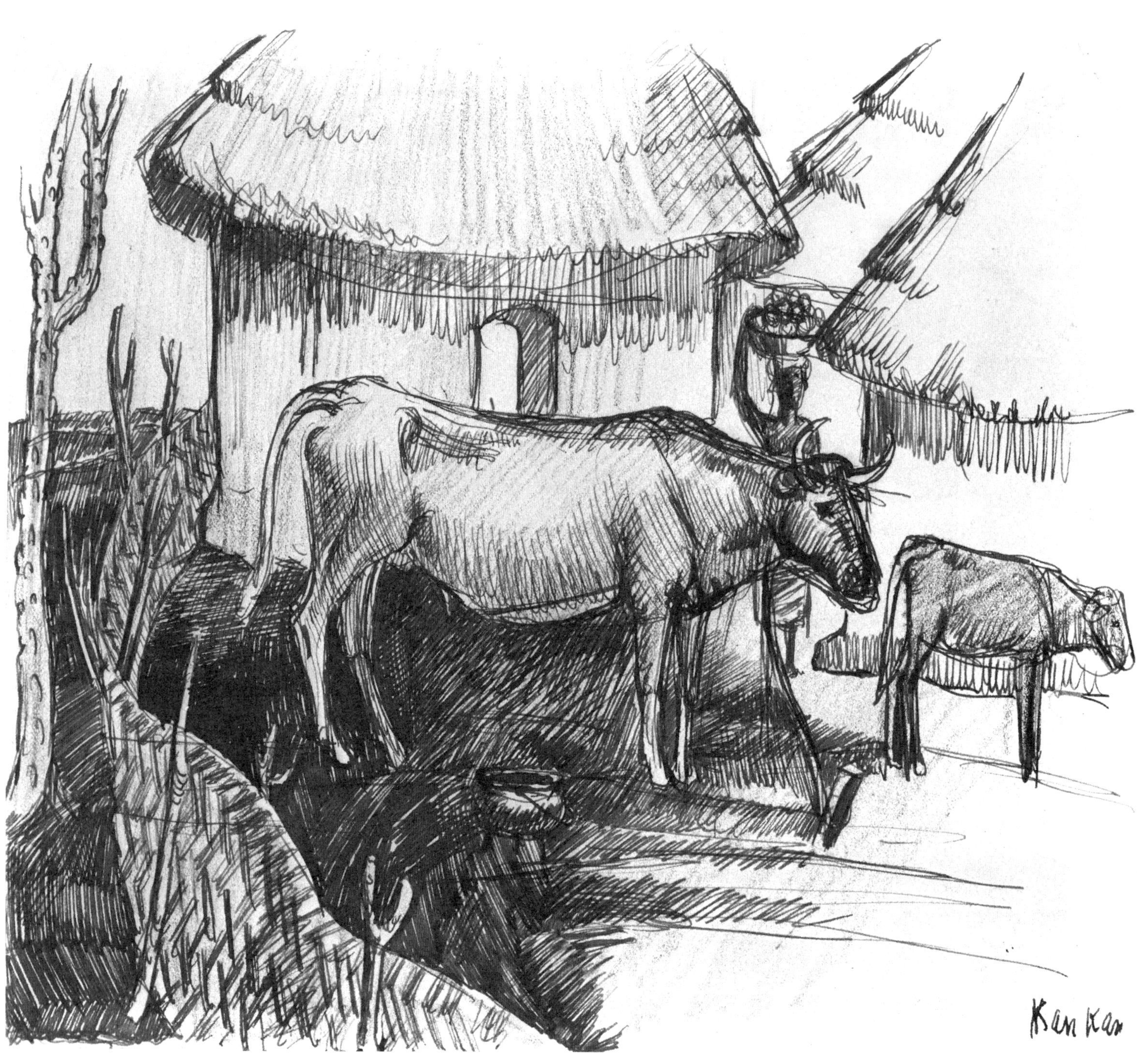

Kan Kan

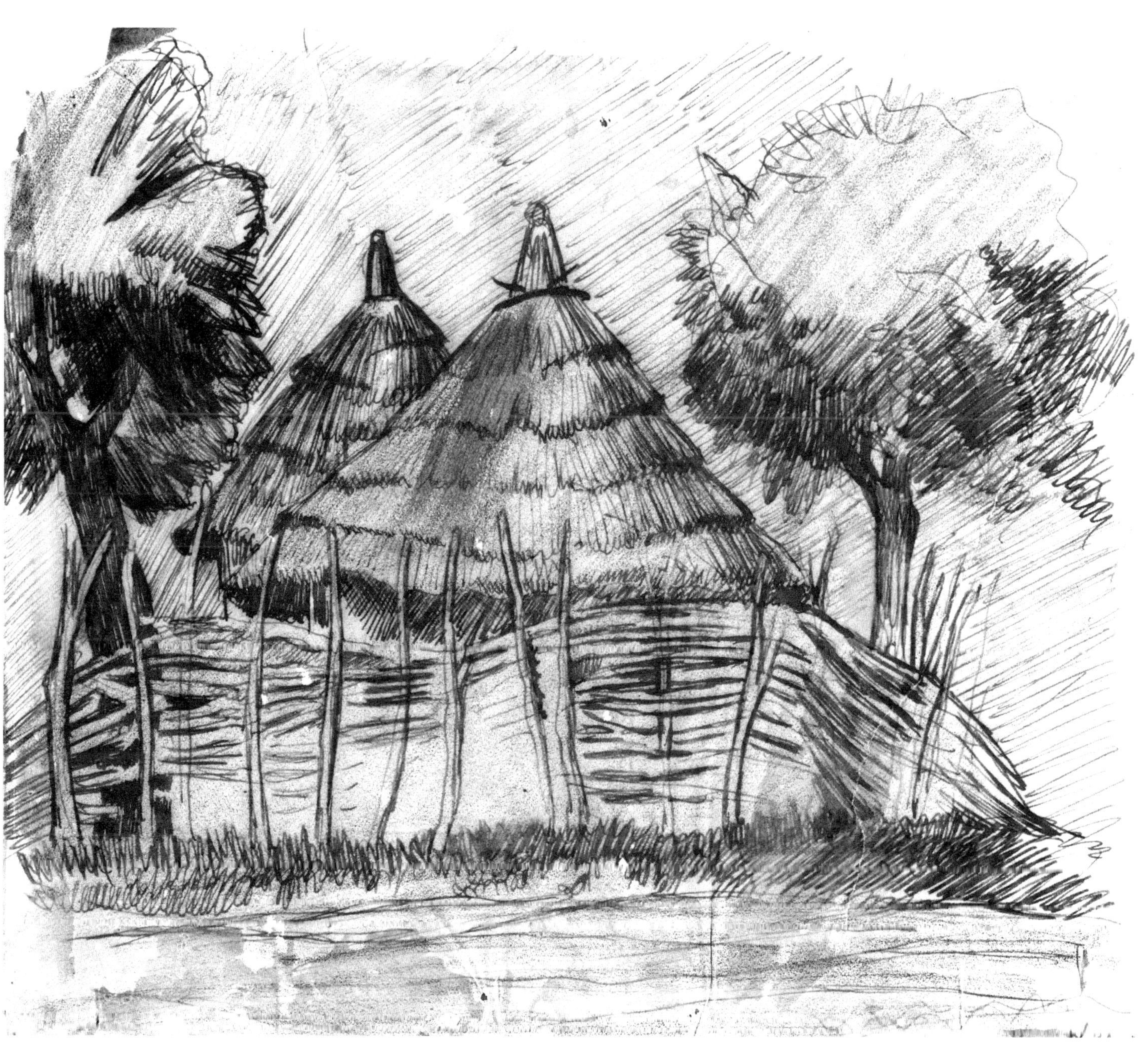

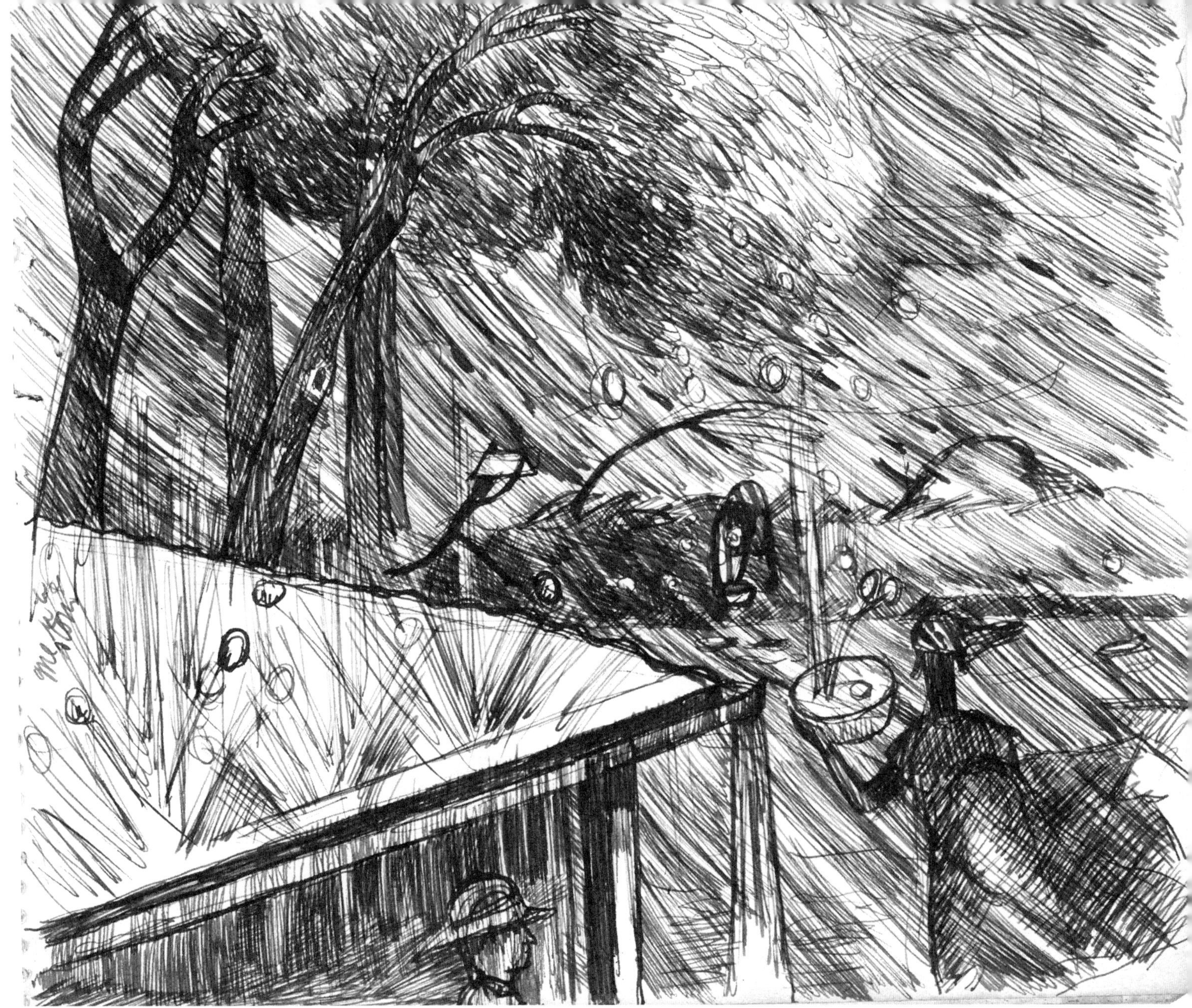

I ALMOST GOT KILLED BY A MANGO

I WAS SCARED IN BED LAST NIGHT. A STORM BLEW UP AND
EVERYTHING WENT FLYING. I LOADED MY GUN BECAUSE I'M AT LEAST
350 FEET FROM ANYONE AROUND AND BESIDES I THOUGHT I HEARD
A SNAKE CRAWLING OVER MY MOSQUITO NET. AND I HEARD THE
AWFULLEST NOISE ABOUT 2 AM. THOSE DAMNED MANGOS DROP-
PING ON MY TIN ROOF. THEY SOUNDED LIKE EXPLOSIONS.

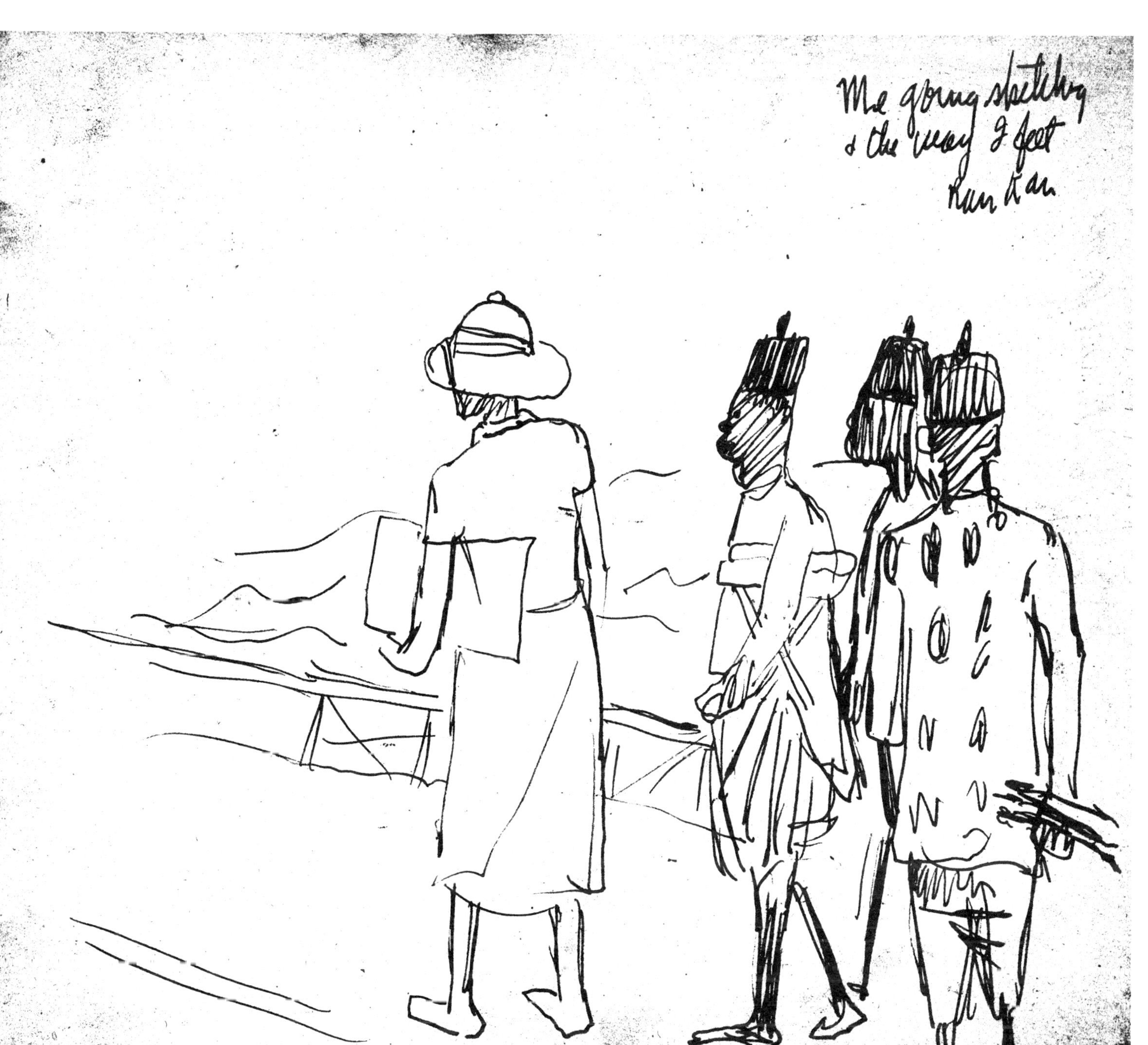

WENT TO THE NIGER RIVER THIS MORNING AND DID

SOME SKETCHES AND A PAINTING. IT'S HOTTERN HELL

HERE. THE WELLS ARE RUNNING DRY. AM NOT FEEL-

ING SO WELL.

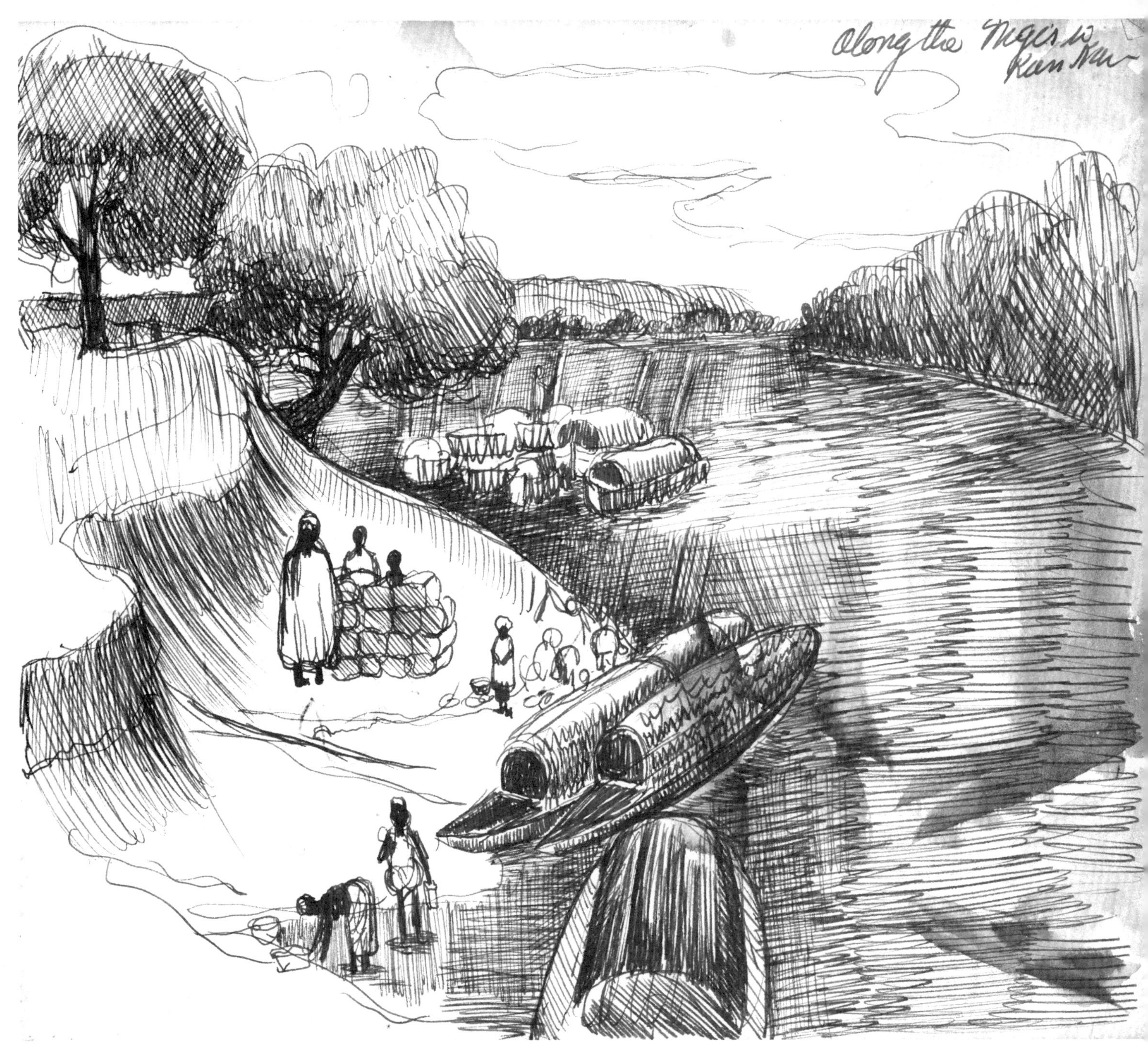

I WENT TO THE RIVER LOOKING FOR CROCODILES. WENT 16 KILOS OUT. SOME WOMEN GAVE ME EGGS, PEANUTS AND TOMATOES. I FOUND A PLACE TO LIE AND EAT. BUILT A BEDLIKE AFFAIR AND WENT TO SLEEP. RODE MY BIKE TO ANOTHER TOWN AND NAPPED IN A NATIVE BED. THEN WENT WADING IN THE STREAM WHERE CROCODILES INHABIT. SAW PEOPLE WITH AWFUL ULCERS. GOT TERRIBLY SUNBURNT.

WENT TO THE OTHER SIDE OF THE NIGER RIVER TODAY.

A BUNCH OF THE WILDEST NATIVES SURROUNDED ME

AND WAS SORT OF SCARED BUT JUST SAT AND

SKETCHED THEM. HOWEVER THE SKETCH WAS LOUSY.

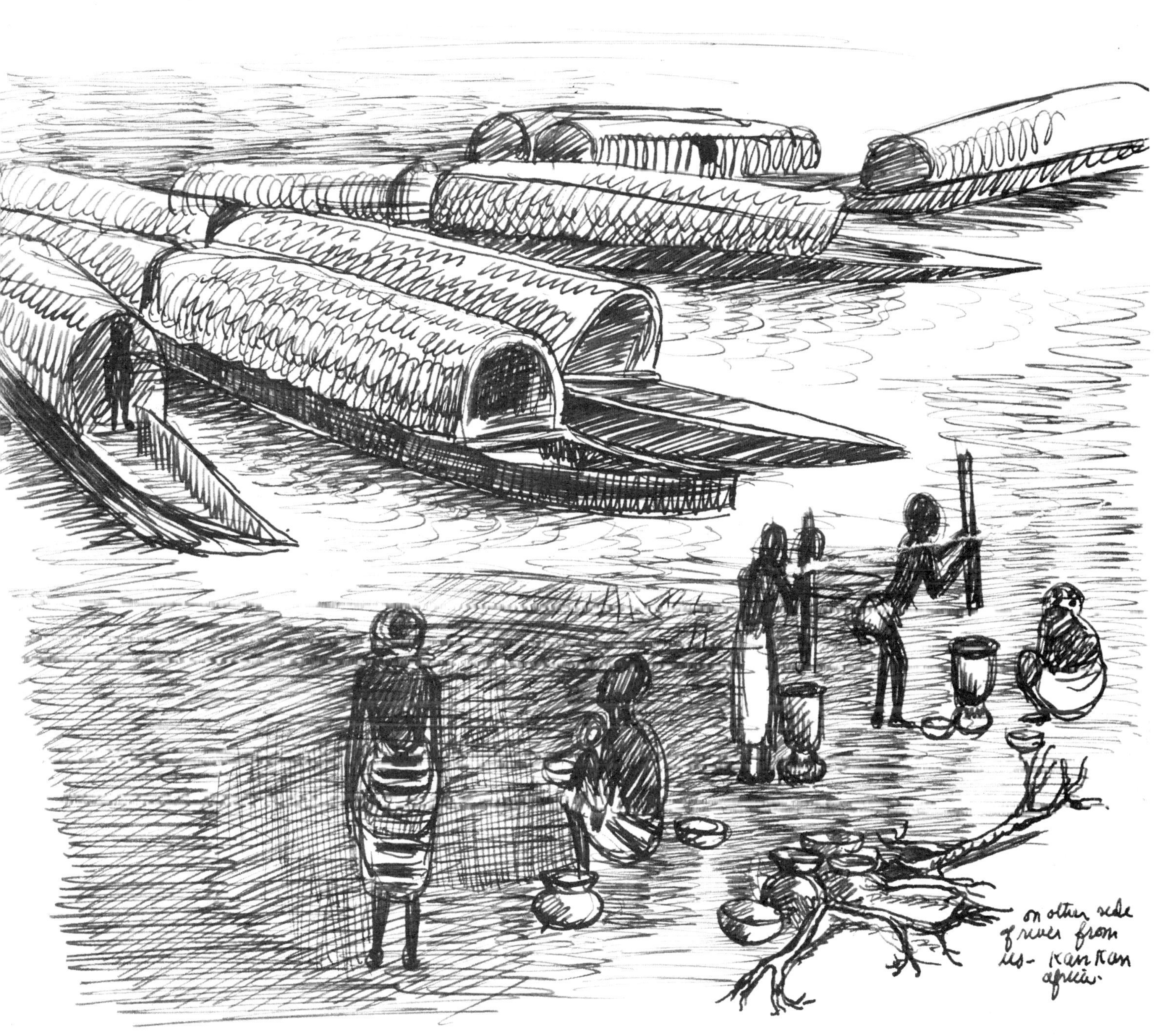

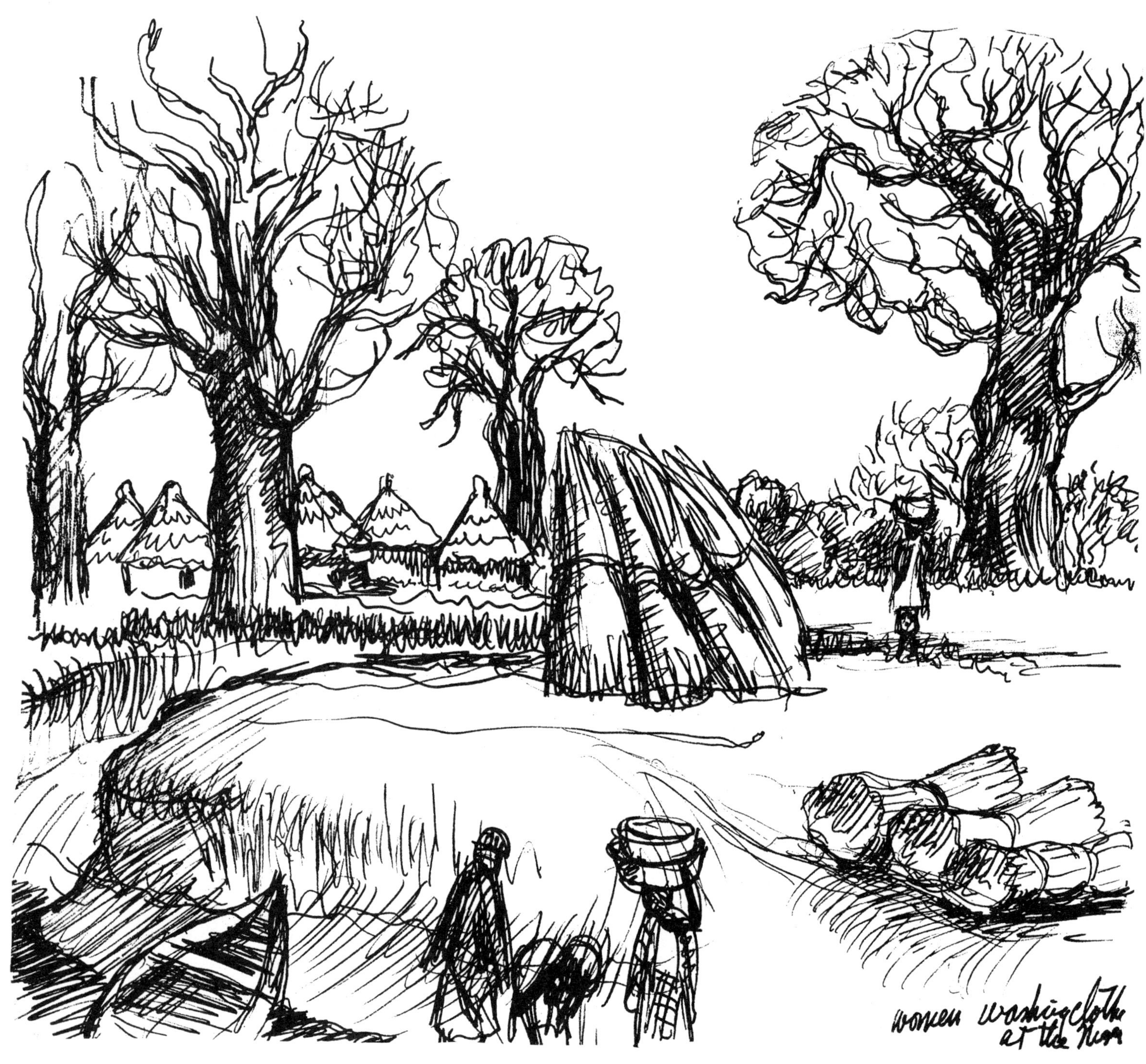

MARCH 27

I TOOK A LITTLE MORE QUININE TODAY AS I
THINK I HAVE MALARIA.

THIS COUNTRY IS KNOWN AS THE WHITE MAN'S GRAVE.

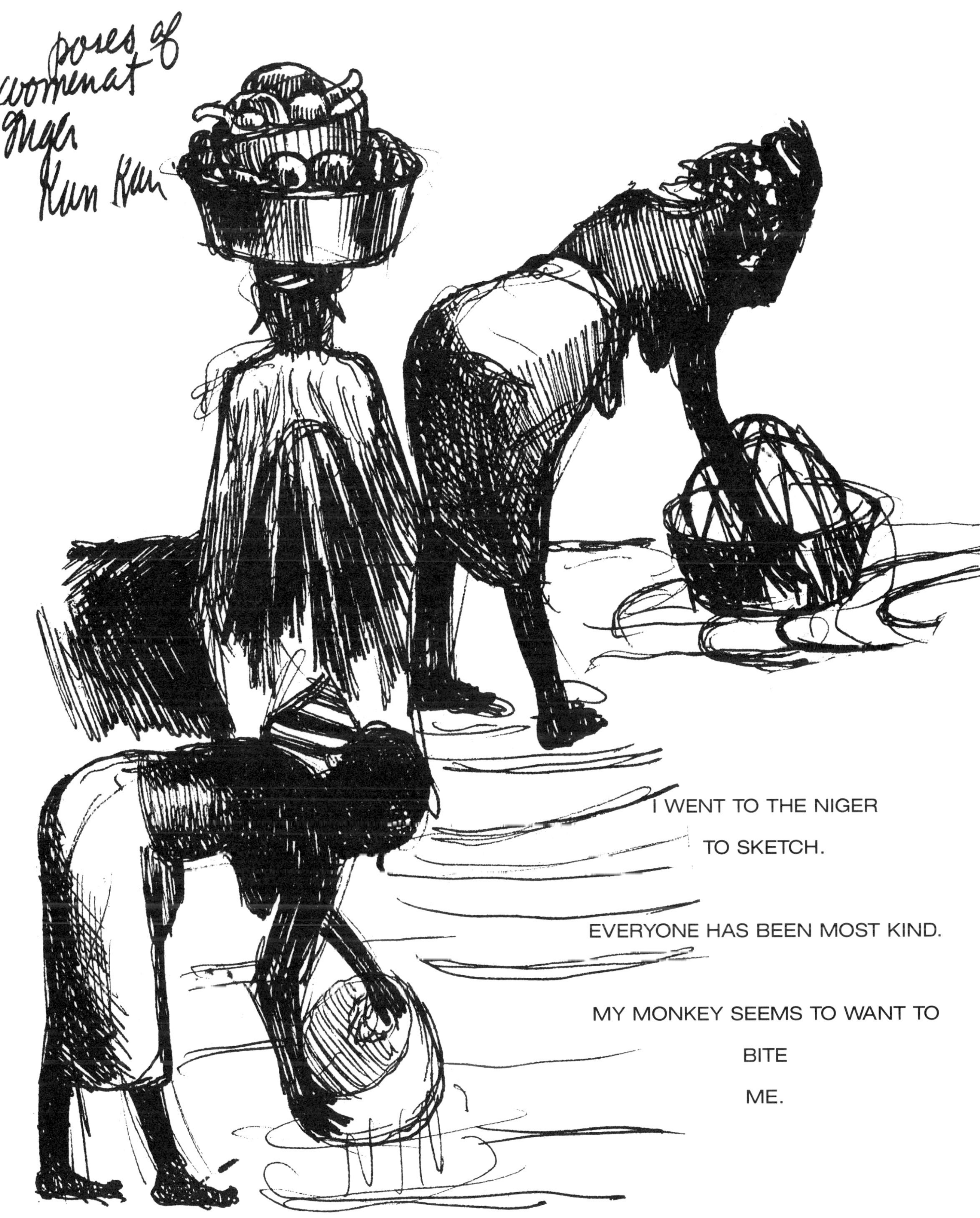
poses of
women at
Niger
Kan Kan
I WENT TO THE NIGER
TO SKETCH.

EVERYONE HAS BEEN MOST KIND.

MY MONKEY SEEMS TO WANT TO
BITE
ME.

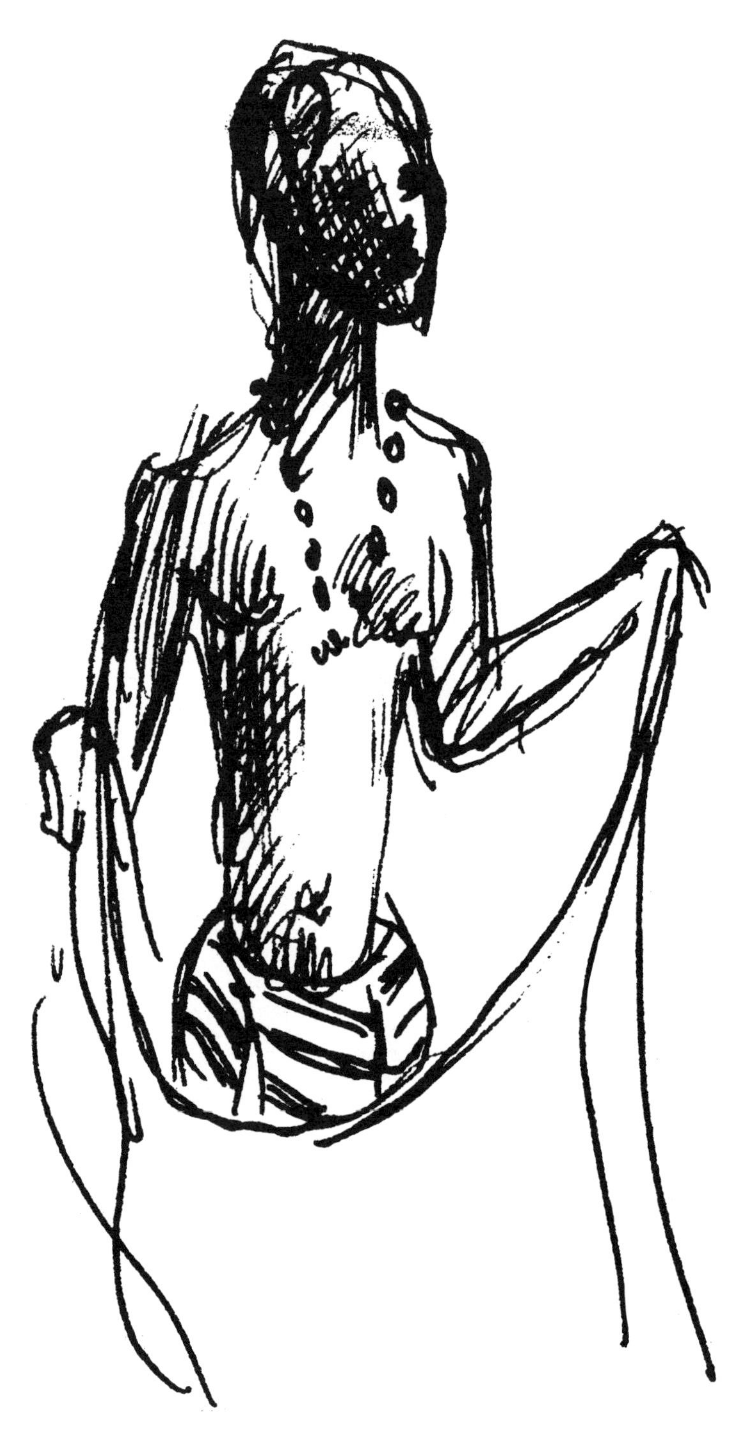

I ASKED A WOMAN TO POSE FOR ME

SHE GOT SCARED

AND RAN AWAY.

MENSTRUATING

WOMEN

MUST LEAVE

THE TRIBE,

GO AWAY

FOR

A

FEW

DAYS.

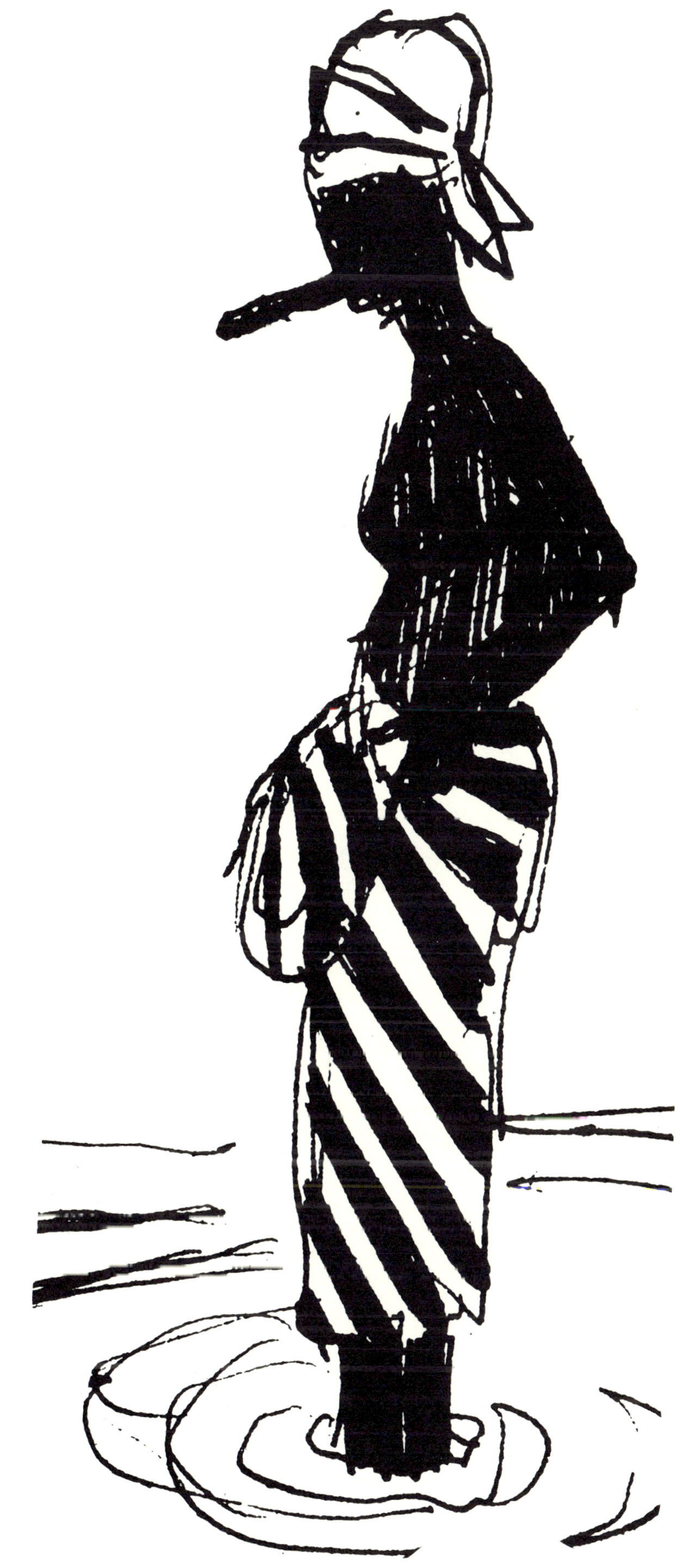

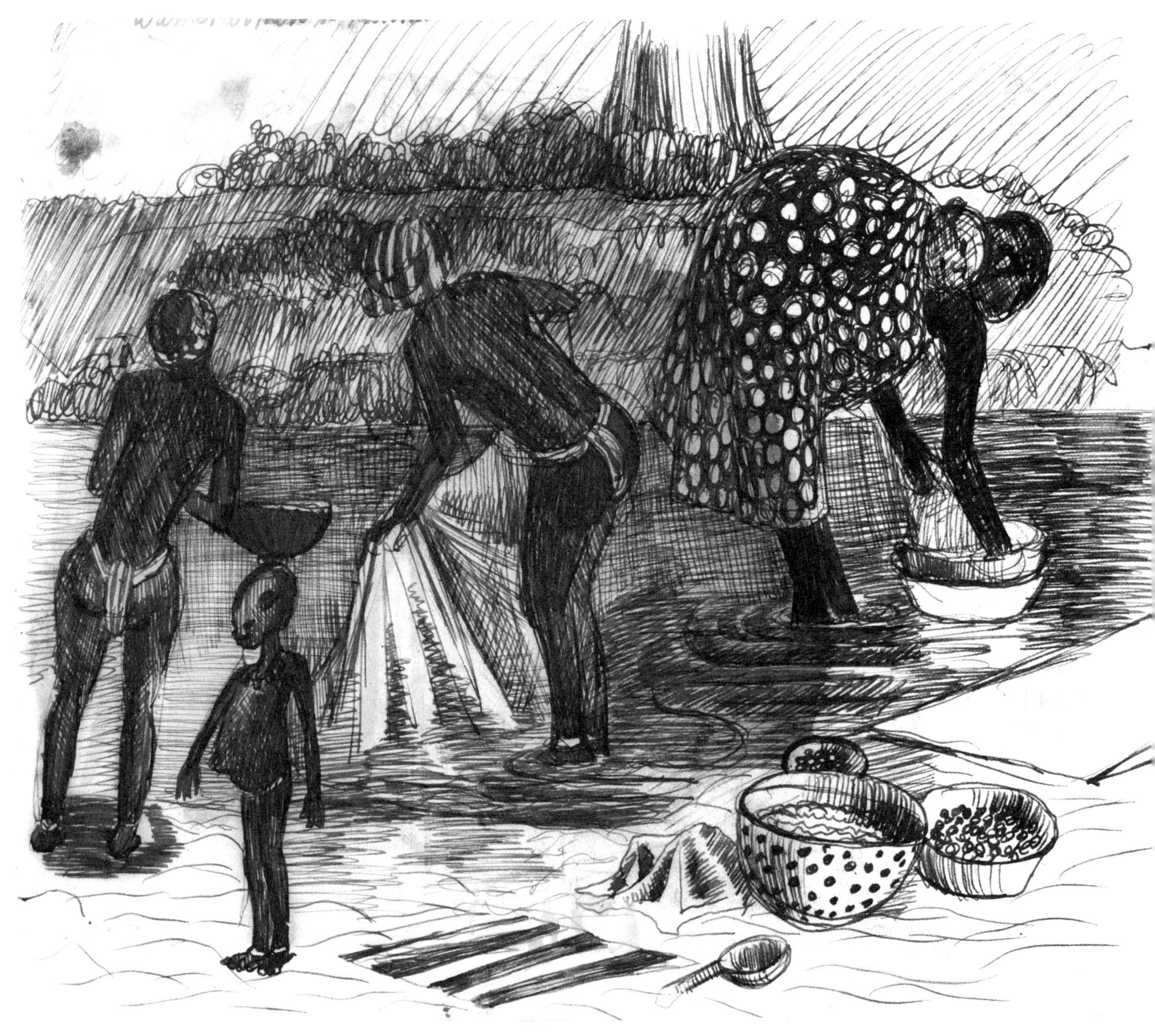

MARCH 31

WOMEN WITH BAWLING CHILDREN TOLD THEM I WOULD TAKE THEM IF THEY DIDN'T STOP CRYING.

HAD TO GET RID OF MONKEY. I THINK IT HAD DISTEMPER. IT BIT ME IN THE LEG.

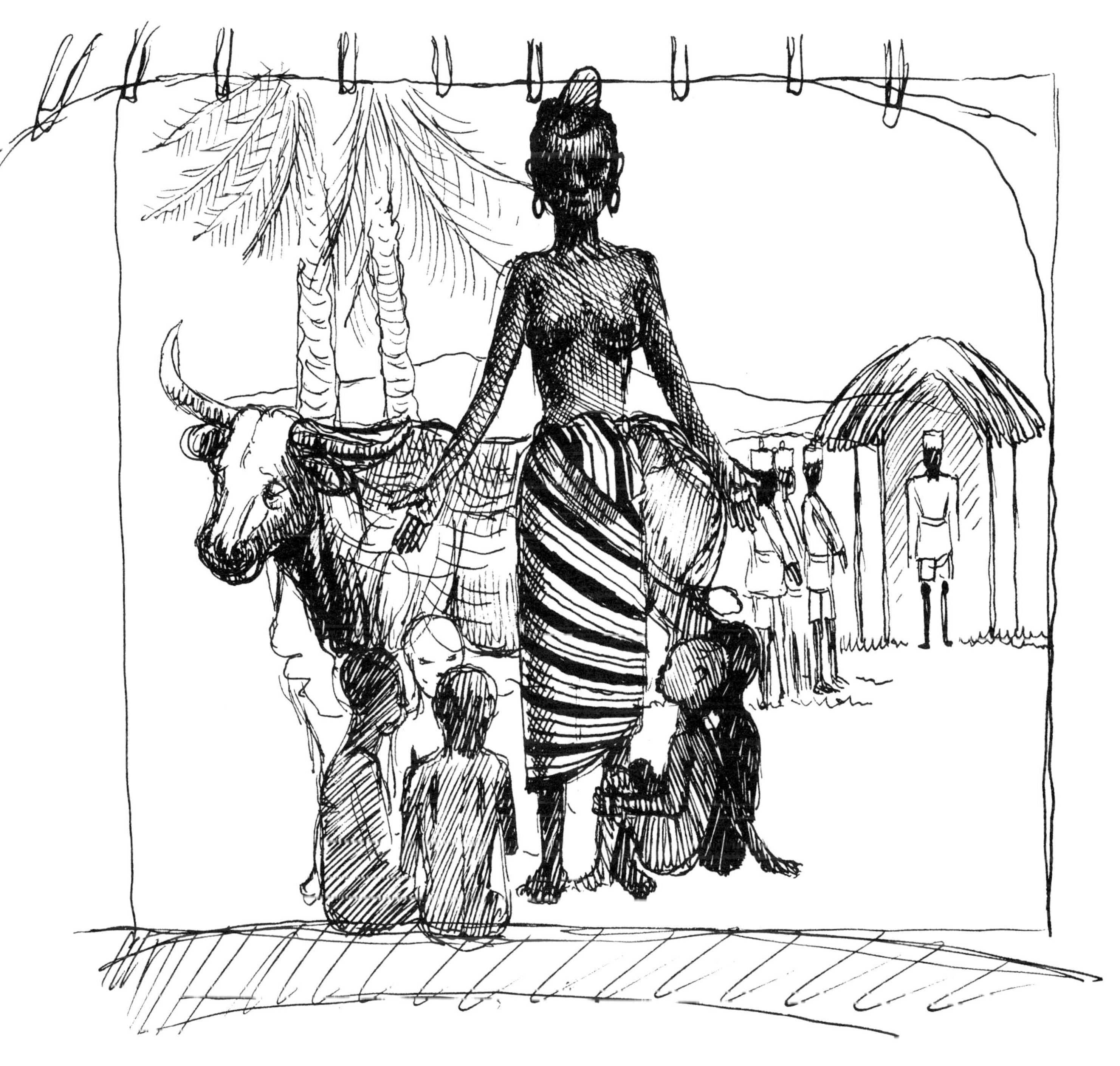

A WOMAN POSED FOR ME WITH HER FIVE BOYS.

ONE WAS ALBINO.

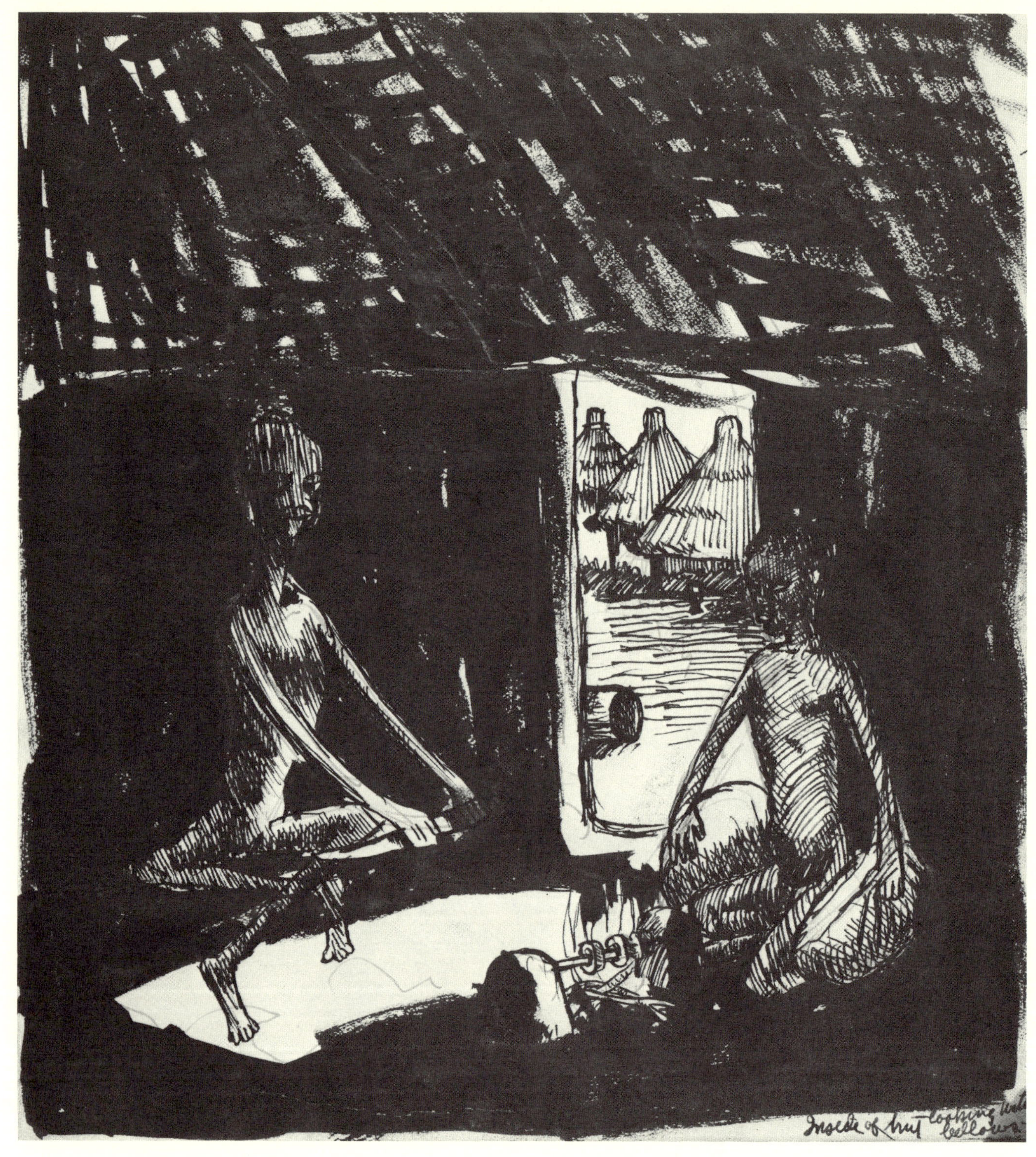

APRIL 8

I HAD BREAKFAST IN A NATIVE HUT. I TOLD THEM I WANTED TO SKETCH. THEY HAD THE MOST BEAUTIFUL GIRL IN THE NEIGHBORHOOD COOK FOR ME SO I COULD DRAW HER.

A LETTER TO CHARLES FABENS KELLEY, DEAN OF THE SCHOOL, THE ART INSTITUTE OF CHICAGO:

IT'S TERRIFICALLY HOT WHERE I AM IN KANKAN, BUT THE NATIVES HAVE GIVEN ME A MUD HOUSE, THATCHED ROOF. I HAVE ONLY TO PAY FOR MY FOOD WHICH IS 7 FRANCS A DAY, ABOUT 35 CENTS. I HAVE NEVER WORKED SO HARD AS DOWN HERE. ALL ONE HAS TO DO IS TO LOOK DOWN THE STREET TO HAVE MURALS WALK RIGHT PAST . . . . THE NATIVES KNOW I AM AN AMERICAN AND THEY THINK AMERICANS CAN DO ANYTHING. THEY ARE VERY POLITE TO ME, BUT IT'S HARD TO WIN THEIR CONFIDENCE. THEY ARE VERY SUSPICIOUS WHEN THEY SEE ME SKETCHING THEM. HOWEVER, NOW I EVEN WALK INTO THE NATIVE HUTS AND THEY DO NOT MIND . . . . THEY GAVE ME A BOY NAMED "BAH" TO COOK FOR ME. WHEN THEY SAW ME COMING THIS MORNING, THEY DRESSED UP THE MOST BEAUTIFUL GIRL IN THE VILLAGE TO COOK PANCAKES AND WHILE SHE WAS DOING IT I COULD SKETCH HER.

THIS IS THE BEST PLACE IN THE WORLD TO PAINT.

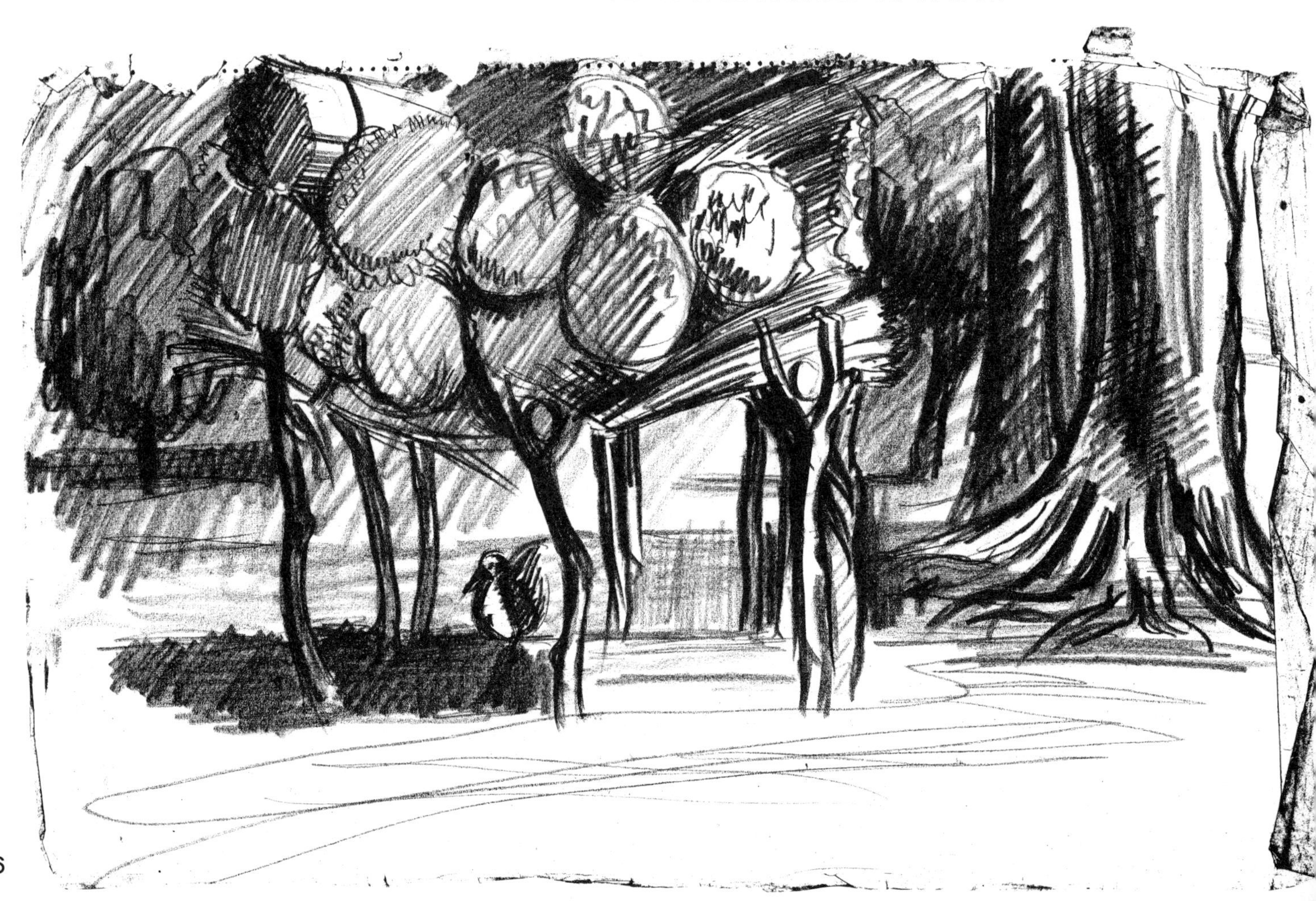

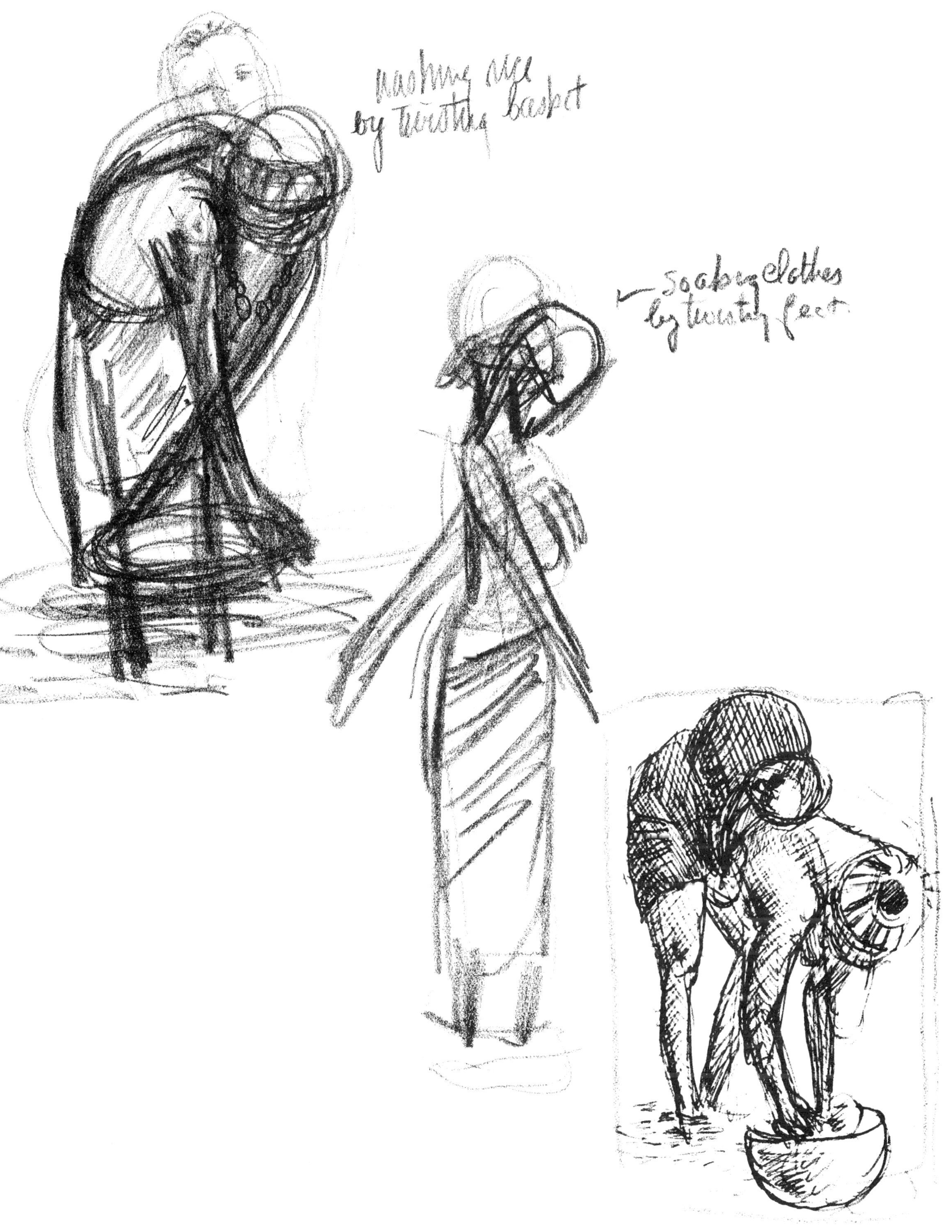

washing rice
by twisting basket

soaking clothes
by twisting feet

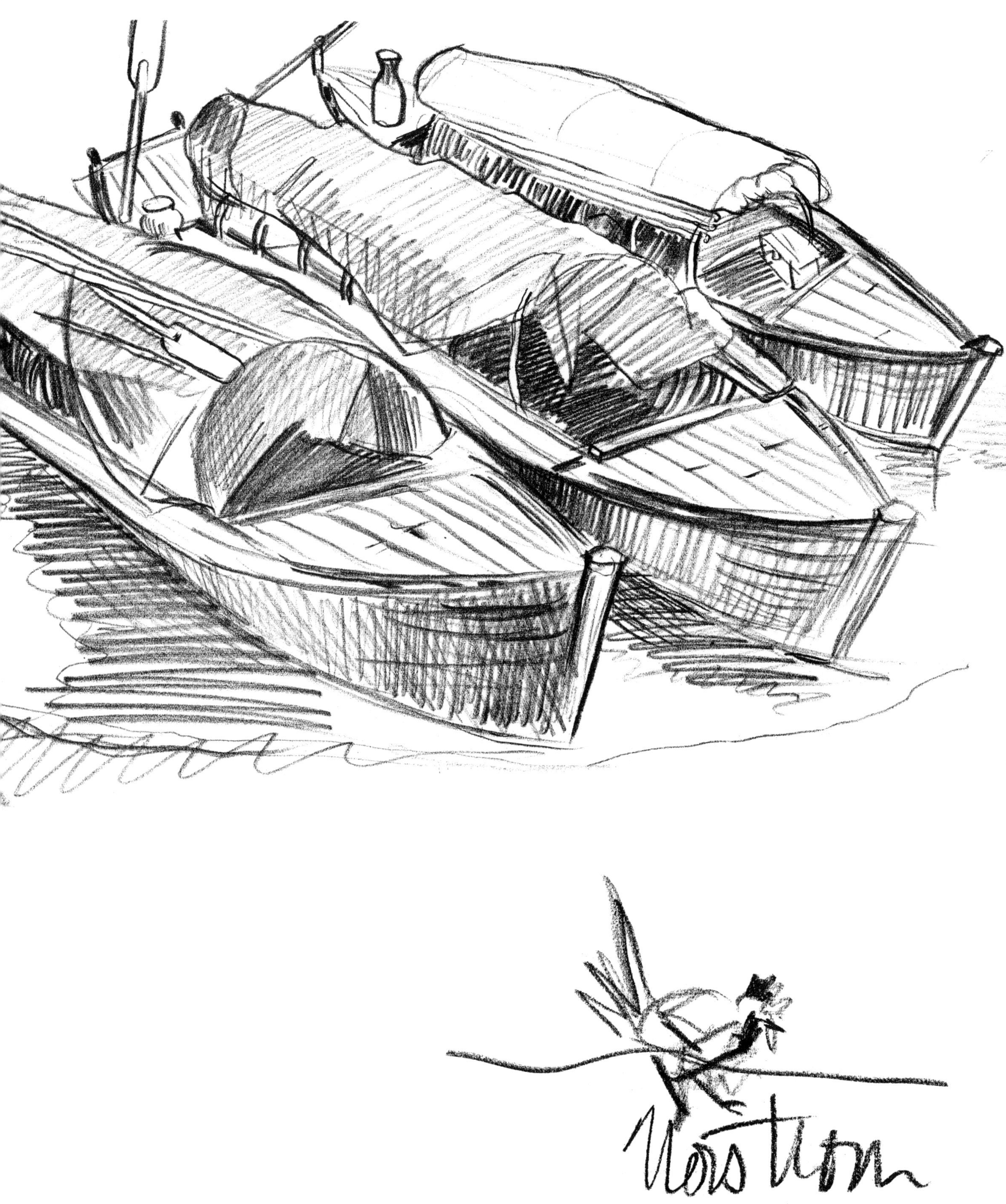

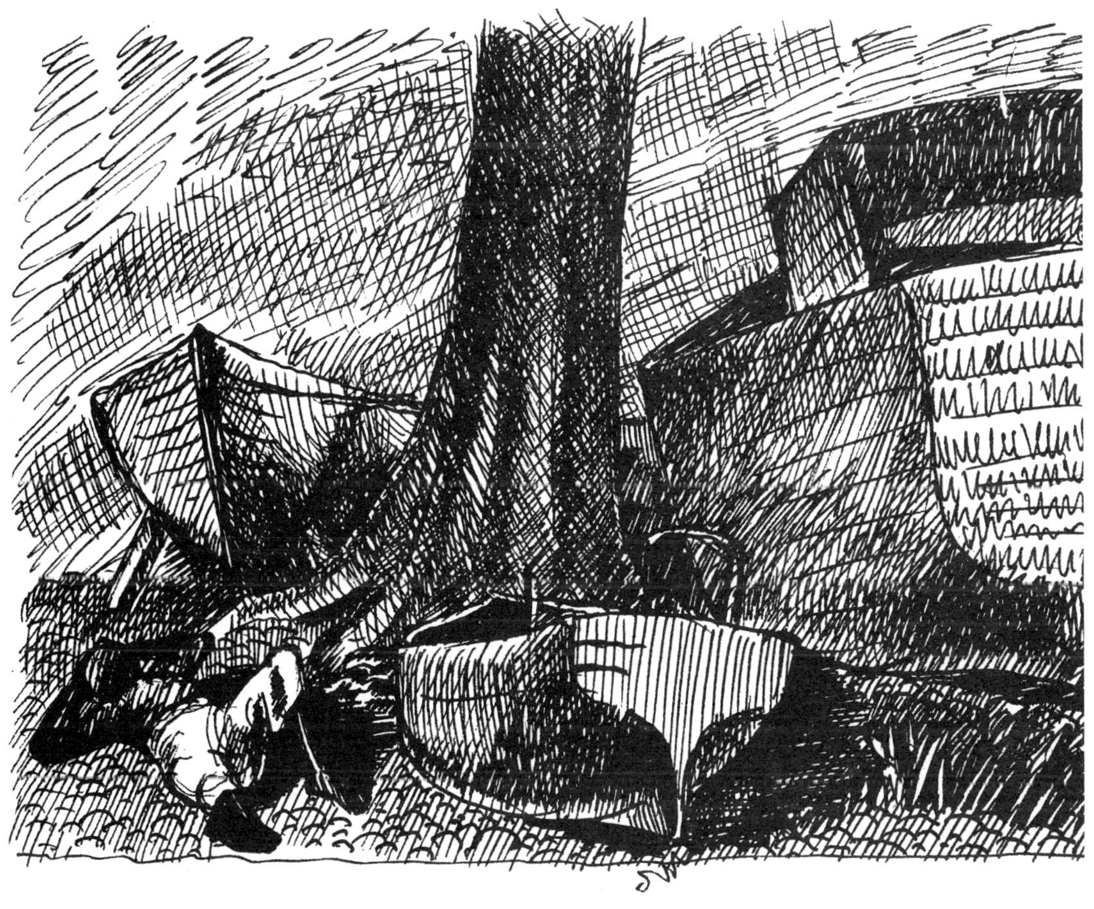

I WENT FOR A WALK IN THE MOONLIGHT. A LOT OF COWS AND BULLS. AFRICA IS LONELY AT NIGHT. WENT TO THE RIVER, SHOWED MY FLASHLIGHT ON THE BOATS. THE LIGHT SHINED ON FACES OF PEOPLE SLEEPING. THEY WERE MAD, BUT IN THE MORNING THEY INVITED ME TO SEE THEM BAKE PANCAKES AND WATCH IVORY CARVERS.

WENT TO ANOTHER FETISH DANCE. BEING THE ONLY WHITE PERSON, THEY ALL POKED ON ME AND MADE FUNNY SALUTES. THEY KEPT GETTING CLOSER AND CLOSER TO ME. I WAS SURE TO GET MOBBED. THE CHIEF DANCER HAD ALL HIS WOMEN DANCE AND THE PEPPIEST WAS MORE IN HIS FAVOR.

SAW A BOY FLOGGED FOR STEALING MANGOS. THEY ARE NOT ALLOWED TO EAT THEM TILL THEY'RE RIPE. THEY GET THREE TRIALS AND THEN ARE FLOGGED AND FINED 15 FRANCS. THIS YOUNG BOY CRIED UN-MERCIFULLY.

I CAN SURE EAT NATIVE FOOD.

THE NATIVES AROUND HERE
HAVE BEEN EYEING ME UP ALREADY
FOR A POTATO STEW.

SAT UNDER A MANGO TREE AND GOT COVERED WITH ANTS. MEN HELPED PICK THEM OFF.

LAST NIGHT I SAW A SNAKE CRAWL OVER MY MOSQUITO NET. THE NET CAME DOWN ON ME. I THOUGHT THE DEVIL HAD ME.

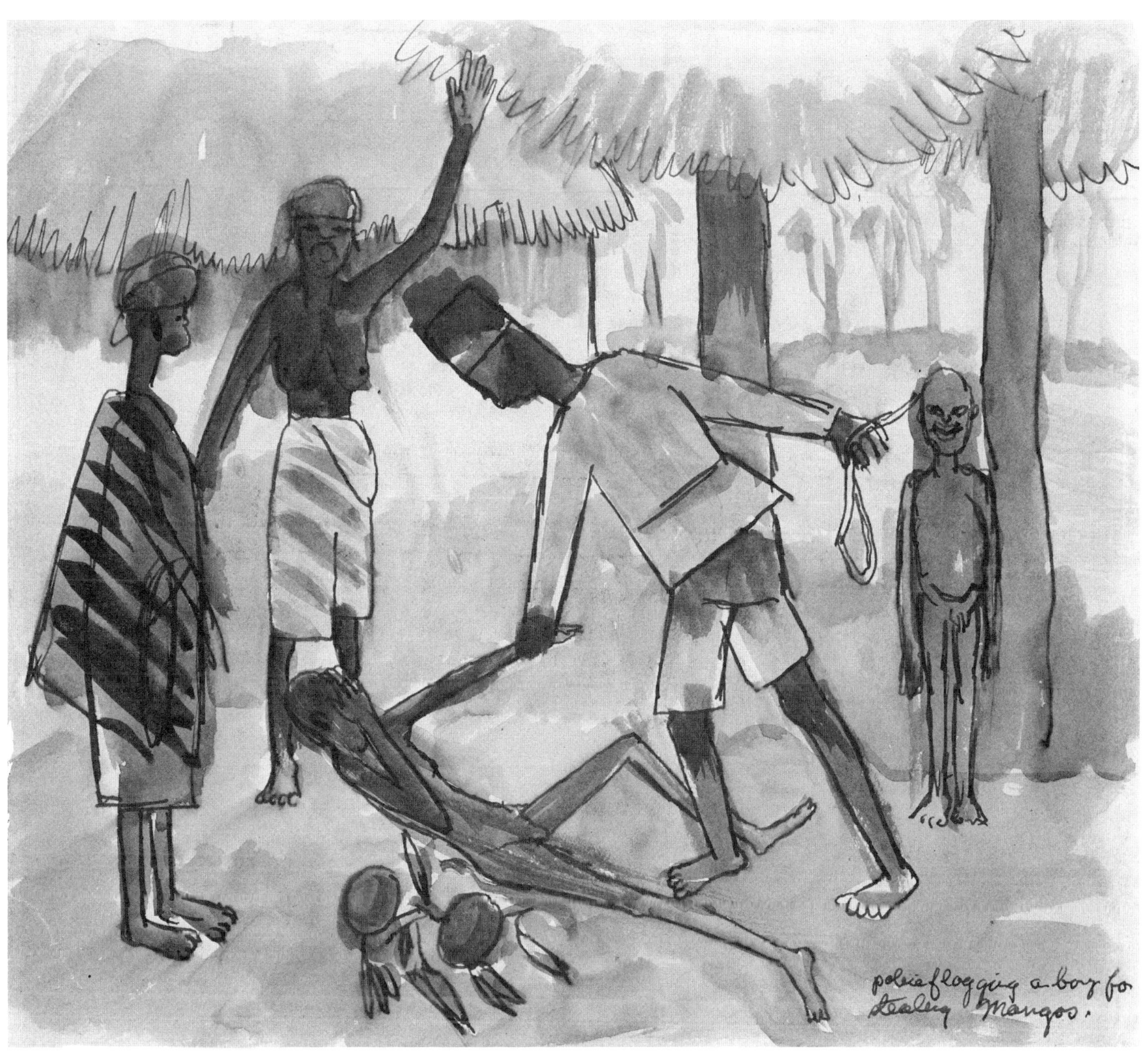

police flogging a boy for
stealing mangos.

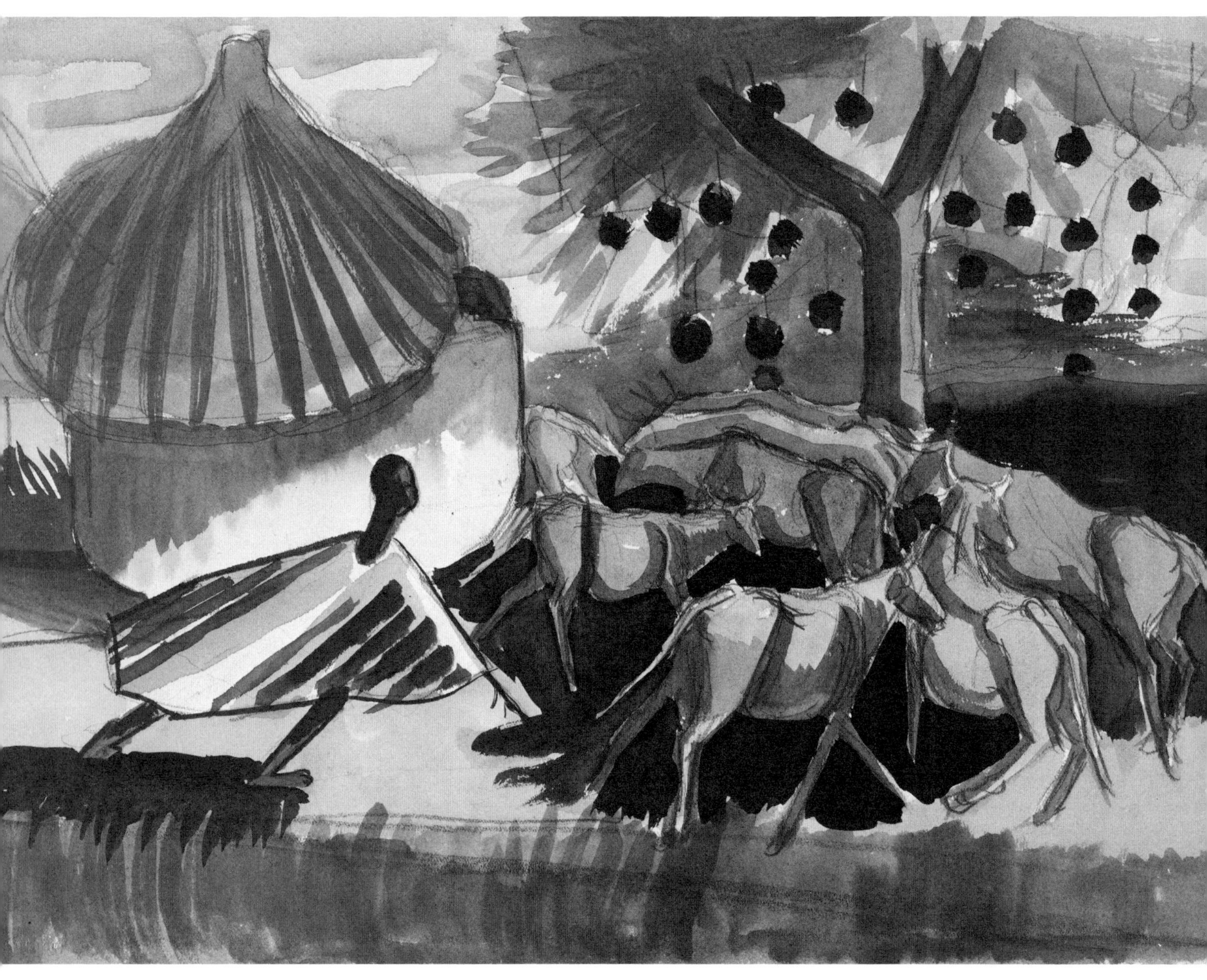

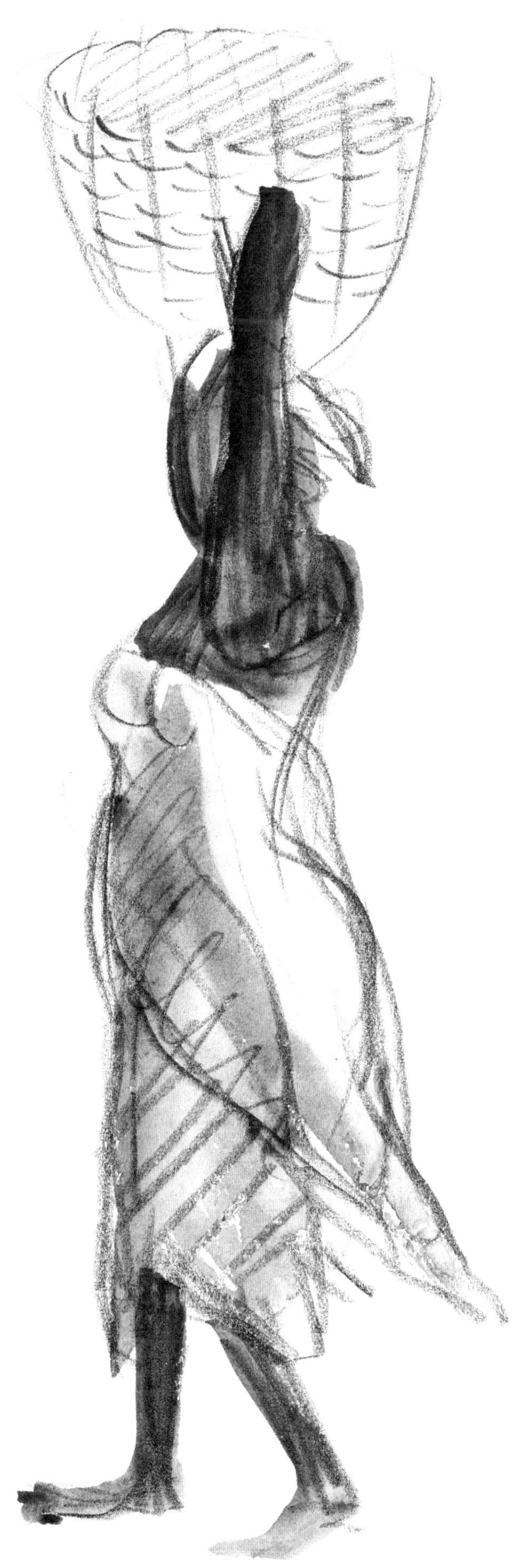

A
LADY
IN
KAN KAN
CAME
TO
SEE
ME.

HER
NAME
IS
MISS
SAYA.

MADE
ARRANGEMENTS
TO
TEACH
SOME
CHILDREN
TO
PAINT.

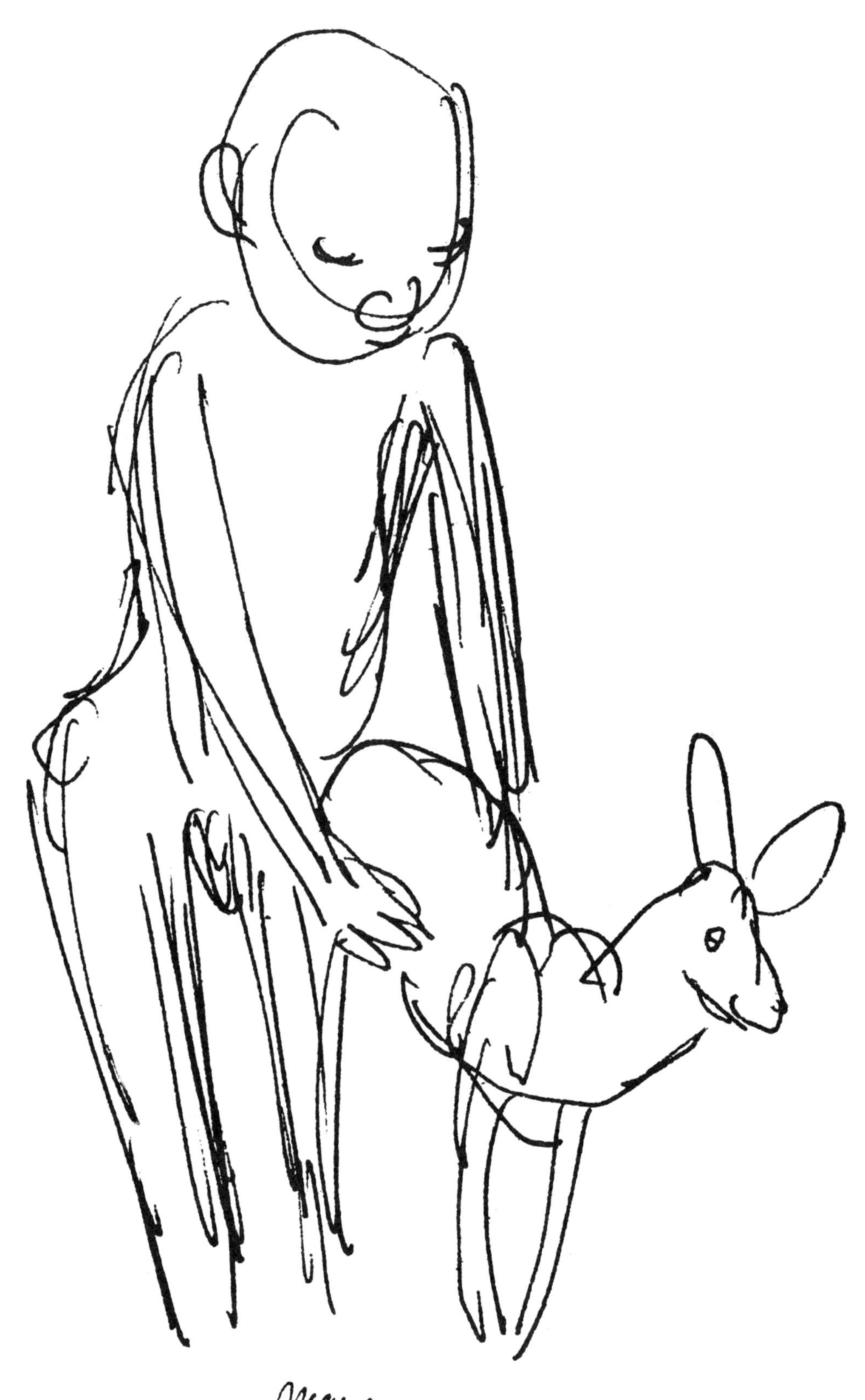

54

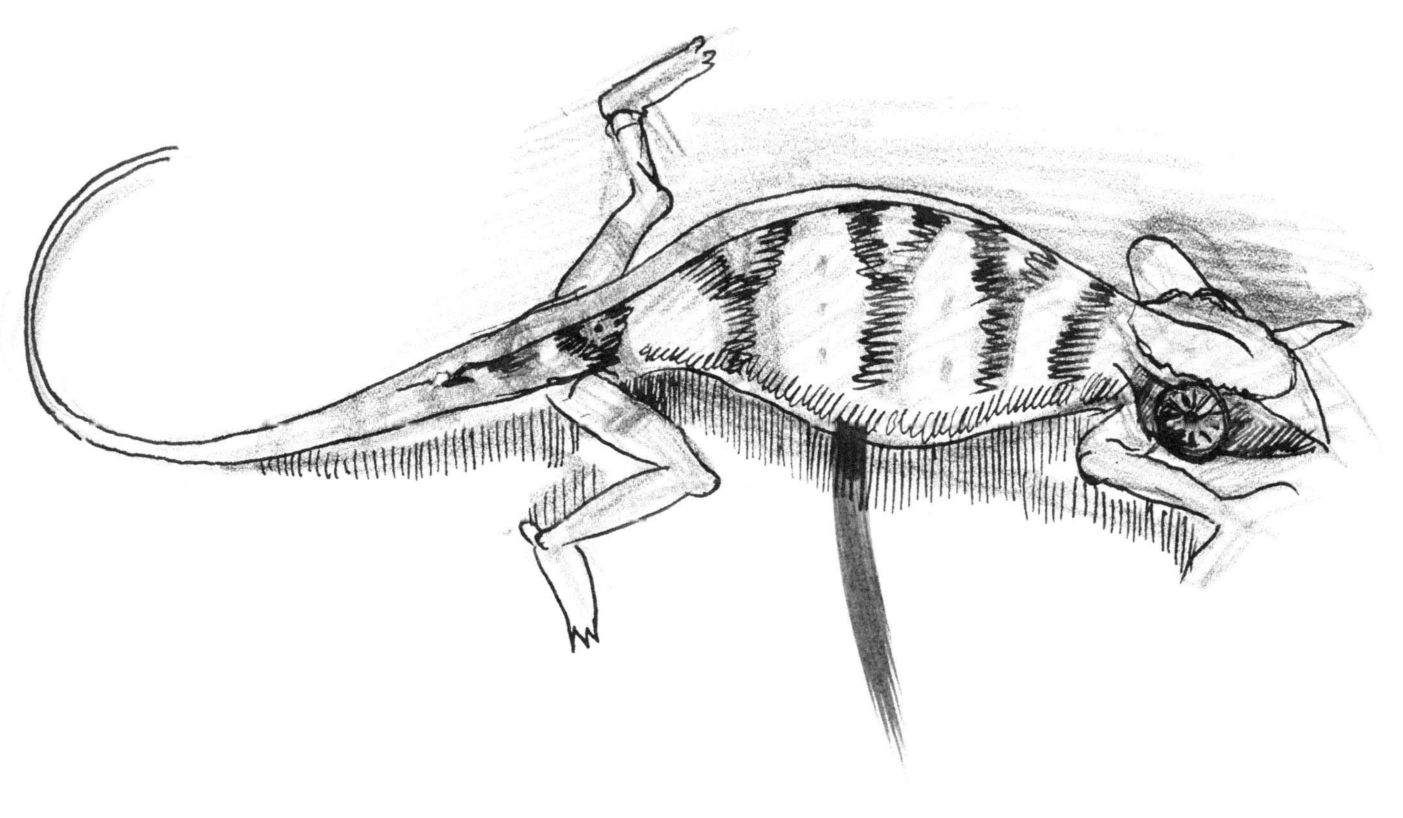

PAMA BROUGHT ME A CHAMELEON

AND A LOT OF INSECTS TO SKETCH.

Having read
the queen - a large worm like termite - if killed -
the other termites can make a queen out of
any of the eggs - how, no one knows - the
queen is about 50 times as large & entirely
different in appearance -

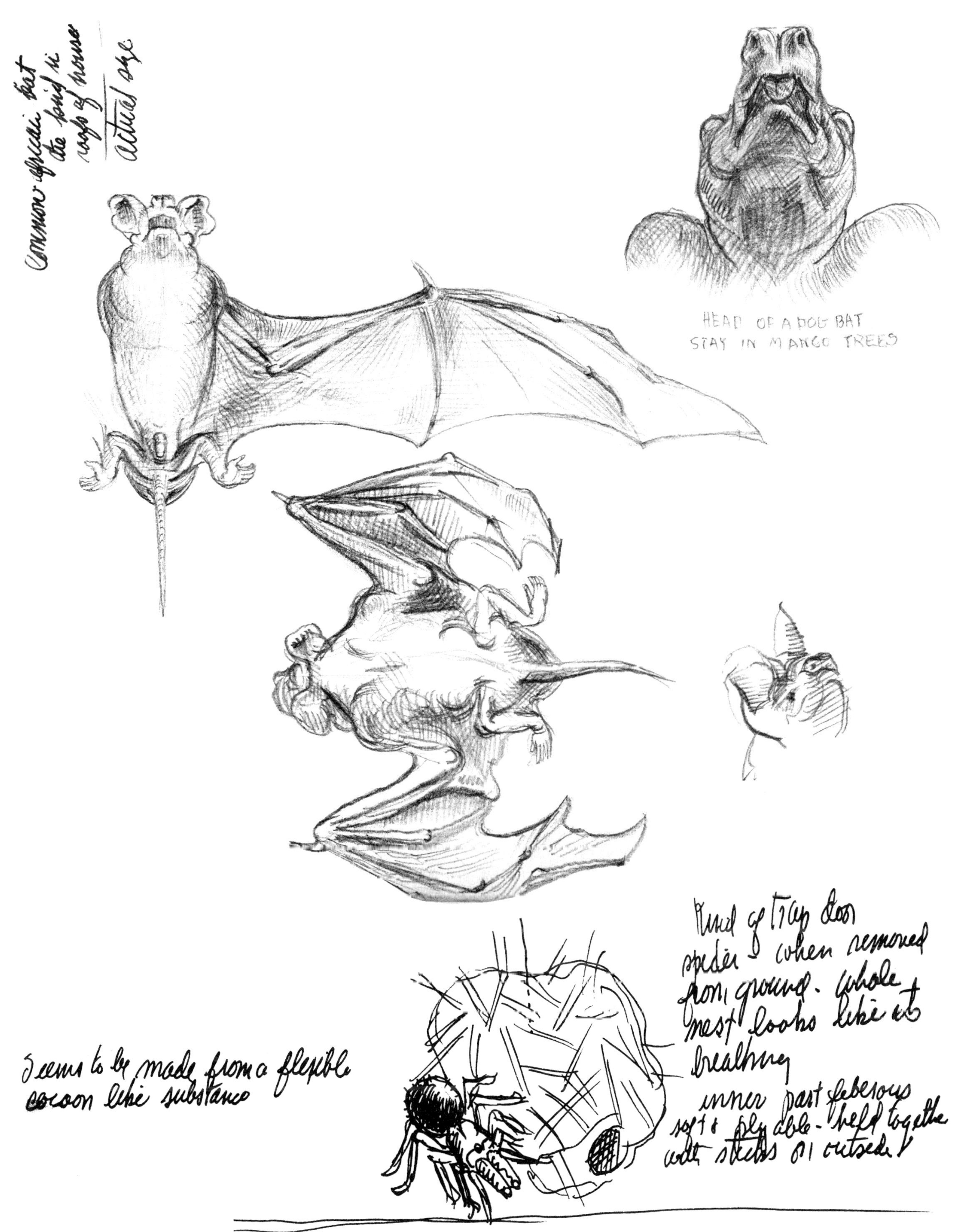

Common african bat that
the hind ti
rays of bones
actual size
HEAD OF A DOG BAT
STAY IN MANGO TREES
Seems to be made from a flexible
cocoon like substance
Kind of trap door
spider - when removed
from ground. Whole
nest looks like its
breathing
inner part feberous
soft & ply able - held togethe
with sticks on outside

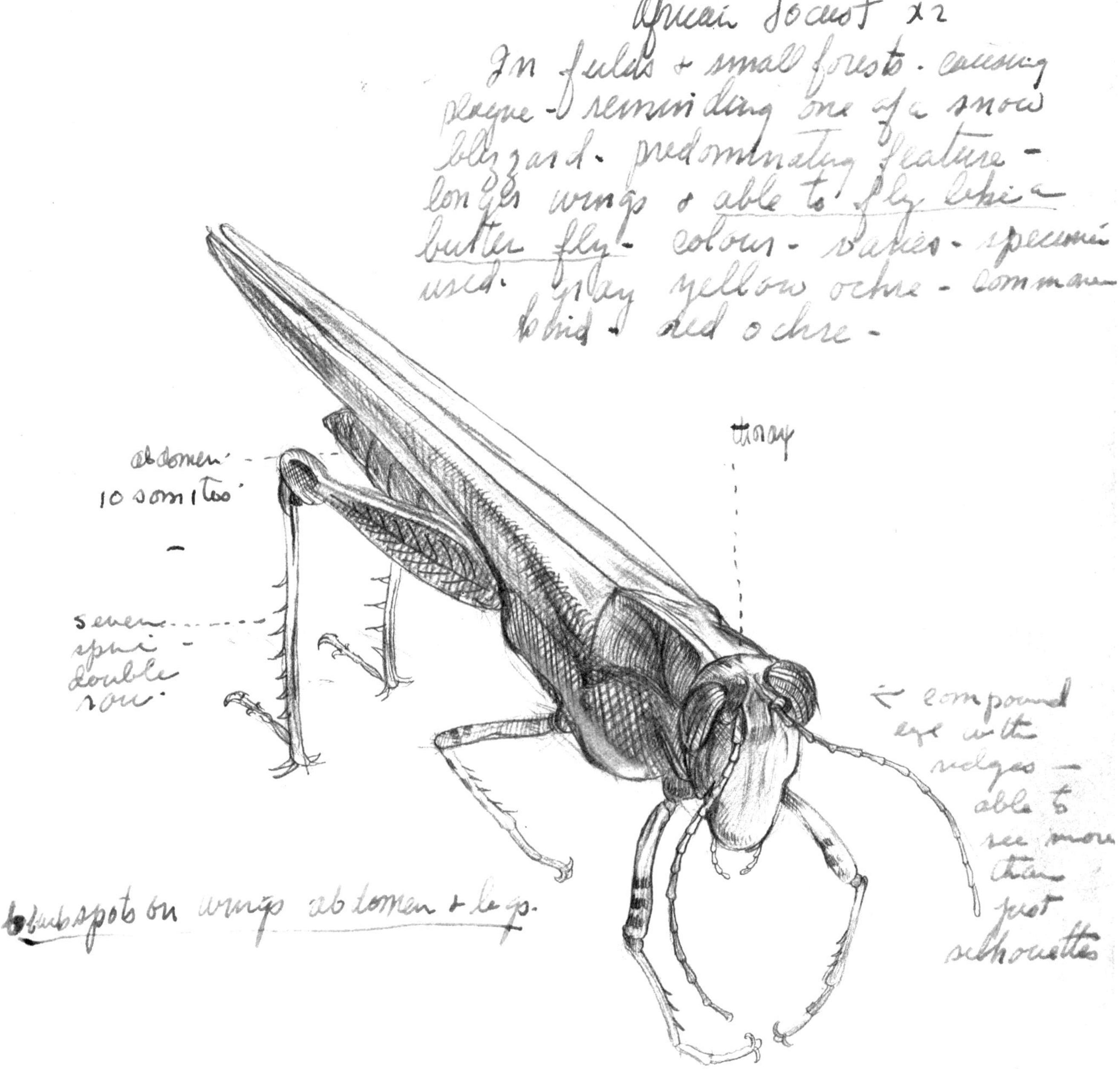

African Locust x2
In fields + small forests. causing
plague - reminding one of a snow
blizzard. predominating feature -
longer wings & able to fly like a
butter fly. colours. varies. specimen
used. grey yellow ochre - common
bird + red ochre -

abdomen
10 somites

seven
spine
double
row

thorax

← compound
eye with
ridges —
able to
see more
than
just
silhouettes

black spots on wings abdomen + legs.

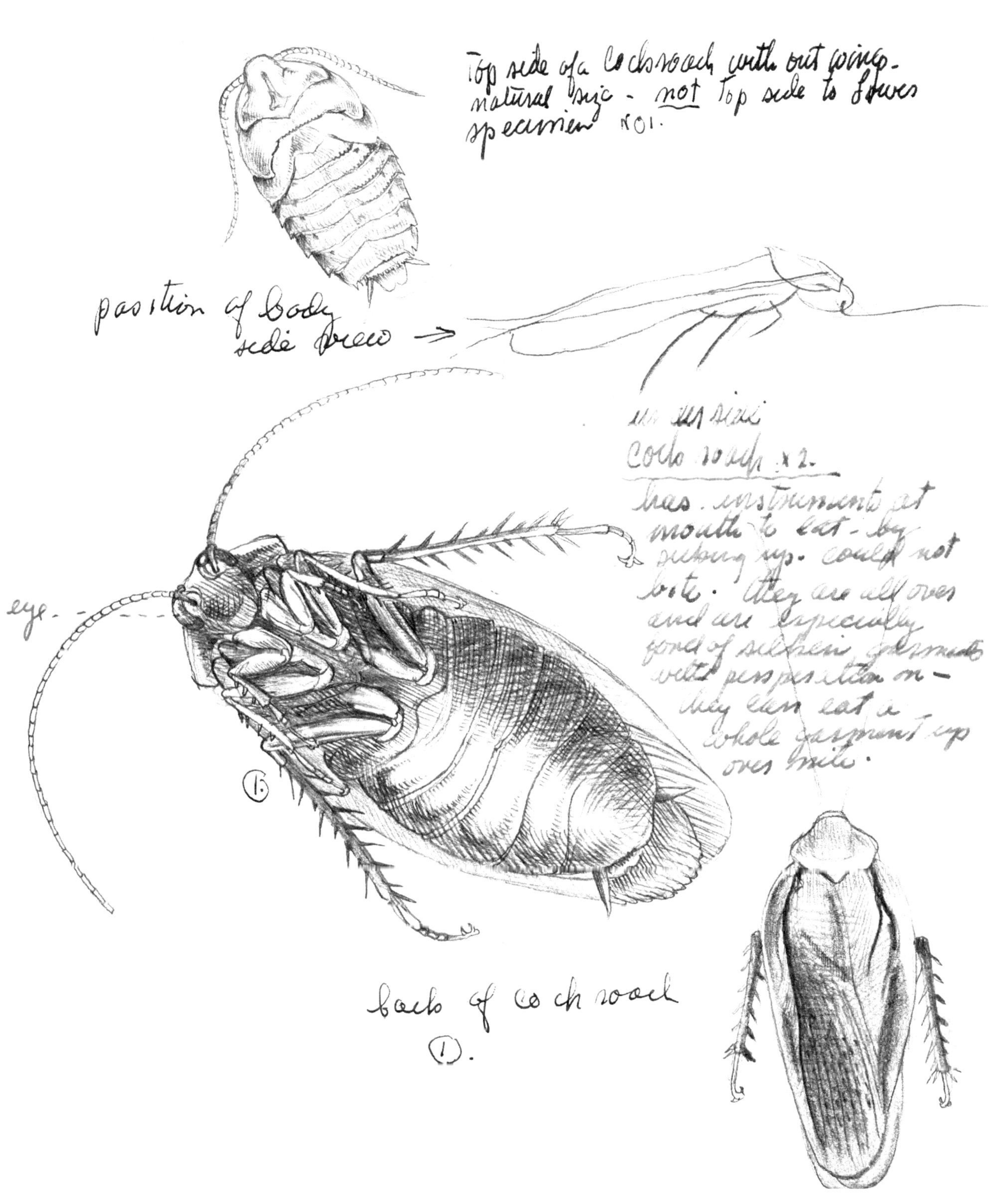

Top side of a Cockroach with out wings. natural size - not Top side to lower specimen No1.

position of body side view →

un ur size Cockroach x 2. has instruments at mouth to eat - by sucking up. could not bite. they are all over and are especially fond of silken garments with perspiration on - they can eat a whole garment up over nite.

eye. -

(b)

back of cockroach (1).

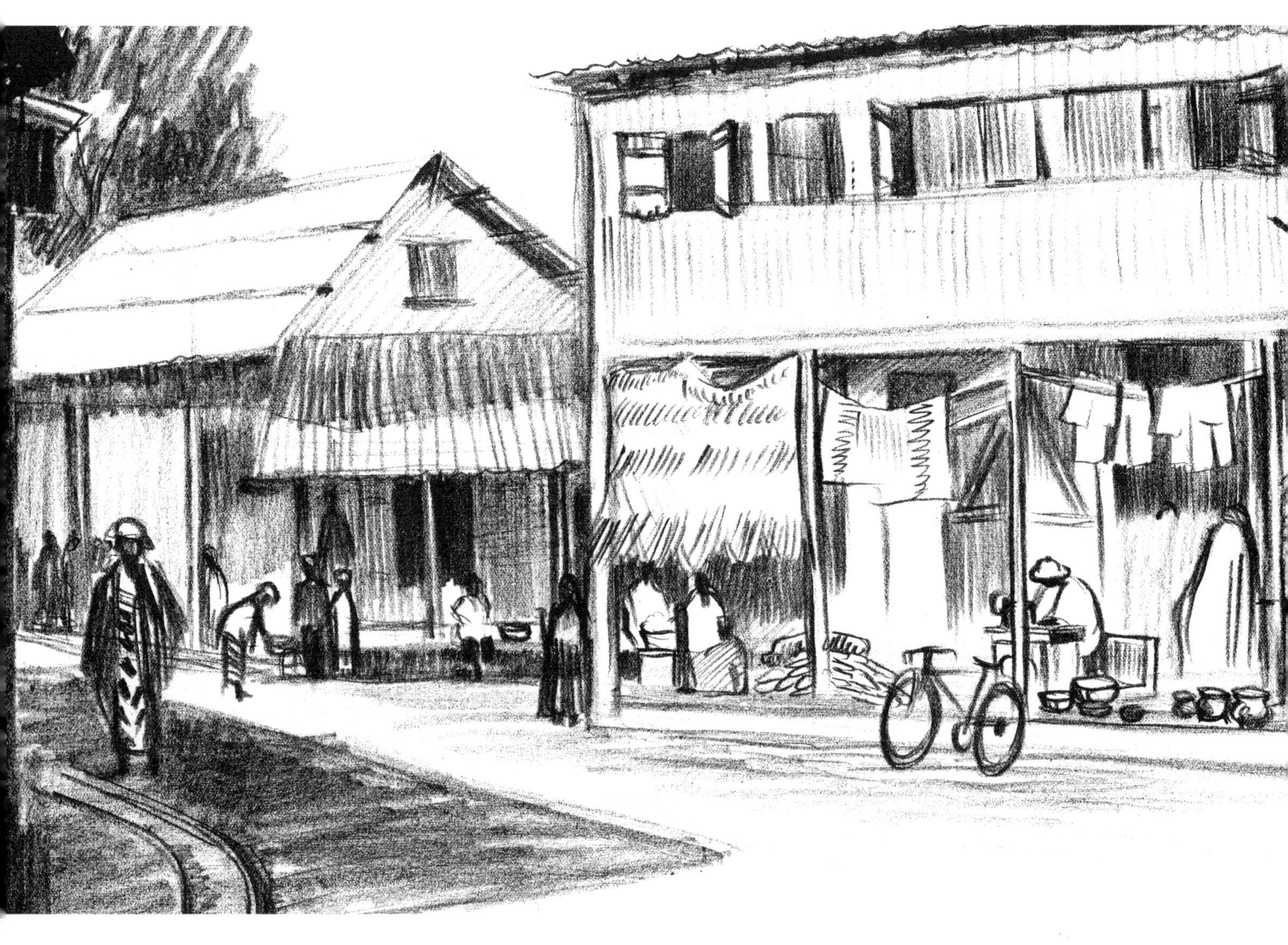

WENT FOR A BIKE RIDE. WHILE GOING UPHILL, A BULL WAS STANDING IN THE ROAD. I WAS SCARED TO PASS HIM, BUT SAW HIM START TOWARD THE BUSHES. I PASSED HIM AND HE REALLY WENT AFTER ME. I RODE STRAIGHT UP THE STEEP HILL AT 30 MILES AN HOUR.

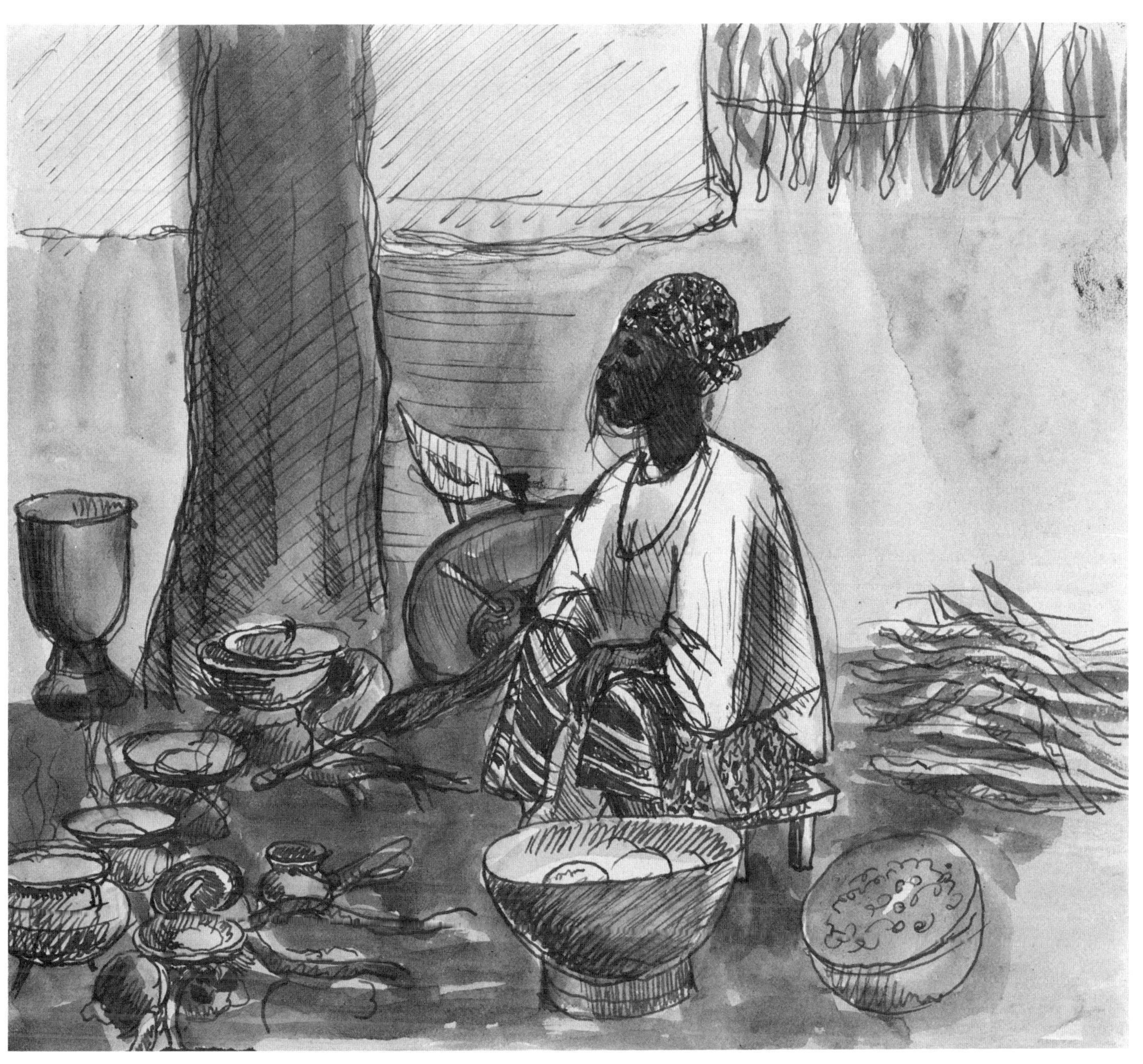

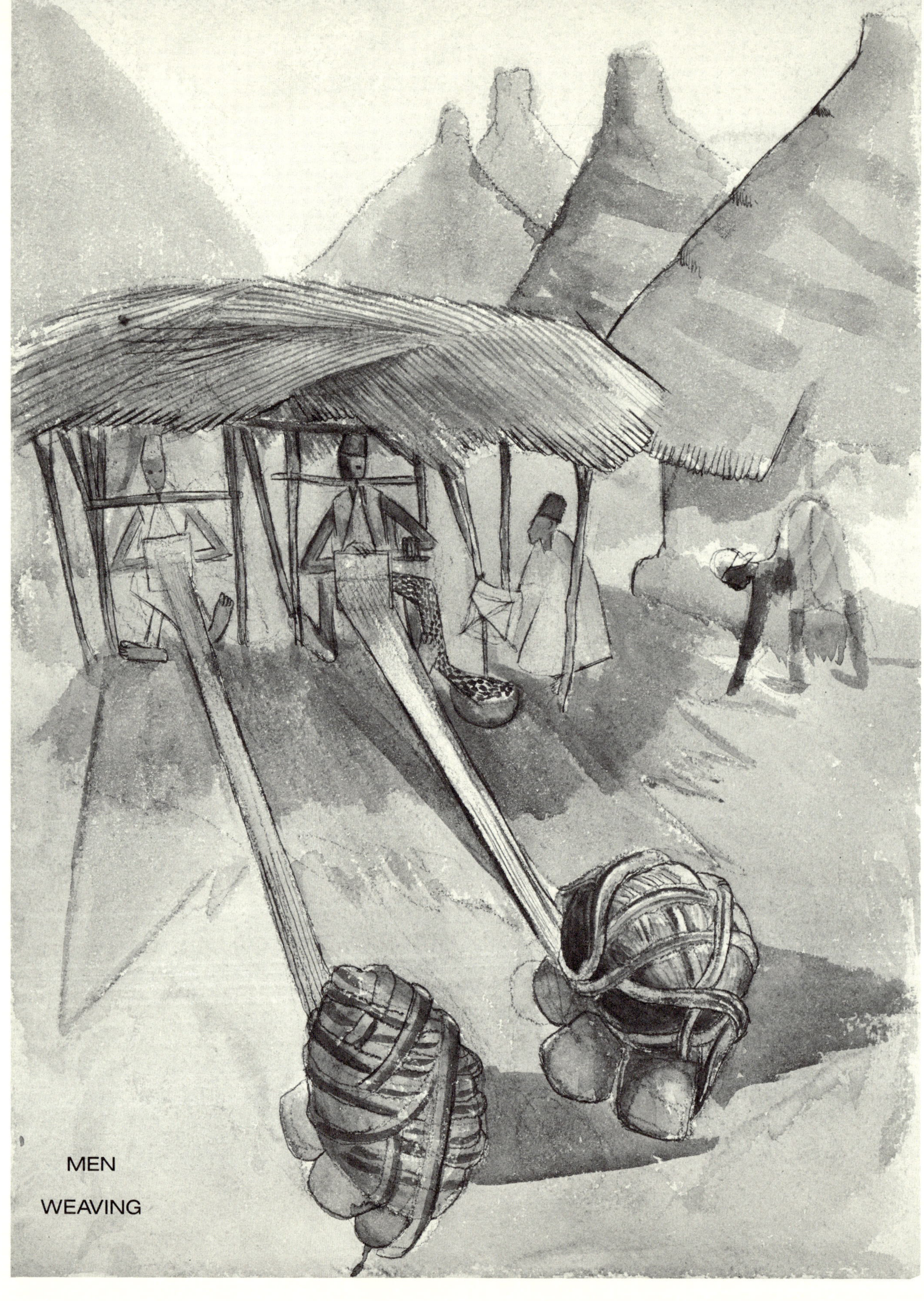

MEN

WEAVING

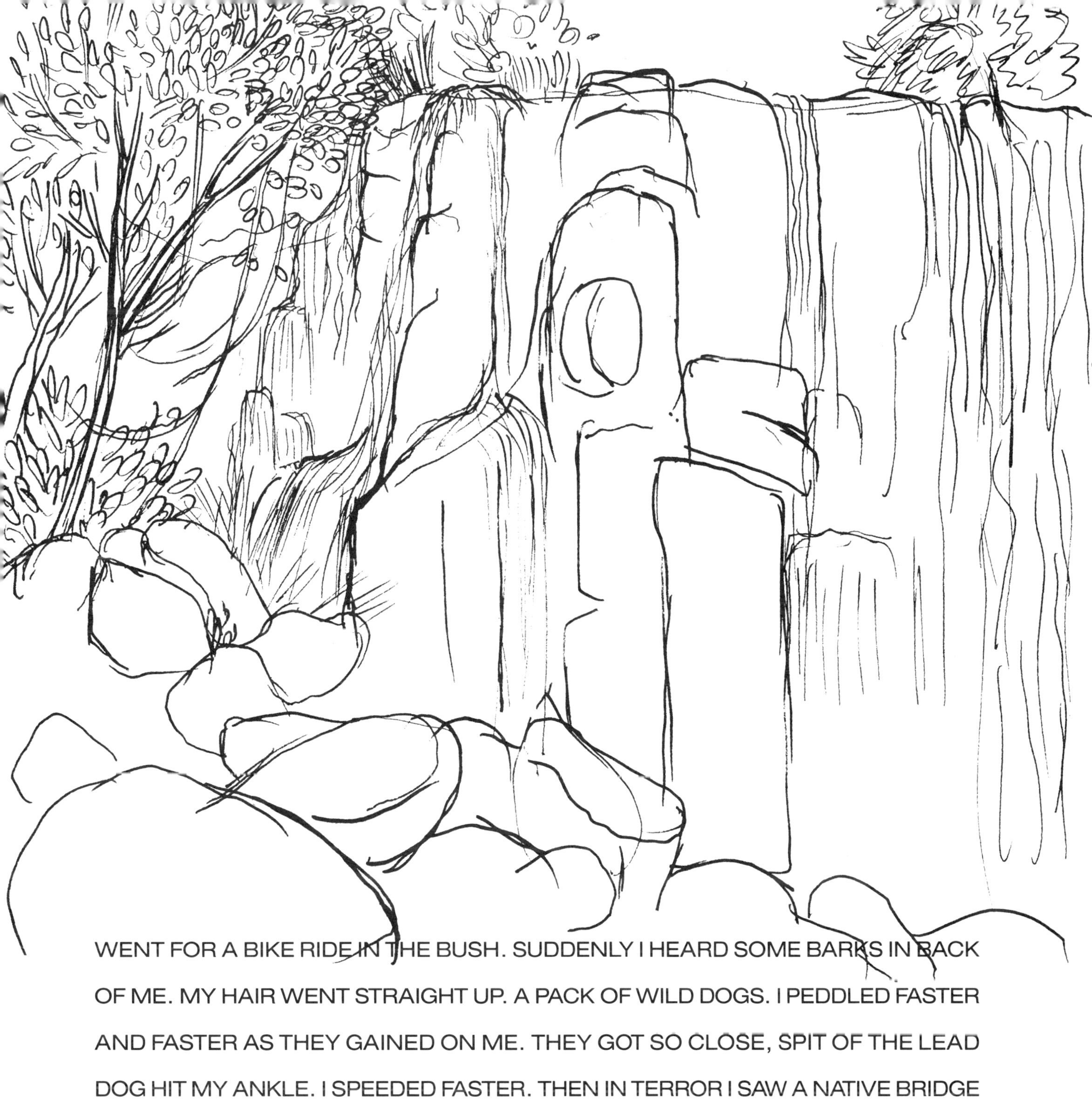

WENT FOR A BIKE RIDE IN THE BUSH. SUDDENLY I HEARD SOME BARKS IN BACK OF ME. MY HAIR WENT STRAIGHT UP. A PACK OF WILD DOGS. I PEDDLED FASTER AND FASTER AS THEY GAINED ON ME. THEY GOT SO CLOSE, SPIT OF THE LEAD DOG HIT MY ANKLE. I SPEEDED FASTER. THEN IN TERROR I SAW A NATIVE BRIDGE OVER A GORGE DIRECTLY IN MY PATH. A LOG LIKE A TIGHT ROPE OVER WHICH NATIVES WALKED. ABOUT 3 INCHES WIDE. WAS GOING SO FAST I WENT STRAIGHT ACROSS AND FELL FLAT ON THE ROCK LEDGE ON THE OPPOSITE SIDE. THE WILD DOGS WERE STOPPED AND HOWLING AND I LAUGHED BUT THE BACK OF MY LEGS STUNG FROM THE SPIT.

APRIL 29

TO GO TO DALABA. EVERYONE CAME TO THE TRAIN TO SEE ME OFF.

APRIL 30

GOT OFF TRAIN AT MAMOU AND GOT A RIDE WITH A MISSIONARY TO DALABA. ALL ROADS OVER CURVES AROUND MOUNTAINS. WE RAN OFF THE ROAD ALMOST OVER A CLIFF — EYES OF ANIMALS SHOWING IN FOREST. ARRIVED ABOUT 10 AND WENT OUT LOOKING AROUND.

MAY 1

VERY COLD THIS MORNING. TOOTHPASTE TASTED LIKE PEPPERMINT ICE CREAM. VALLEY WAS FILLED WITH CLOUDS OF MISTS, THE MOUNTAIN TOPS STICKING OUT LIKE ISLANDS. VERY FOGGY — DEW ON PINE TREE. WENT OUT TO VISIT SOME NATIVES IN THEIR HUTS. DID A WATER COLOR.

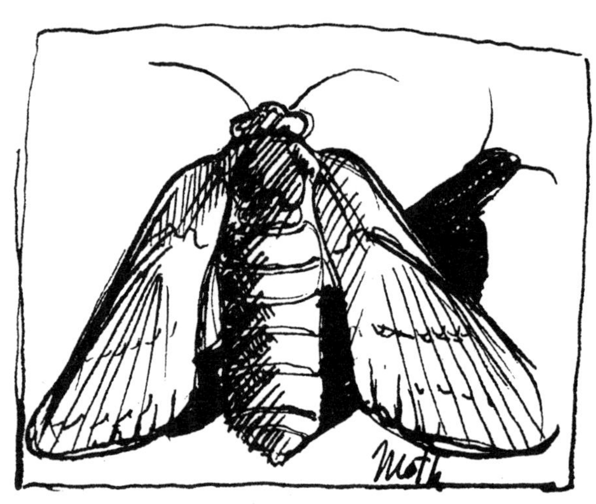

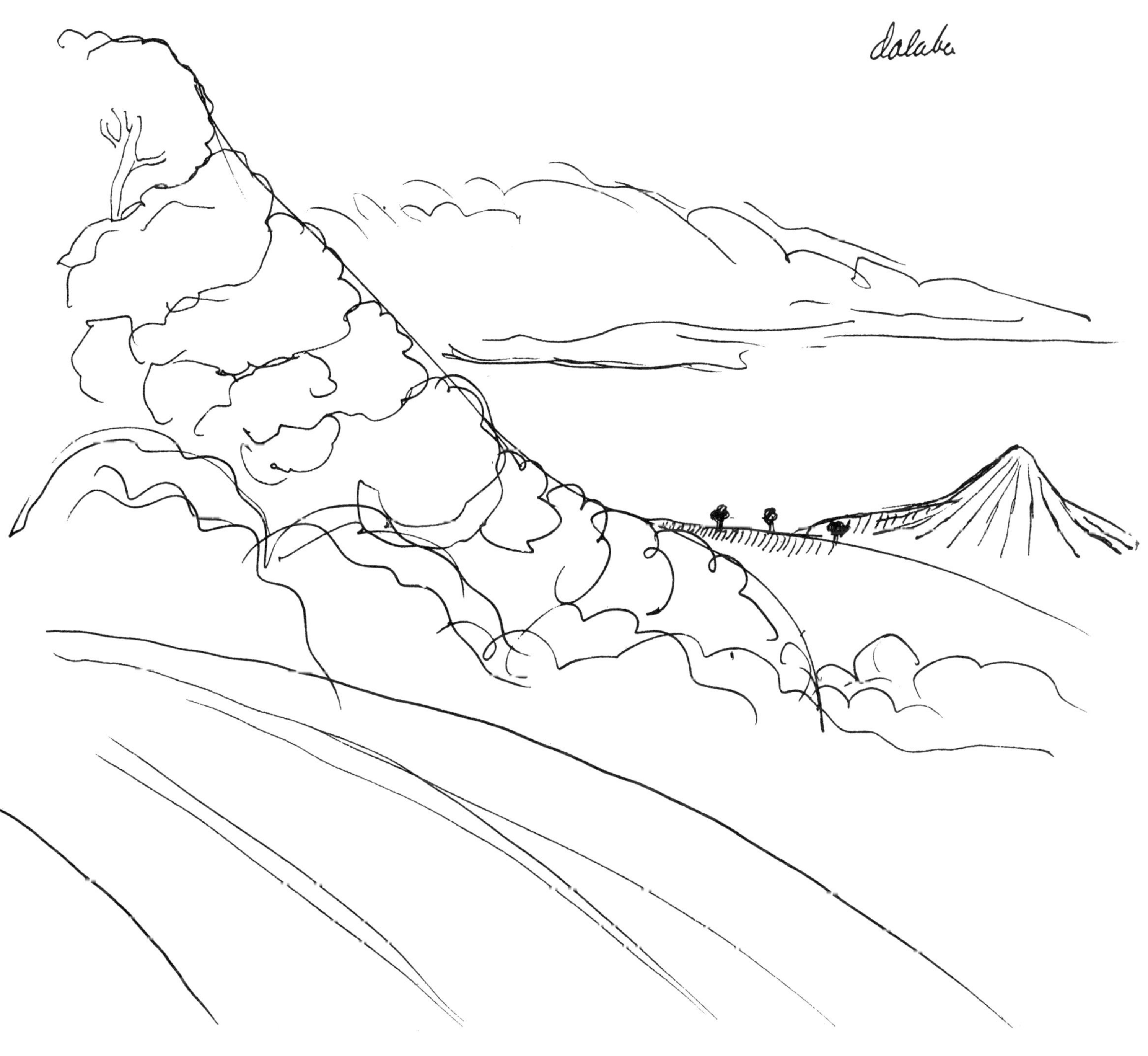

dalaba

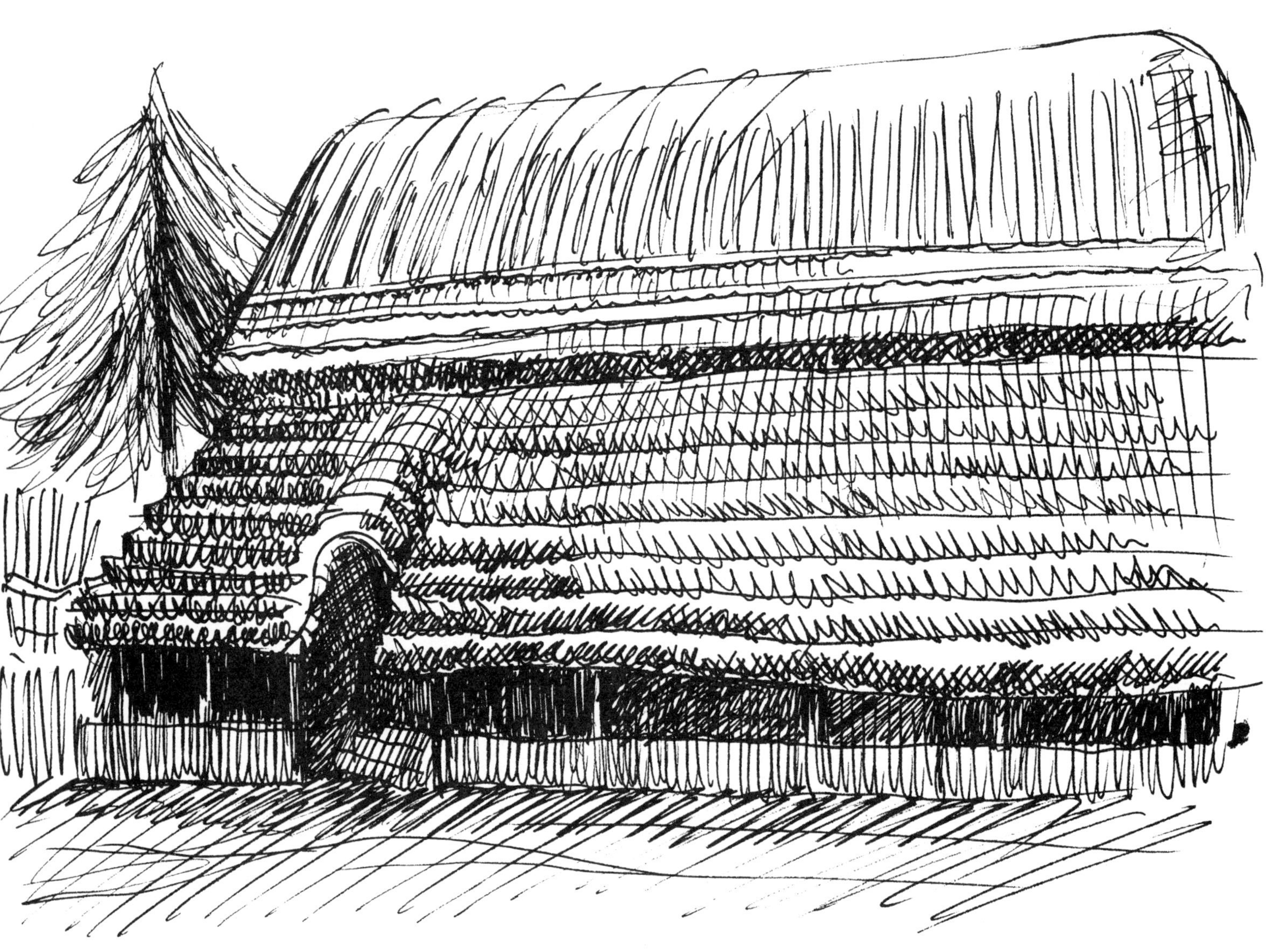

MET A RICH CHIEF. WENT INTO THE ROOMS OF HIS WIVES. BEAUTIFULLY DECORATED WITH BLUE AND RED DESIGNS. ONE OF HIS WIVES WAS A KNOCKOUT. SUN GOT TOO HOT SO WENT DOWN TO THE KING'S ORCHARD AND STOLE SOME ORANGES. HAD FUN KNOCKING THEM DOWN.

THE CHIEF NAMED A MOUNTAIN PEAK AFTER ME.

HE'S A RASCAL.

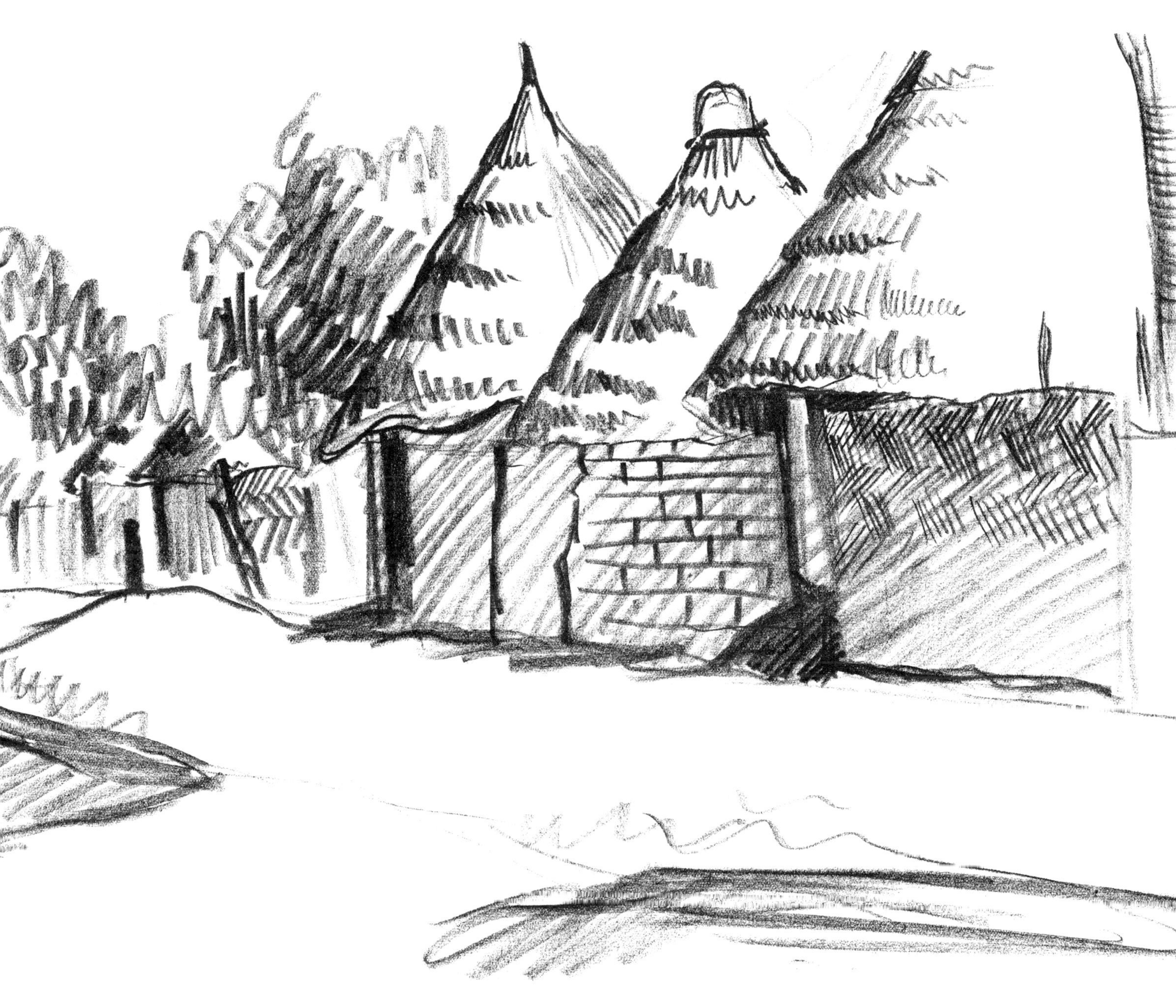

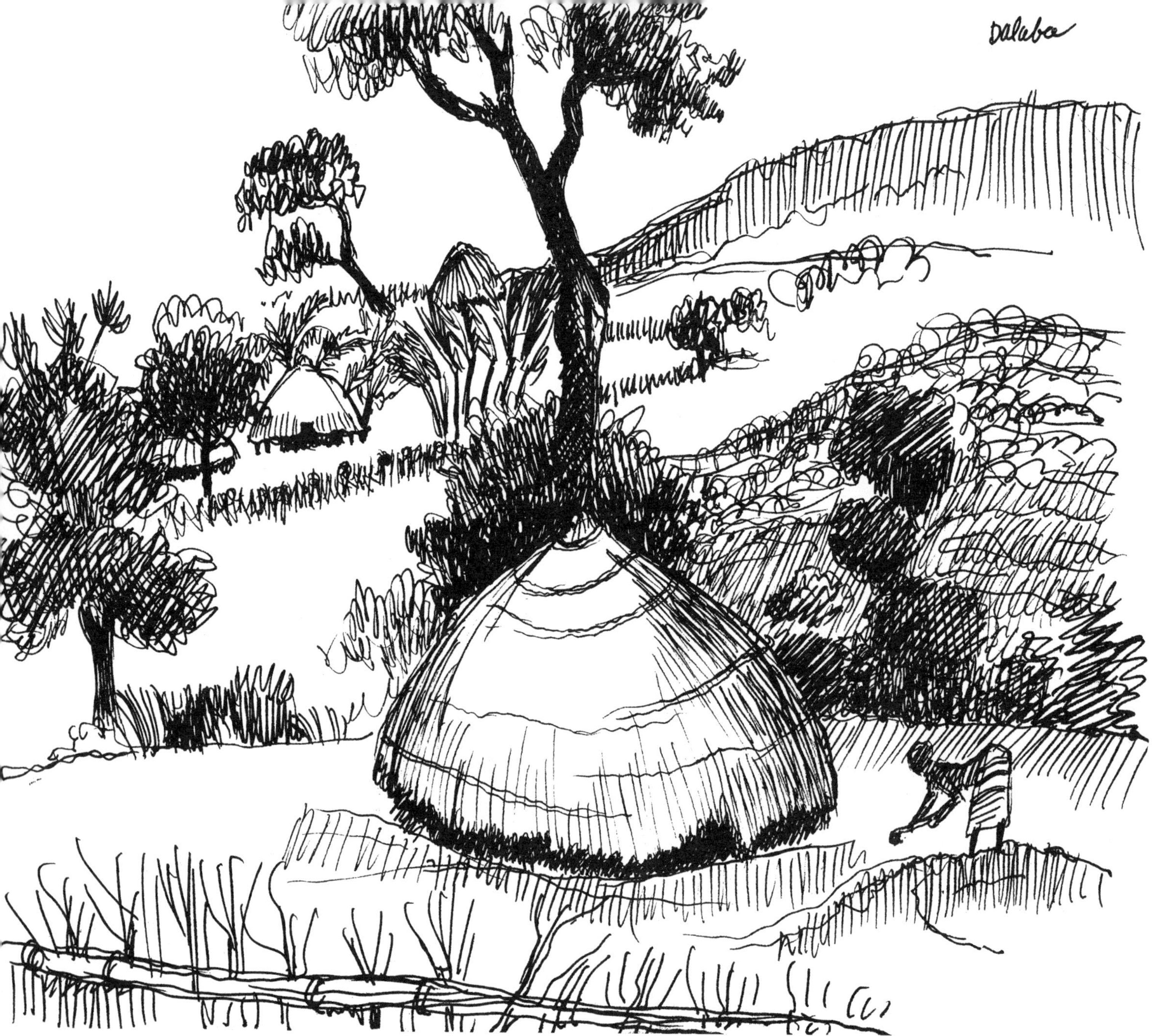

I'M IN THE WILDS NOW, LIVING ON A MOUNTAIN 4,000 FEET ABOVE SEA LEVEL OVERLOOKING THE VALLEY OF DALABA. IT GETS COLD AT NIGHT. COLD HERE IS ABOUT 70. THIS IS FULA COUNTRY. YOU LOOK DOWN AND SEE LITTLE FULA HUTS. THE VALLEY IS MILES IN AREA. THE FULA WOMEN WEAR THEIR HAIR IN BRAIDED THIN STRINGS AND SMEARED WITH BUTTER. A NATIVE WOMAN HAS HER HAIR DONE ONCE A MONTH SO OF COURSE SHE HAS PLENTY OF LICE.

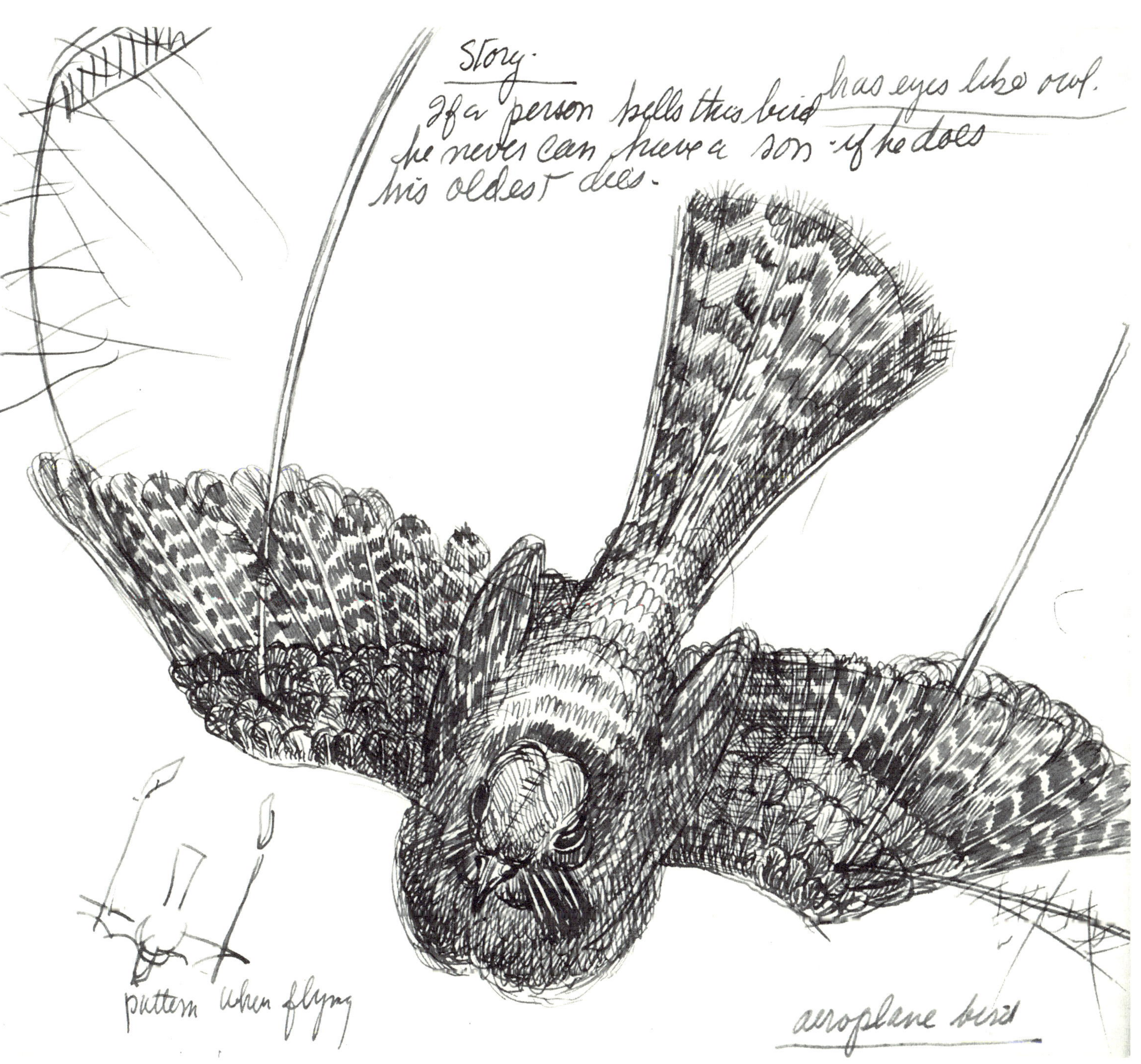

Story.
If a person kills this bird has eyes like owl.
he never can have a son · if he does
his oldest dies.
pattern when flying
aeroplane bird

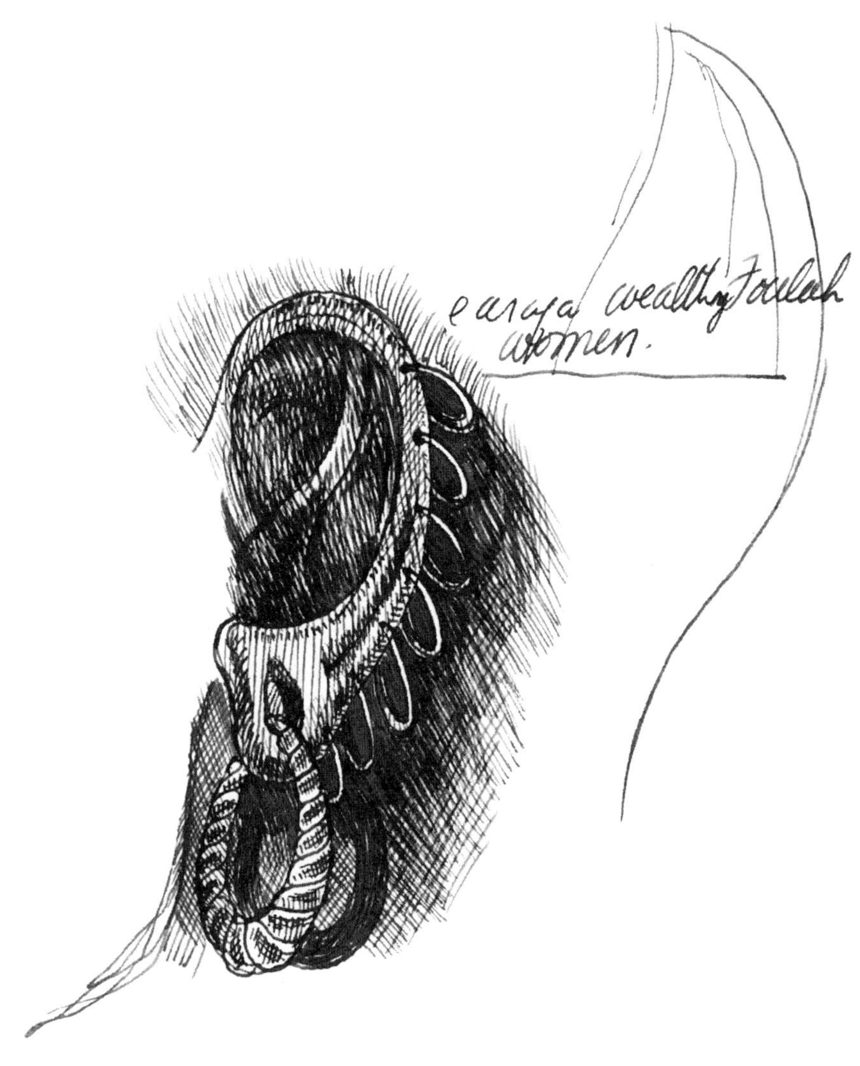

WENT TO SEE SOME NATIVE FRIENDS. THEY ALL THOUGHT I WAS A NICE GIRL AND FELT MY BREASTS TO SEE IF I WAS DEVELOPED ENOUGH TO GET MARRIED. THEY ALL THOUGHT I WAS DEVELOPED ENOUGH TO GET MARRIED.

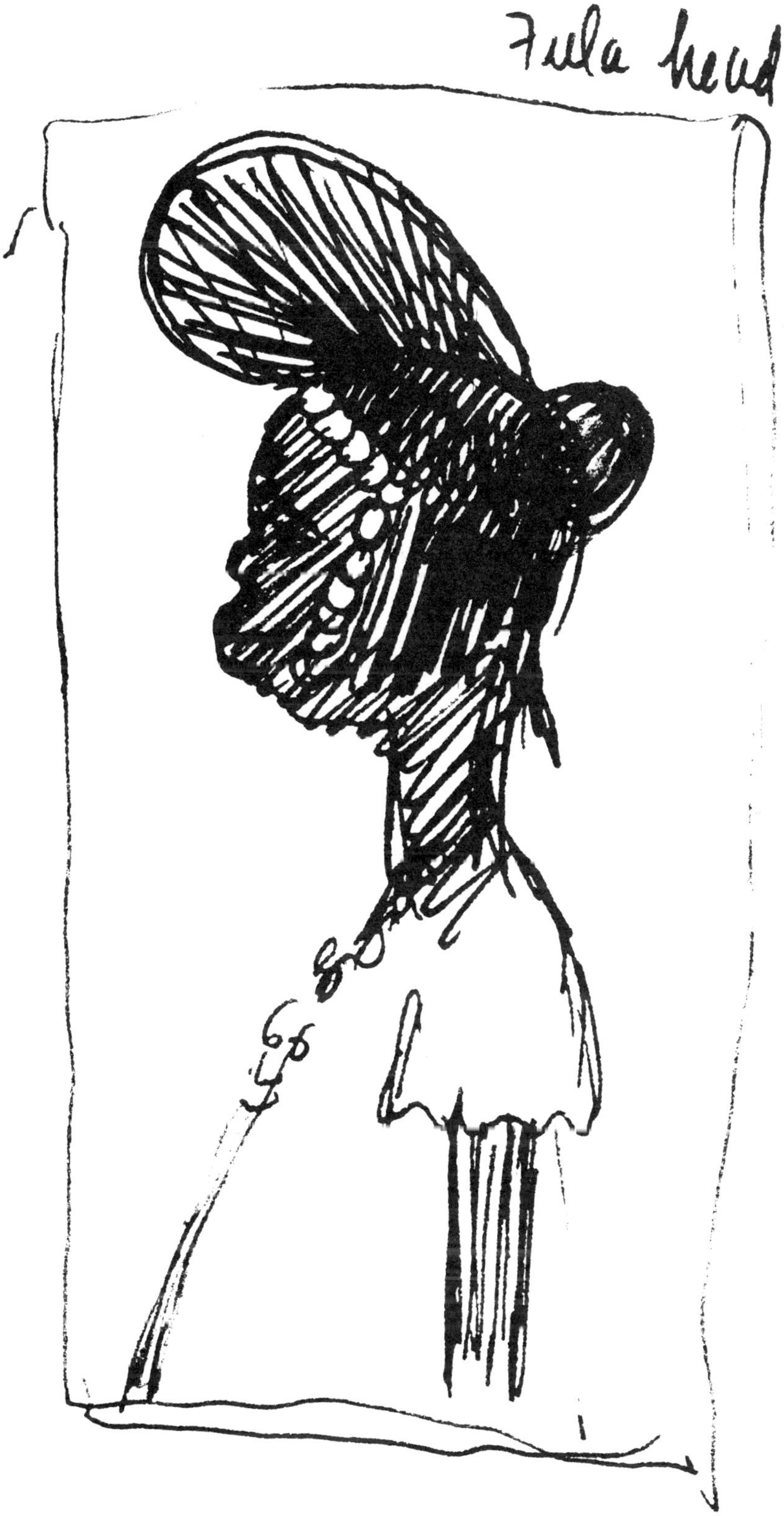

DID A WATERCOLOR

OF A

LITTLE FULA GIRL

IN

ELABORATE HEADDRESS

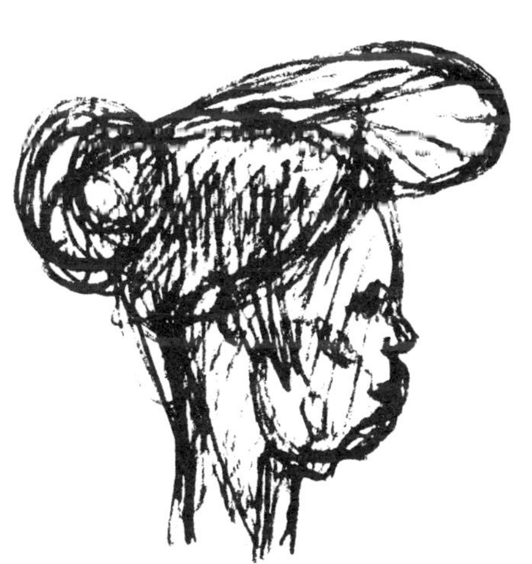

DEAR MA,

I LIKE NEGROES AND CAN'T UNDERSTAND CLASS DISTINCTION. I SAY "BONJOUR" TO THEM AND THEY SEEM VERY HAPPY.

I'M A GOOD TRAVELER—WHERE MOST PEOPLE WOULD BE SCARED AND NERVOUS I JUST THINK IT'S LOT OF FUN.

I HANG AROUND IN THE SUNLIGHT AND SKETCH AND WORK LIKE HELL AT NIGHT ON MURAL SKETCHES.

MY HOUSE IS FULL OF WASPS AND BEES, BUT THE ONLY THING TO DO IN AFRICA IS TO IGNORE STUFF AS BEST AS POSSIBLE. IF YOU GO TO THE CAN AND SIT ON A TARANTULA, YOU IGNORE IT. IF YOU HAVE BEES IN YOUR BED AT NIGHT. YOU IGNORE THEM. AFRICA IS SURE THE PLACE. BEAUTIFUL BIRDS FLY IN MY HUT AT NIGHT AND BUILD NESTS.

IF ONE RESISTS DISEASE HERE, IT'S THE SAFEST COUNTRY IN THE WORLD. A GIRL CAN GO OUT ANY PLACE DAY OR NIGHT ALONE AND NEVER BE MOLESTED. IT SURE IS SWELL GOING ANYWHERE WITH NO FEAR.

THERE ARE SO MANY QUEER INSECTS AND FLOWERS AND BEAUTIFUL BIRDS. IT'S JUST LIKE HEAVEN.

IT WILL TAKE A COUPLE OF MONTHS TO GET THE FEVER OUT OF MY SYSTEM. BUT I FEEL FINE. YOU SEE, MALARIA IS SUCH A SUBTLE THING. YOU TAKE QUININE REGULARLY AND DON'T GET SICK, BUT IT'S IN YOUR SYSTEM.

BOY, WHEN I GET HOME I'M GONNA DOWN 20 ICE CREAM CONES, POP, CANDY.

THE NATIVES IN THE BUSH PRESENTED ME WITH PEANUTS, EGGS AND TOMATOES. A COUPLE OLD LADIES DANCED FOR ME—REAL CRAZY LIKE—SAYING I MADE THEM HAPPY SO THEY'D MAKE ME HAPPY.

DON'T WORRY.

WANDA

I DON'T KNOW WHAT FEAR IS ANY MORE.

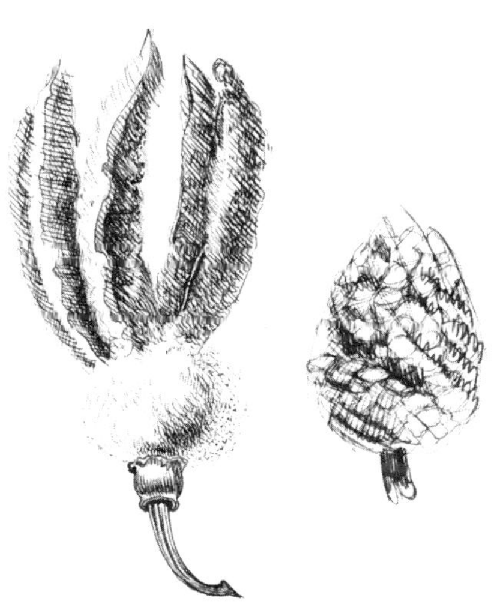

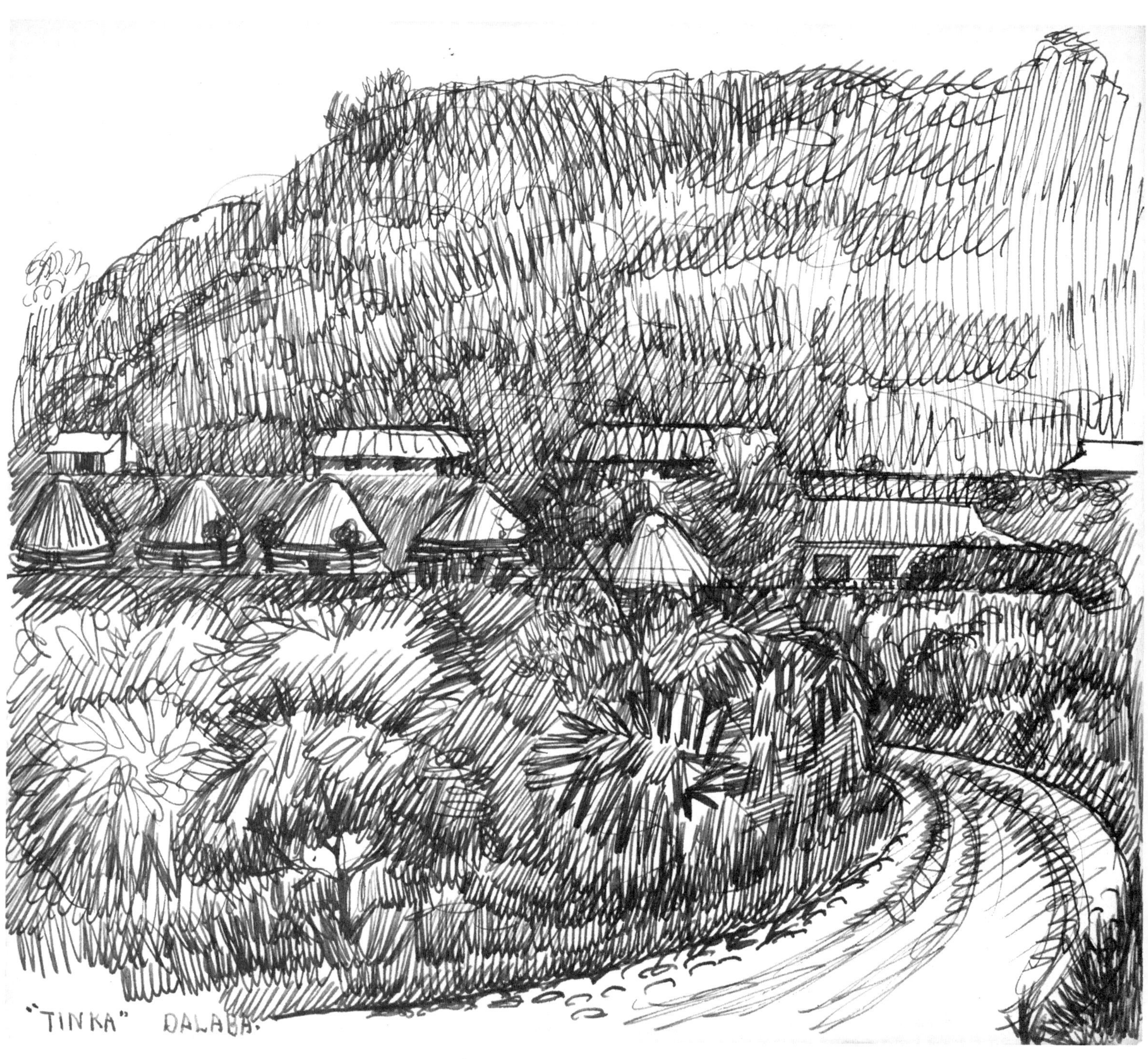

A REAL AFRICAN STORM

THE GROUNDS WERE JUST ONE LAKE.

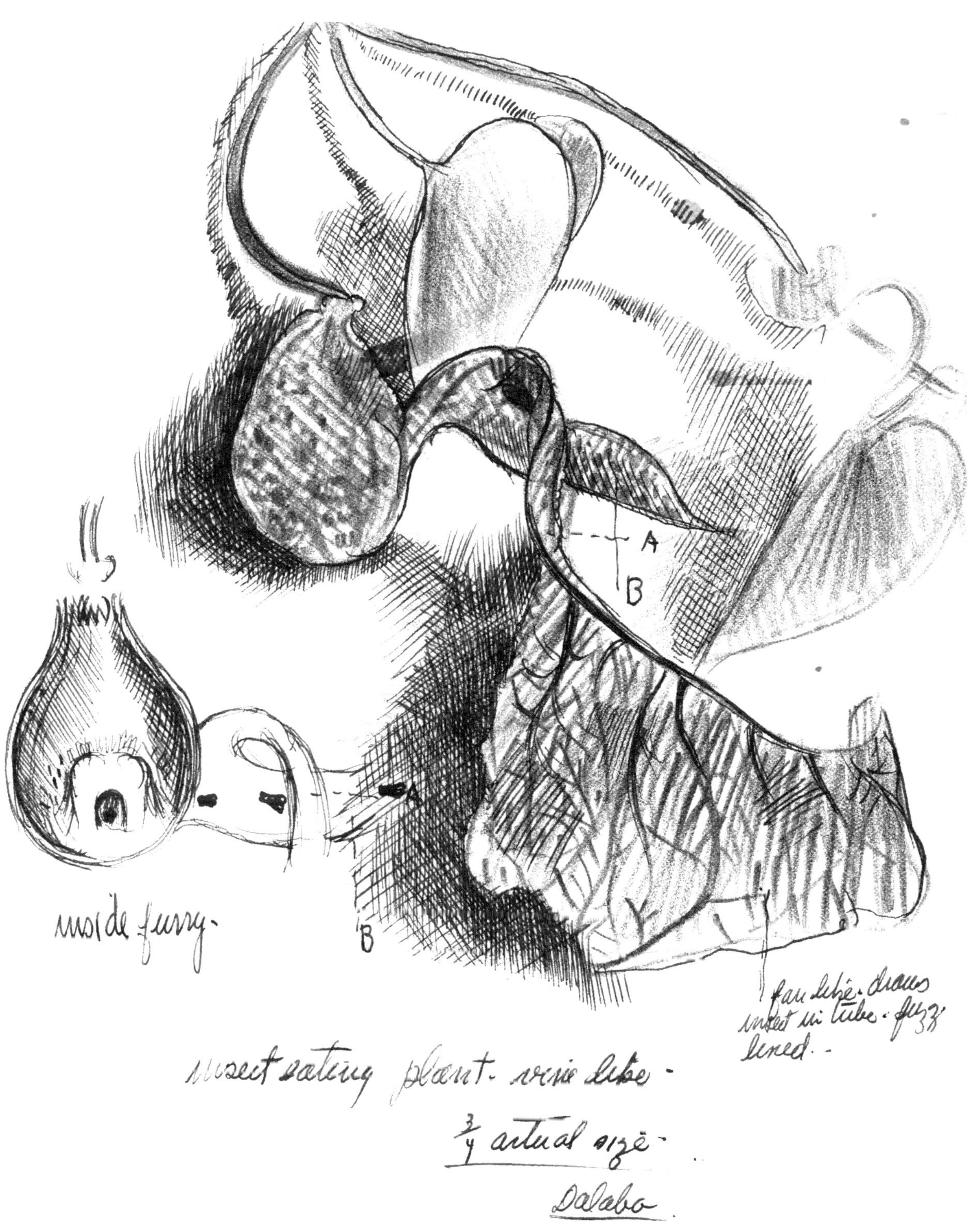

inside furry.
A
B
B
fan like. draws
insect in tube. fuzz
lined. -
insect eating plant. vine like -
¾ actual size.
Dalaba

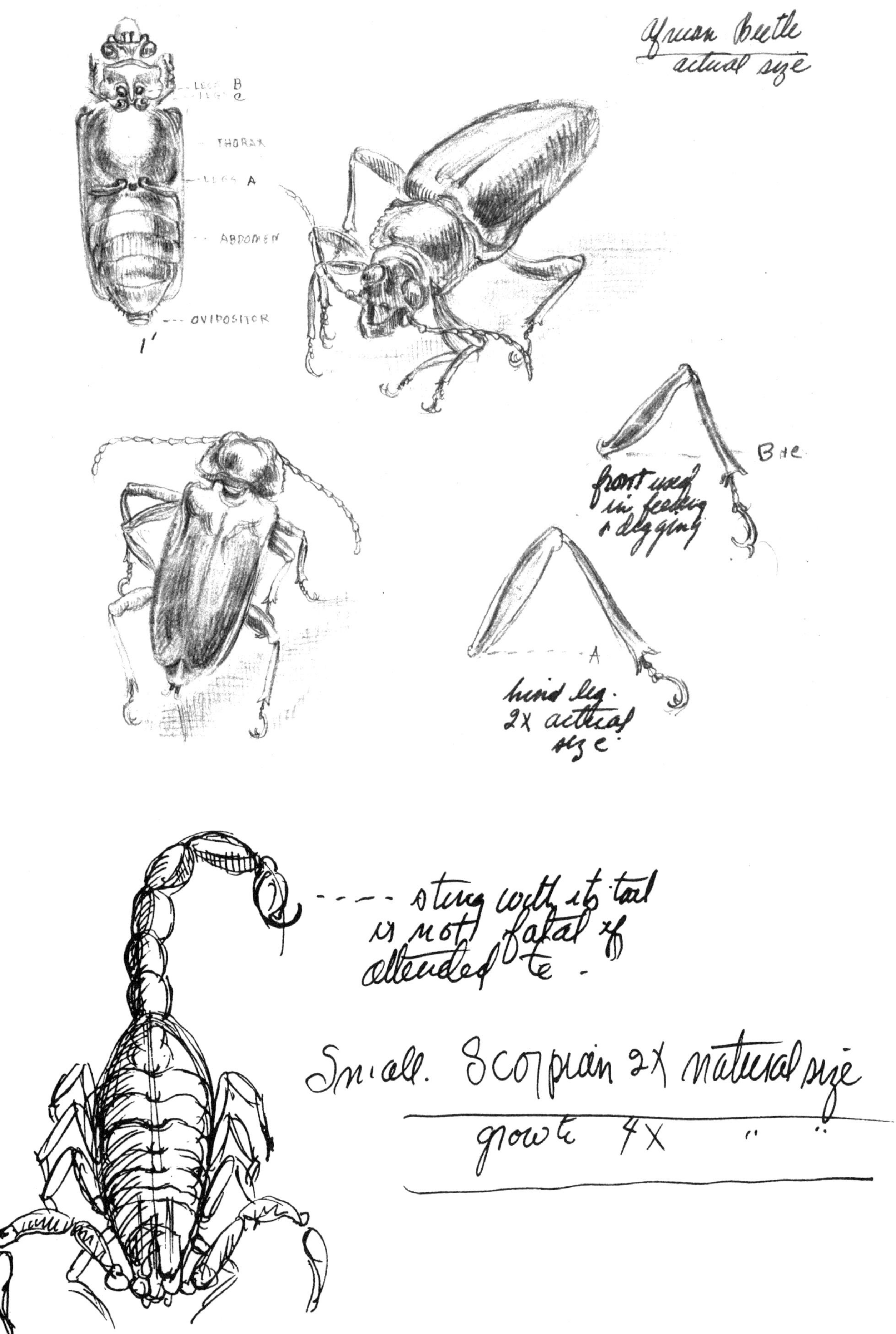
African Beetle
actual size
LEGS B
LEGS C
THORAX
LEGS A
ABDOMEN
OVIPOSITOR
1"
B+c
front used in feeding & digging
A
hind leg. 2x actual size.
sting with its tail is not fatal if attended to.
Small Scorpian 2x natural size
growth 4x

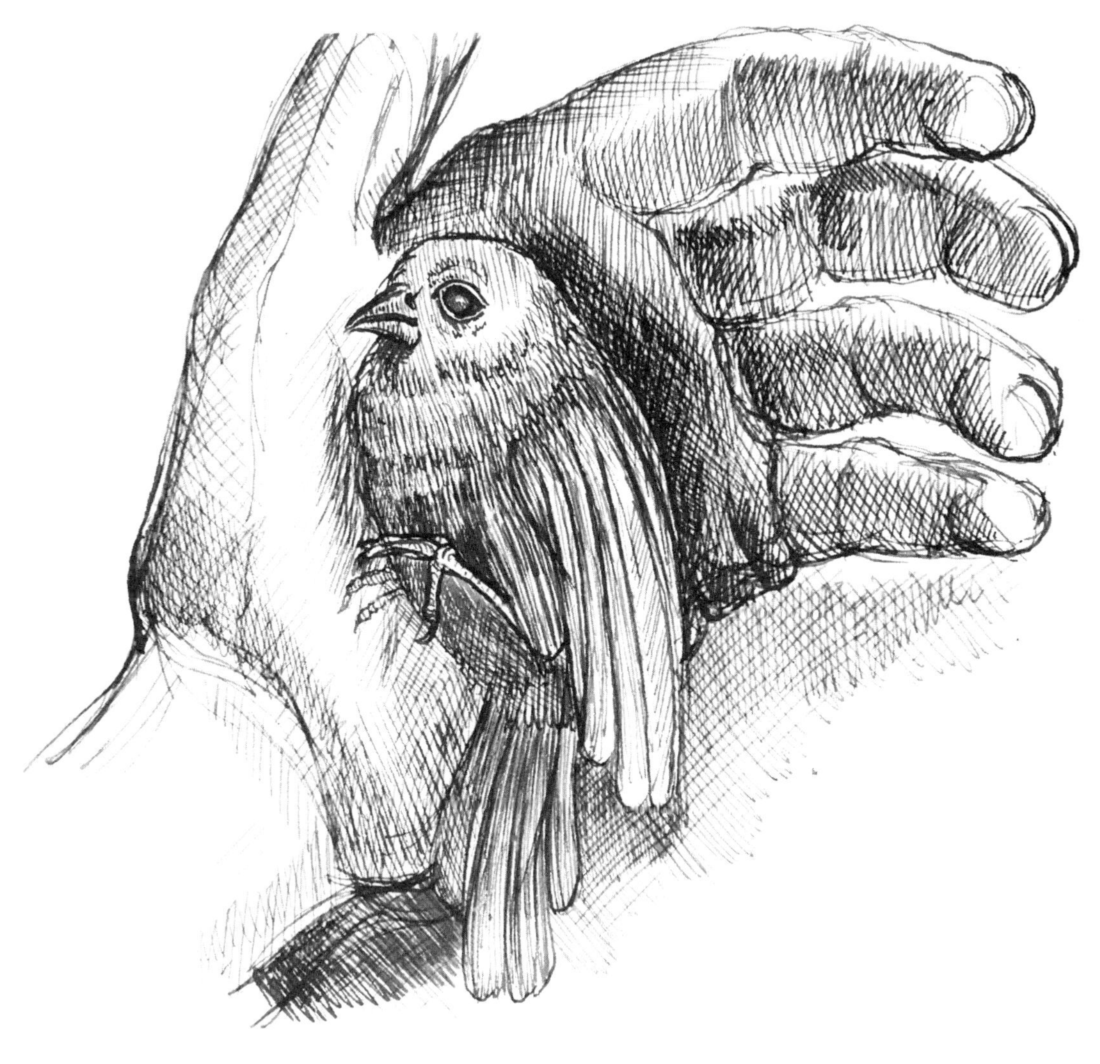

FOUND A BIRD WITH A BROKEN LEG.

PUT SPLINTS ON IT.

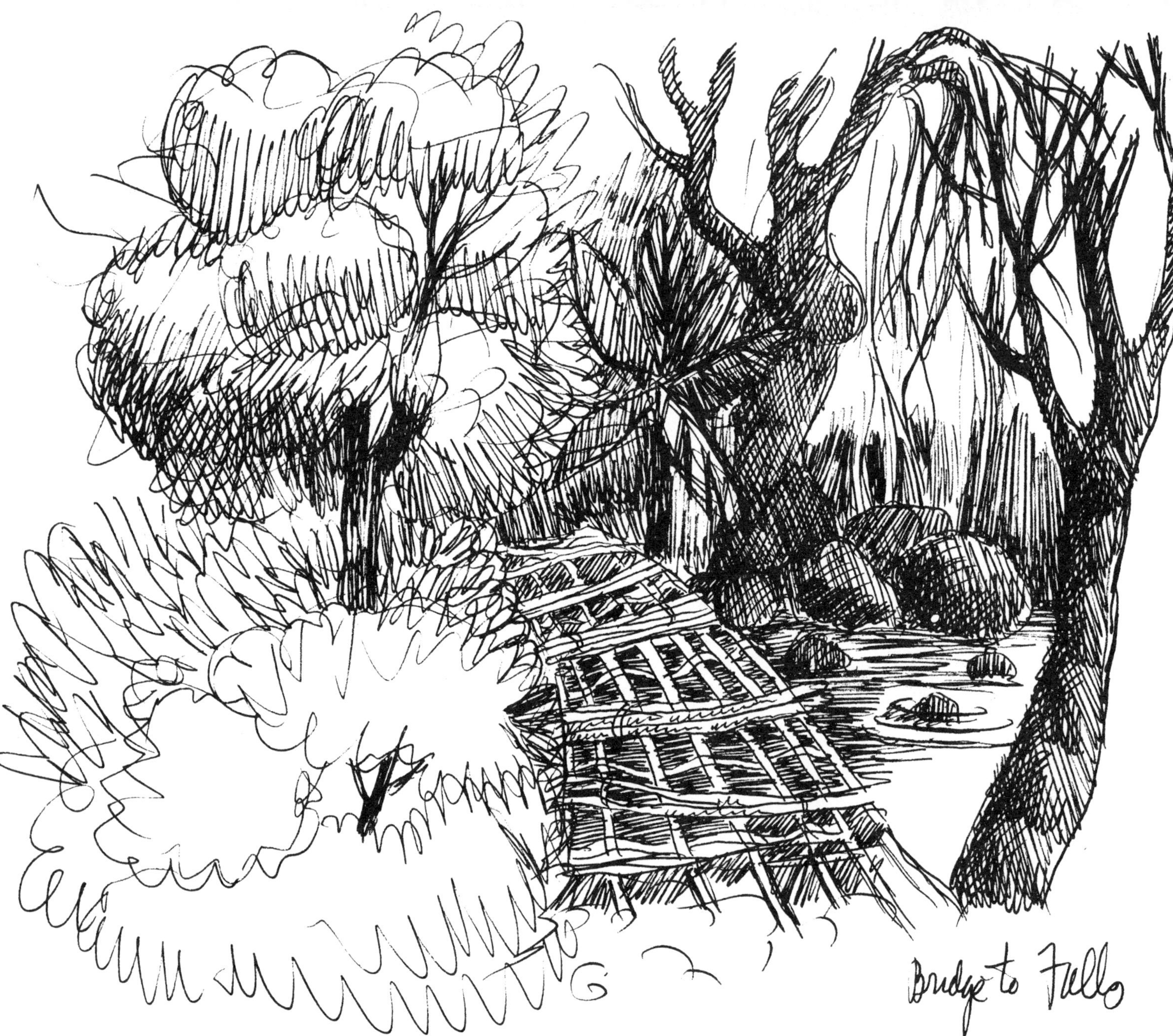

THIS COUNTRY IS MARVELOUS. WALKED THROUGH
BEAUTIFUL MOUNTAINOUS COUNTRY. CAME TO A
TYPICAL NATIVE BRIDGE —ALMOST FELL AS IT HAD BIG
HOLES IN IT. CLIMBED UP TO THE TOP OF THE FALLS
AND DESCENDED OVER ROCKS TO BOTTOM—CLUNG
ONTO ROOTS AND VINES—SLIPPED ON ROCKS— IT WAS
FINE CLIMBING BACK UP AGAIN.

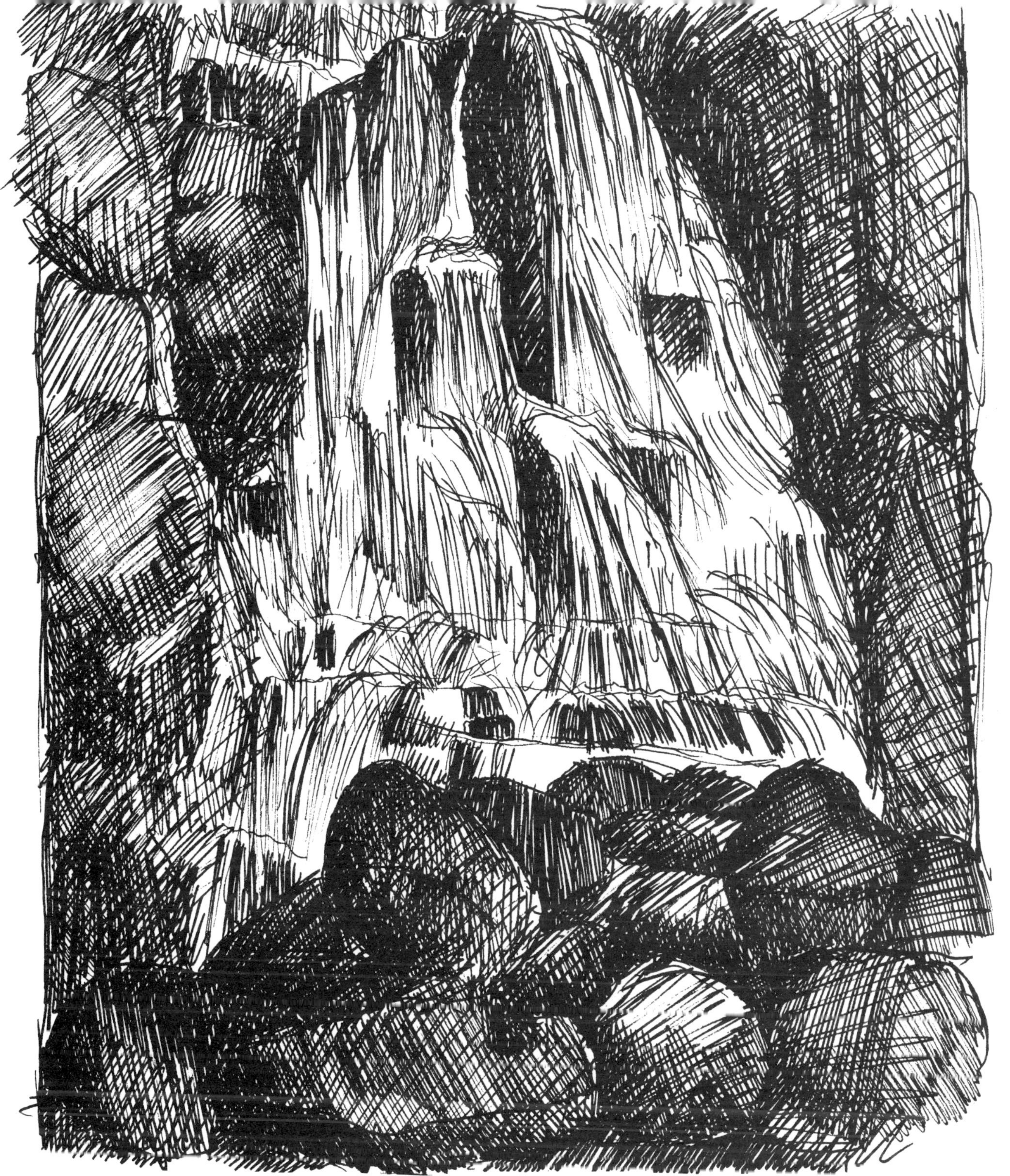

HAD LUNCH, GREEN ORANGES AND BANANAS. DID A
WATERCOLOR IN NOONDAY HEAT. MET A BUNCH OF
NATIVES WITH BOWS AND ARROWS. THEY TOLD ME
THE BRIDGE BACK WAS OUT.

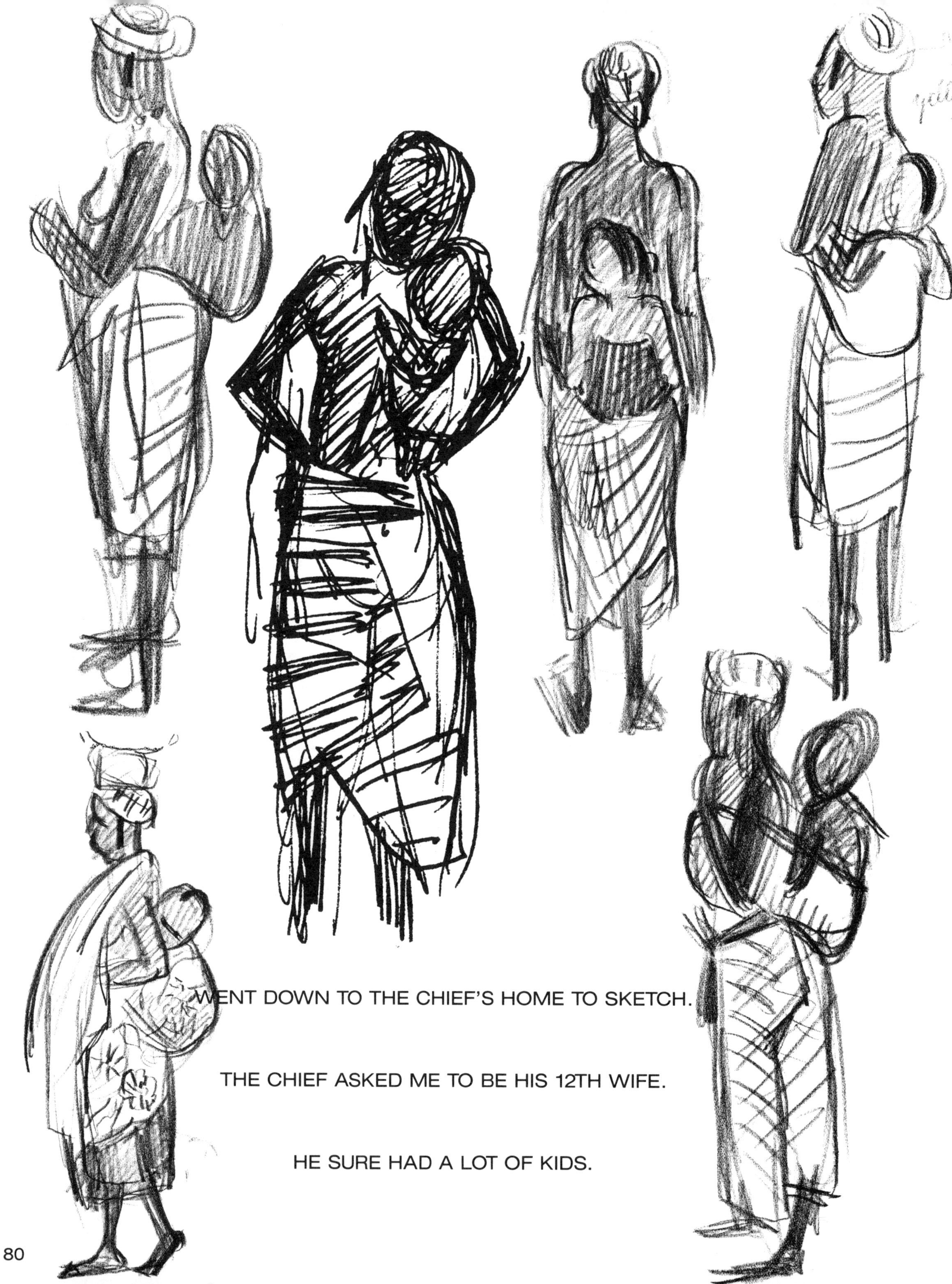

WENT DOWN TO THE CHIEF'S HOME TO SKETCH.

THE CHIEF ASKED ME TO BE HIS 12TH WIFE.

HE SURE HAD A LOT OF KIDS.

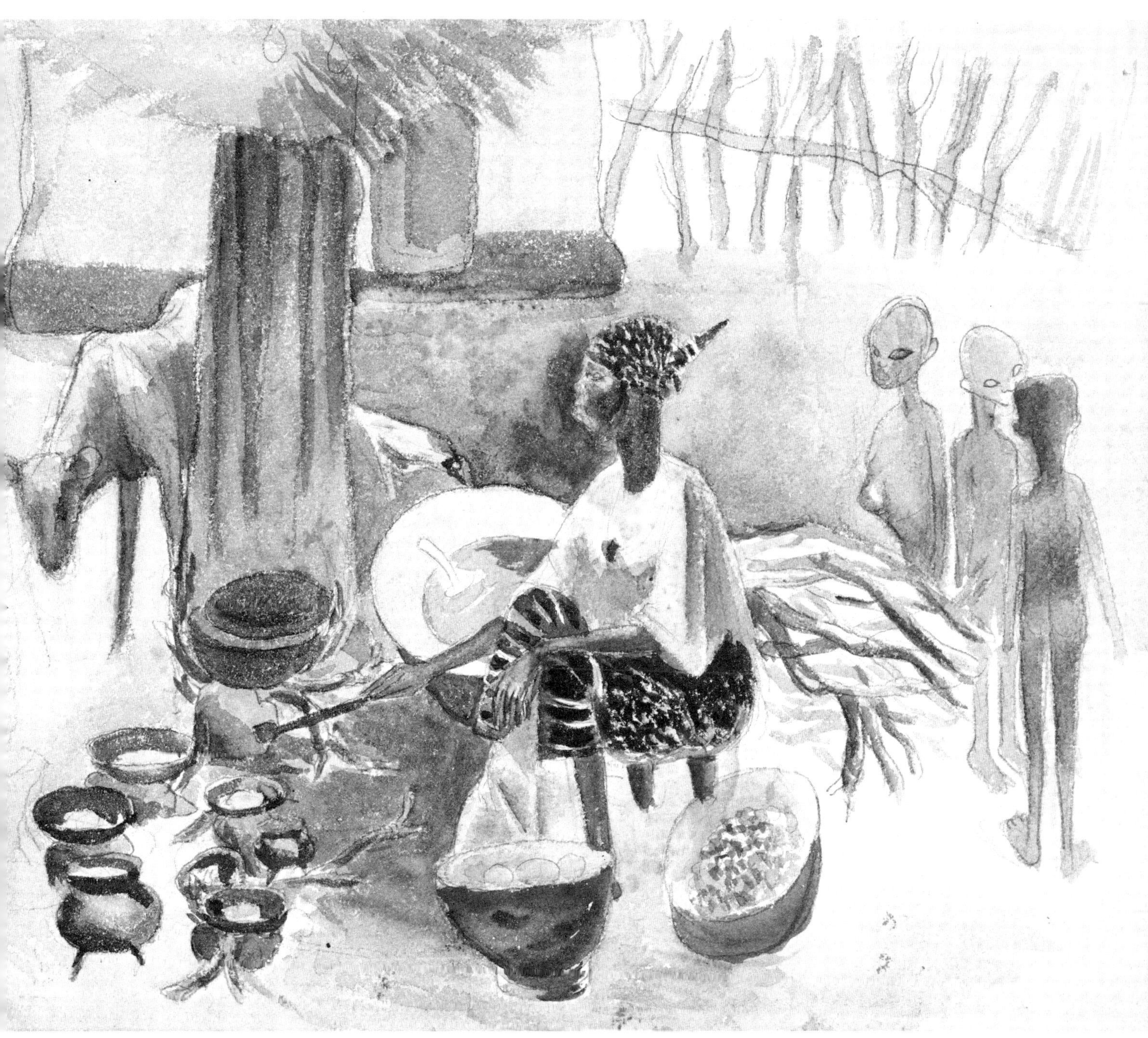

WENT FOR A LONG WALK IN THE AFTERNOON. SAW MORE ALBINOS AGAIN. WATCHED A WOMAN DRESSING ULCERS. I PUT WORD OUT TO GET ME A SNAKE. COLORED BIRDS ARE LOVELY, BRIGHT REDS, GREENS AND YELLOWS. HAVE LOVELIEST VIEW OF VALLEY OVERLOOKING NATIVE HUTS. IT SURE IS SWELL HERE. A LOT OF INTERESTING FOLIAGE.

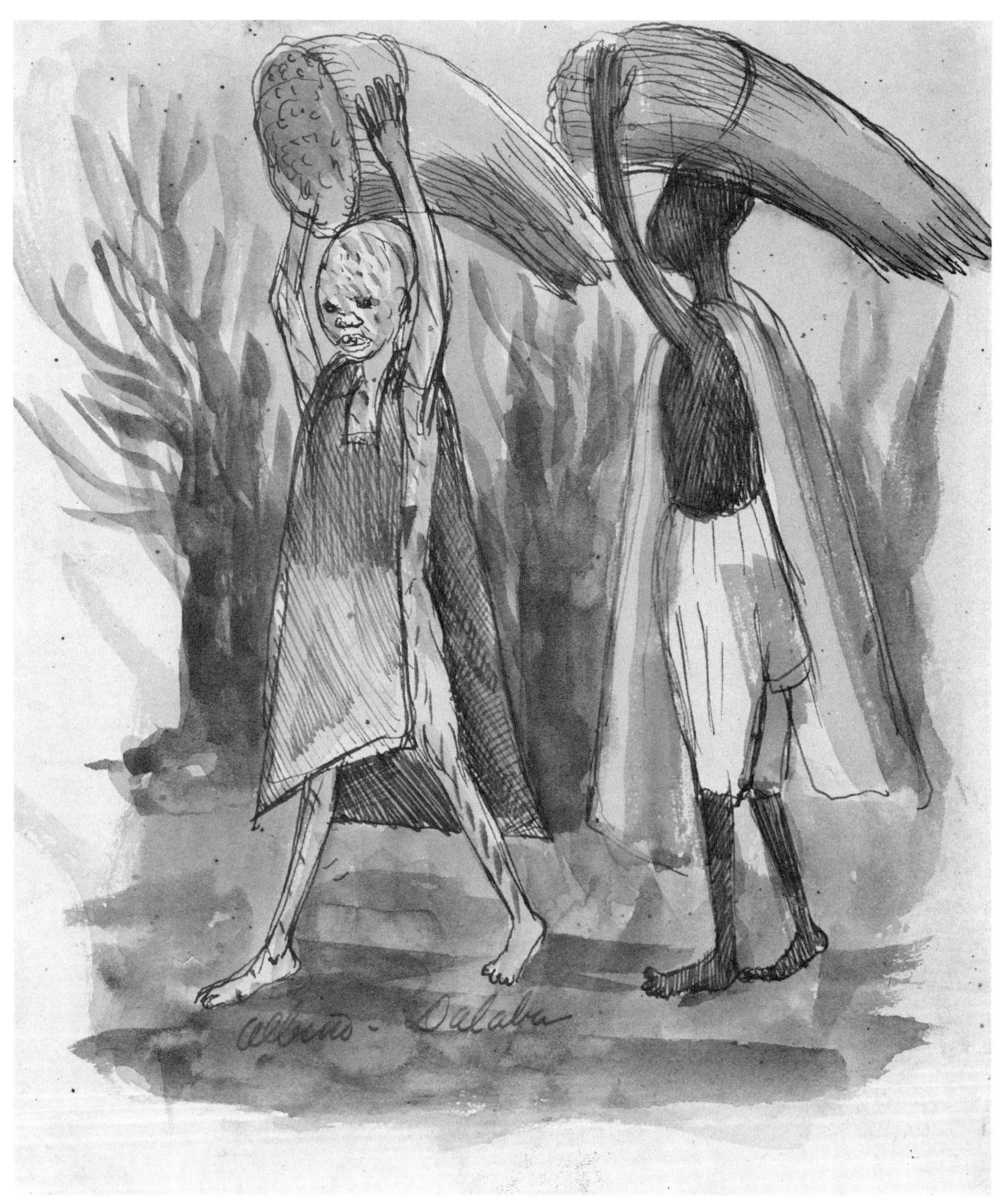

WENT FOR A WALK 6 KILOS OUT. SAT ON A ROCK FOR AN HOUR TRYING TO COAX MONKEYS OUT OF TREES. EVERY TIME I GOT ONE TO COME DOWN, NATIVES CARRYING THATCH FOR ROOFS WOULD GO BY AND SCARE THEM.

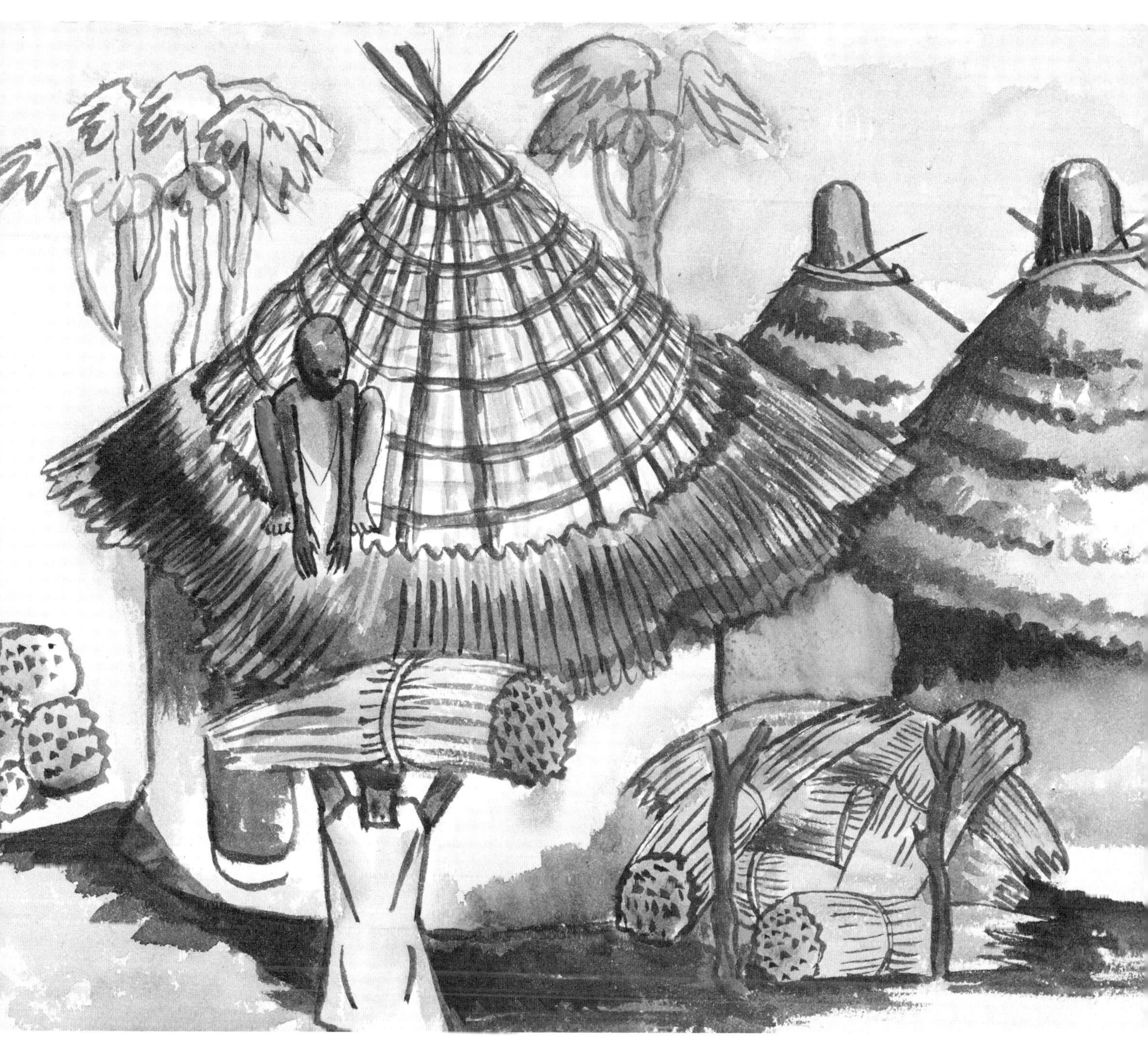

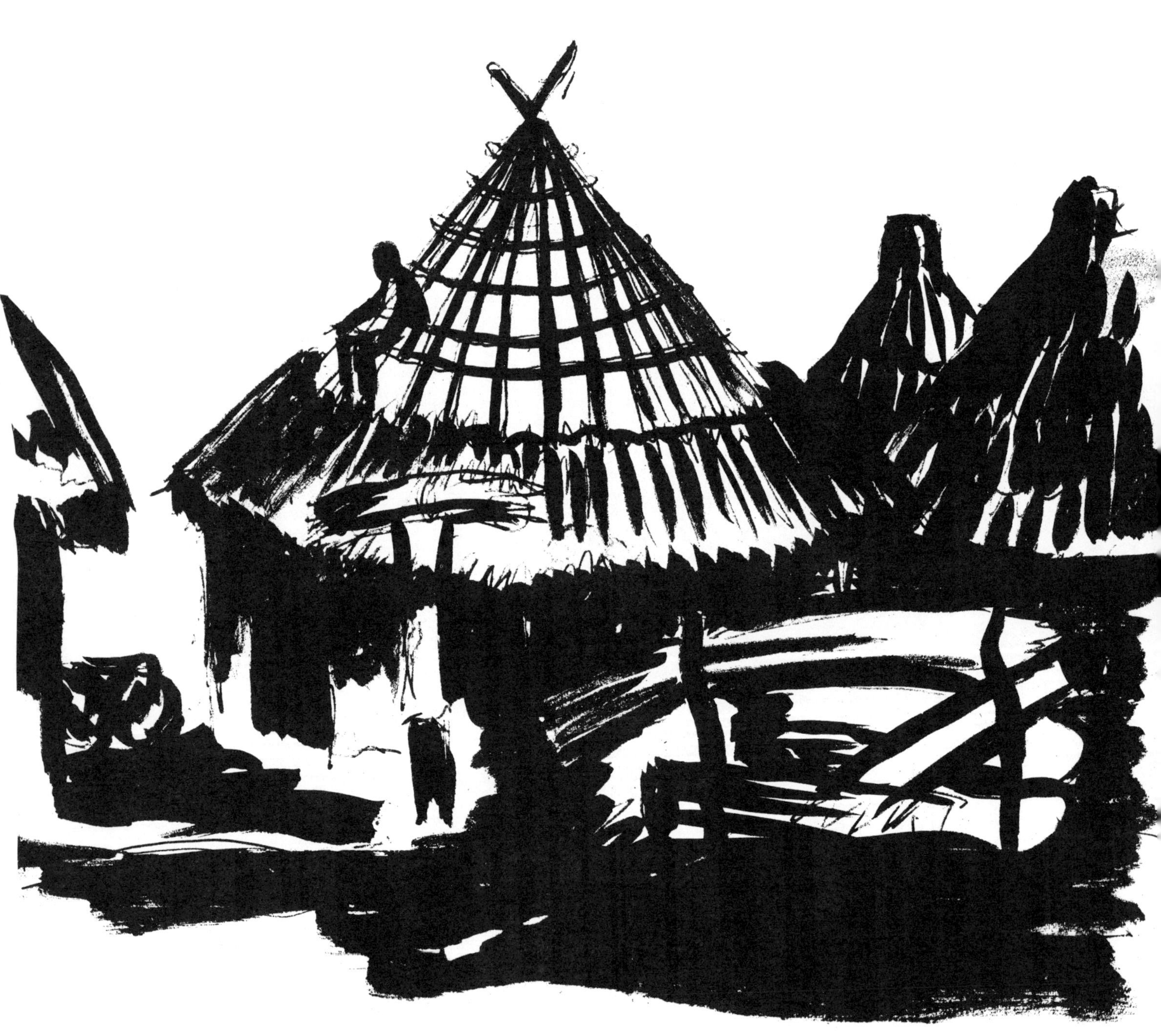

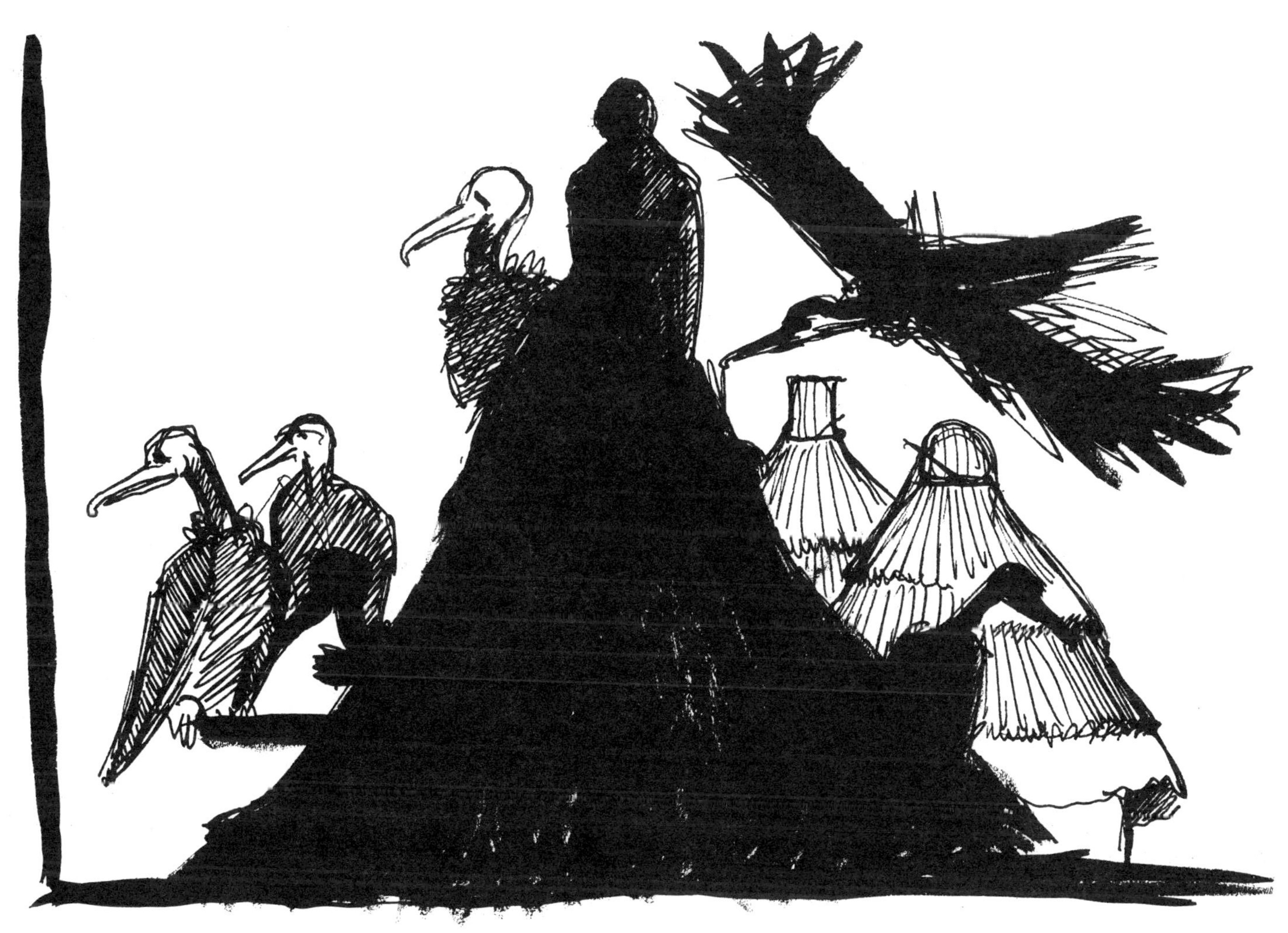

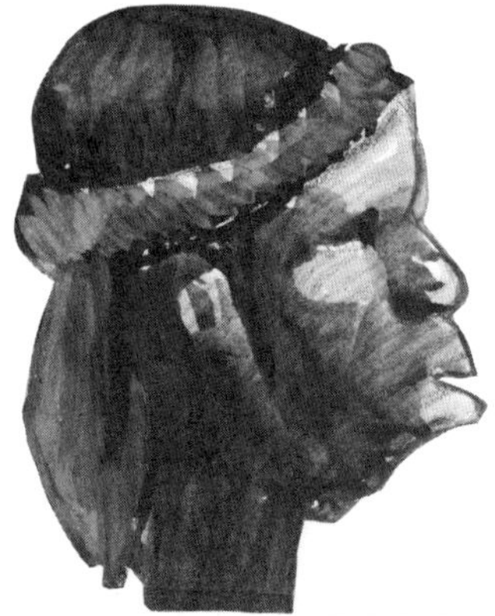

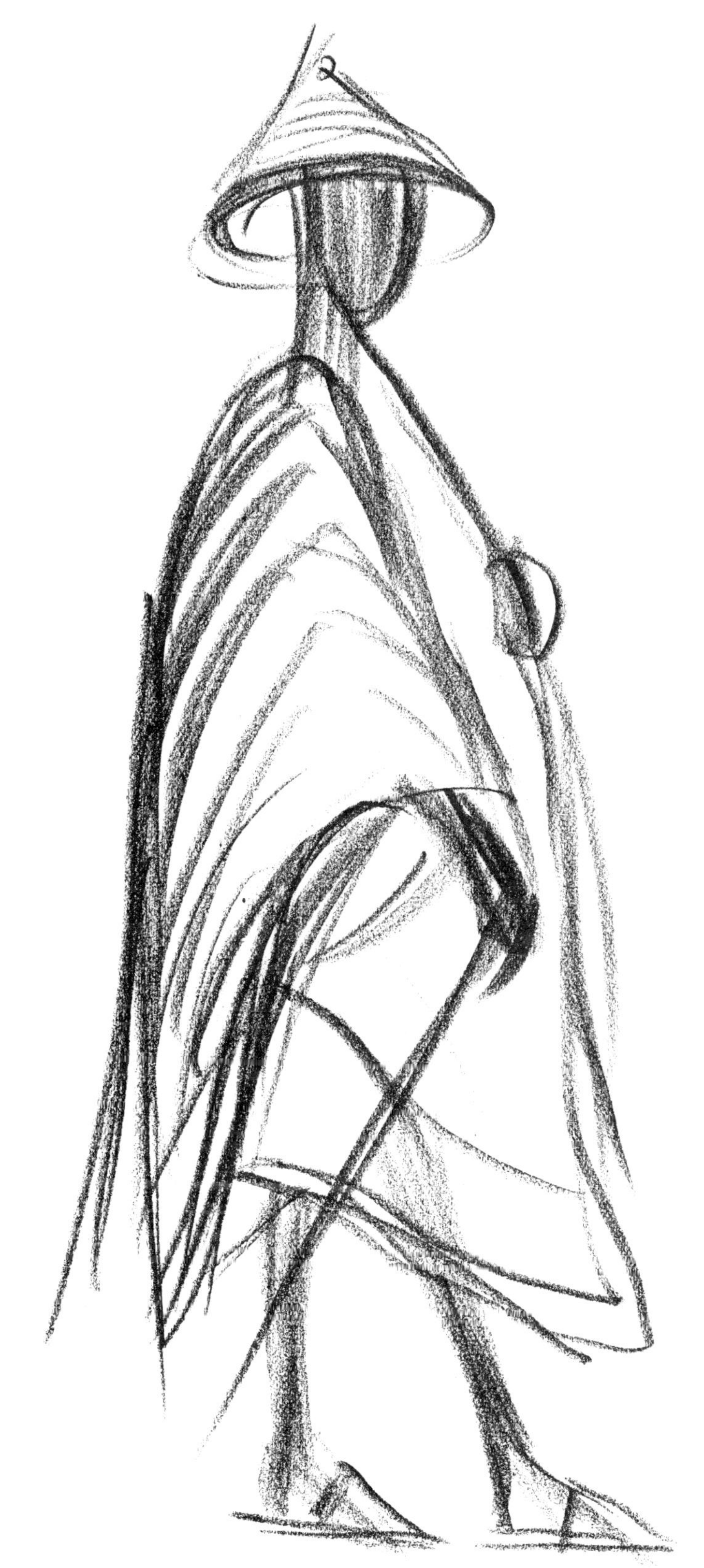

A WITCH DOCTOR PREDICTED SOMETHING ABOUT MY DEATH.

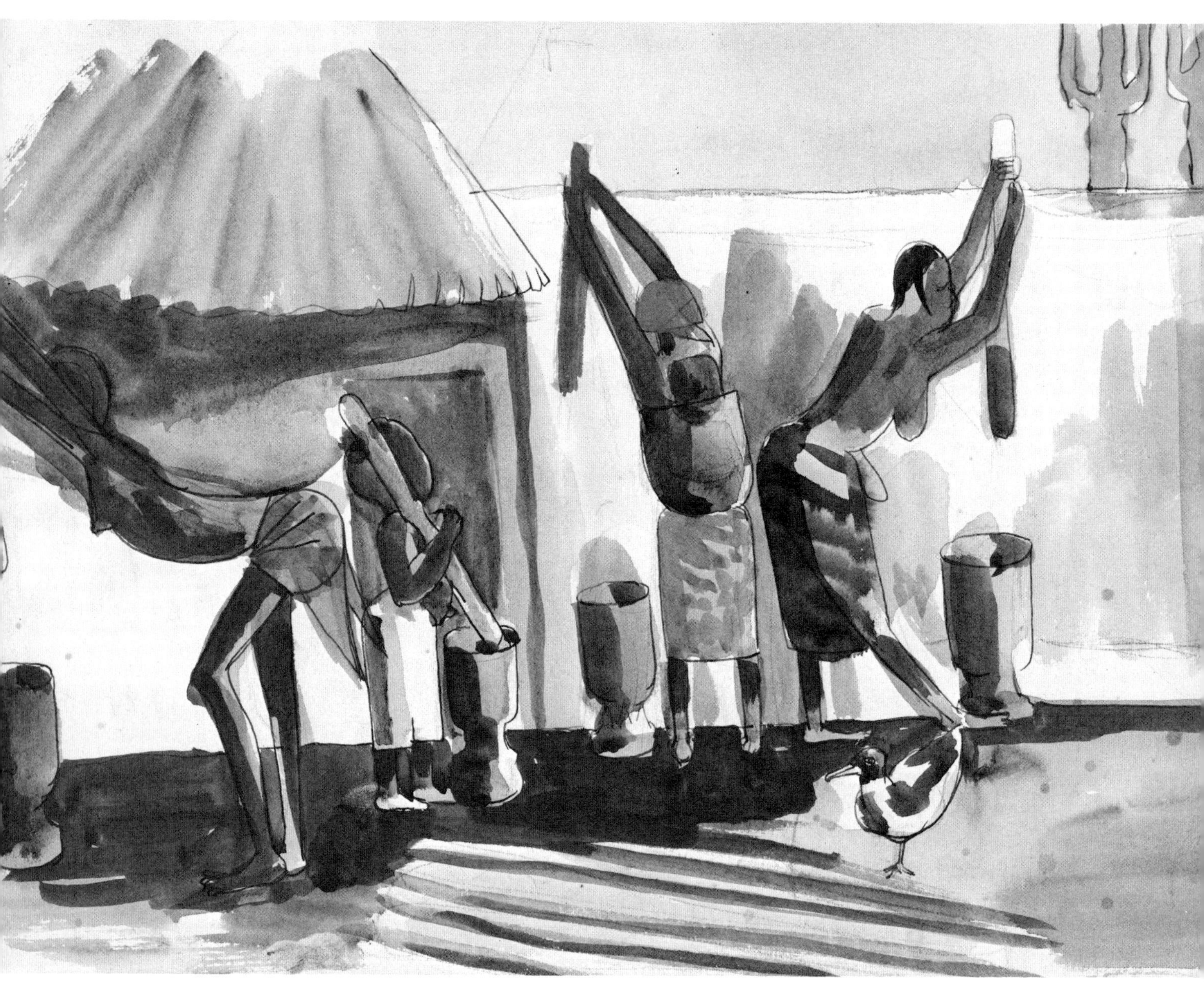

HE SAID

I WOULD BE WALKING ALONG

A BEACH

AT NIGHT

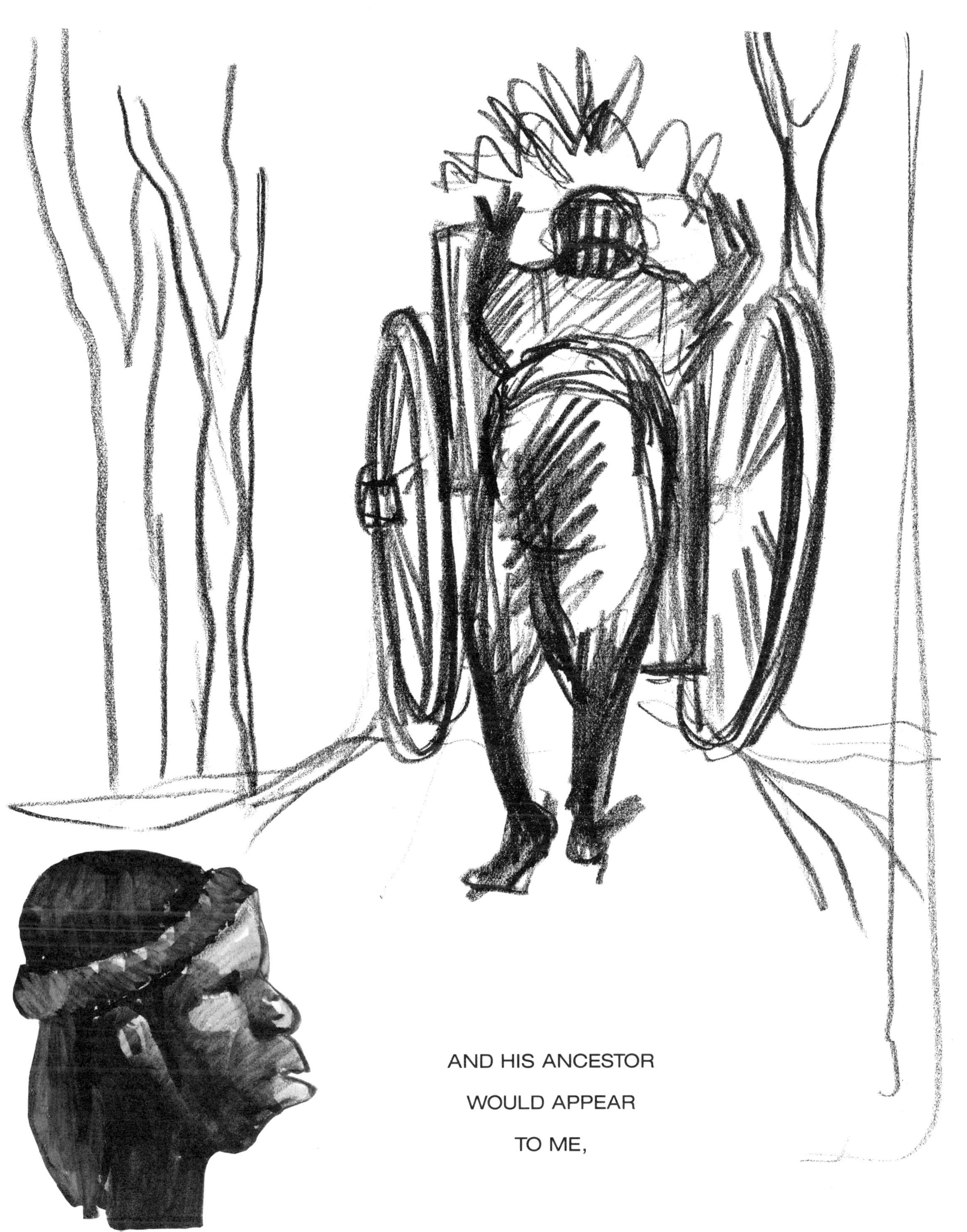

AND HIS ANCESTOR

WOULD APPEAR

TO ME,

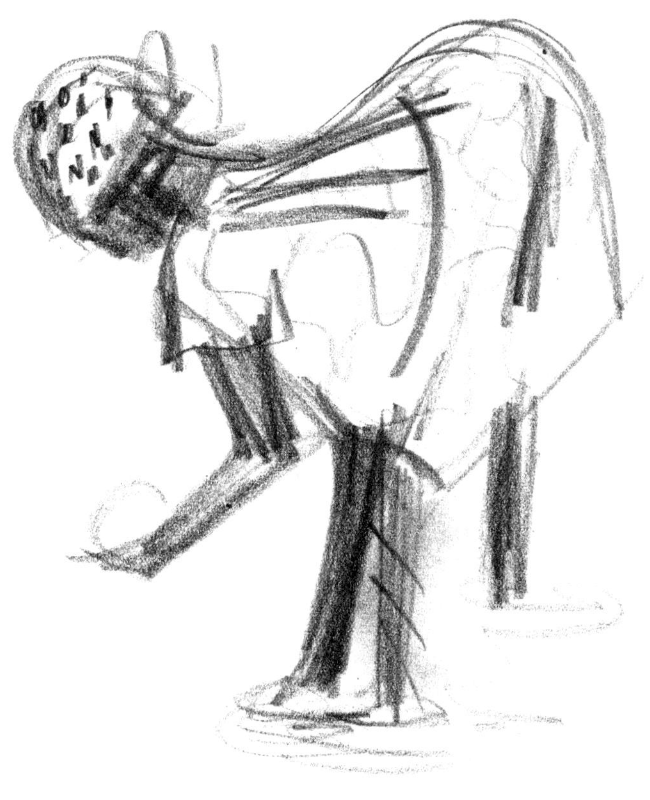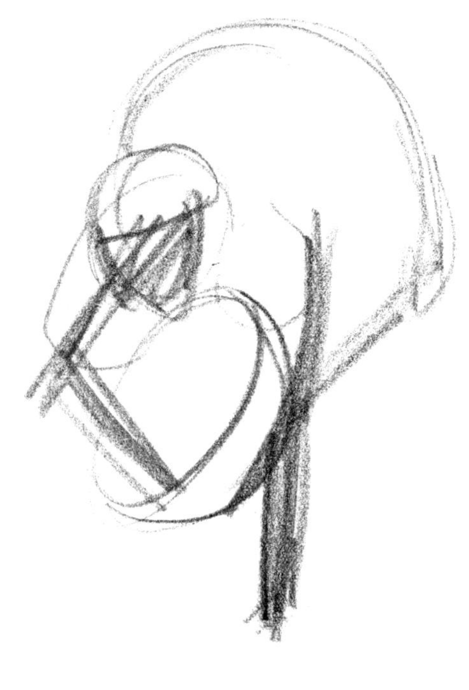

AND BECKON ME

TO FOLLOW HIM

INTO THE OCEAN,

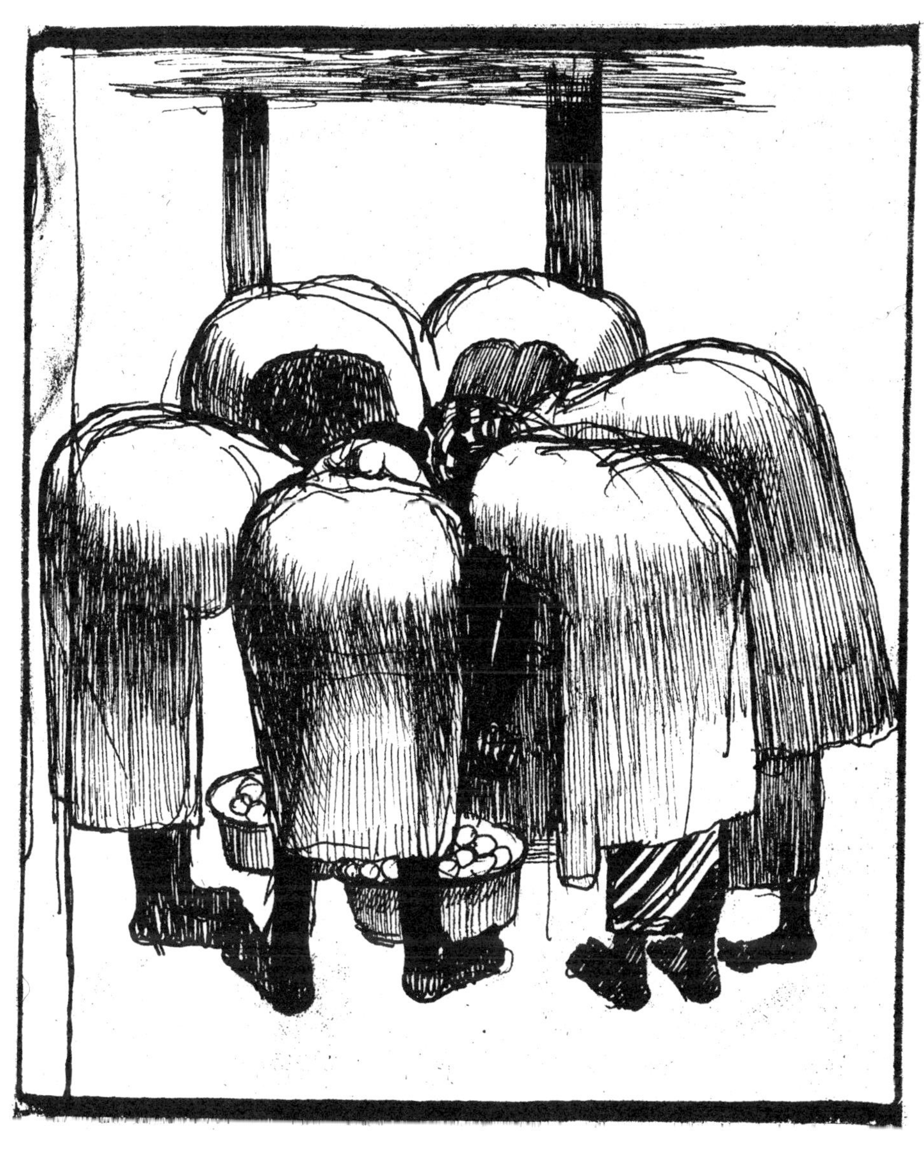

BUT I WOULD NOT GO WITH HIM.

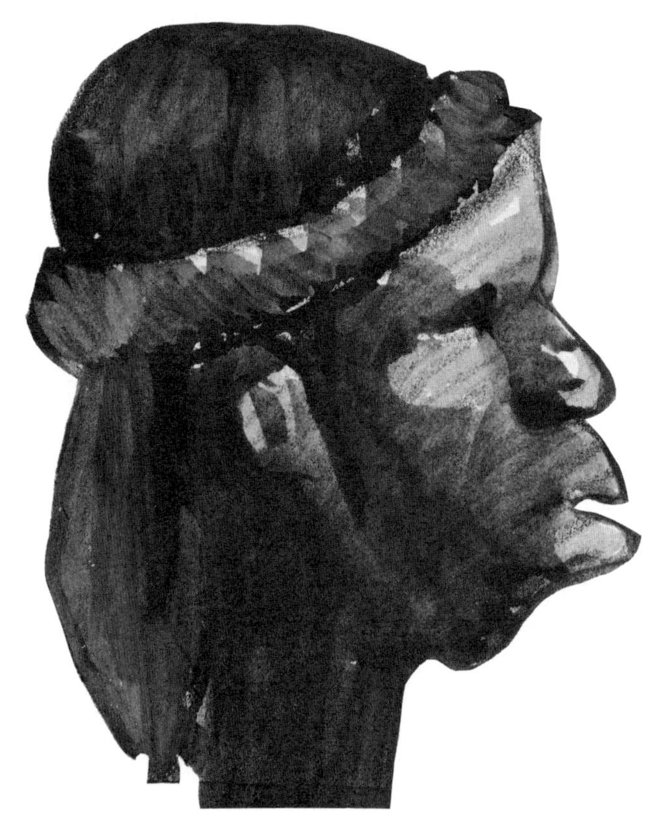

HE SAID

HIS ANCESTOR WOULD APPEAR A SECOND TIME

ON A BEACH AGAIN AND BECKON ME AGAIN.

THIS WOULD BE FIVE YEARS LATER.

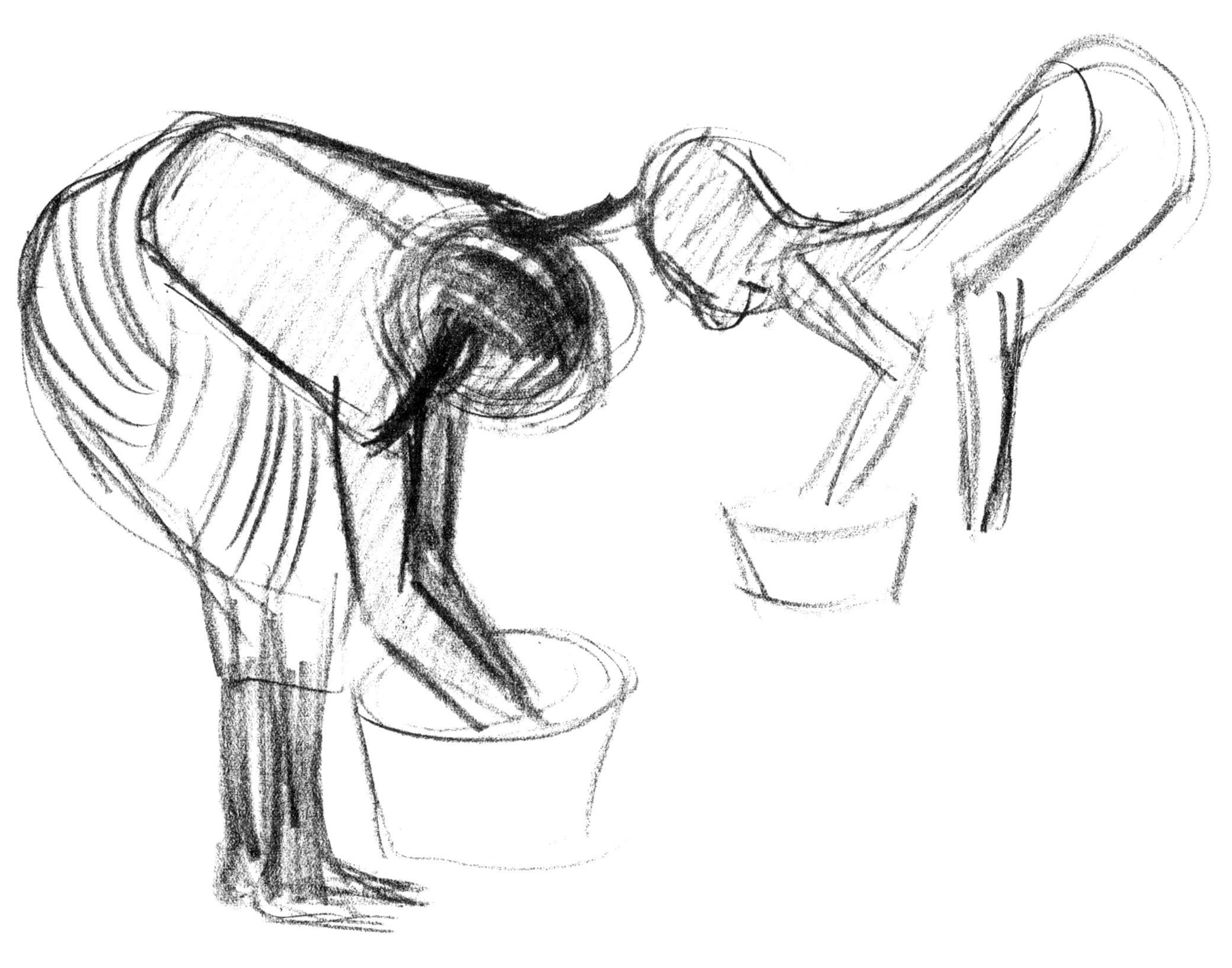

AGAIN I WOULD NOT GO WITH HIM.

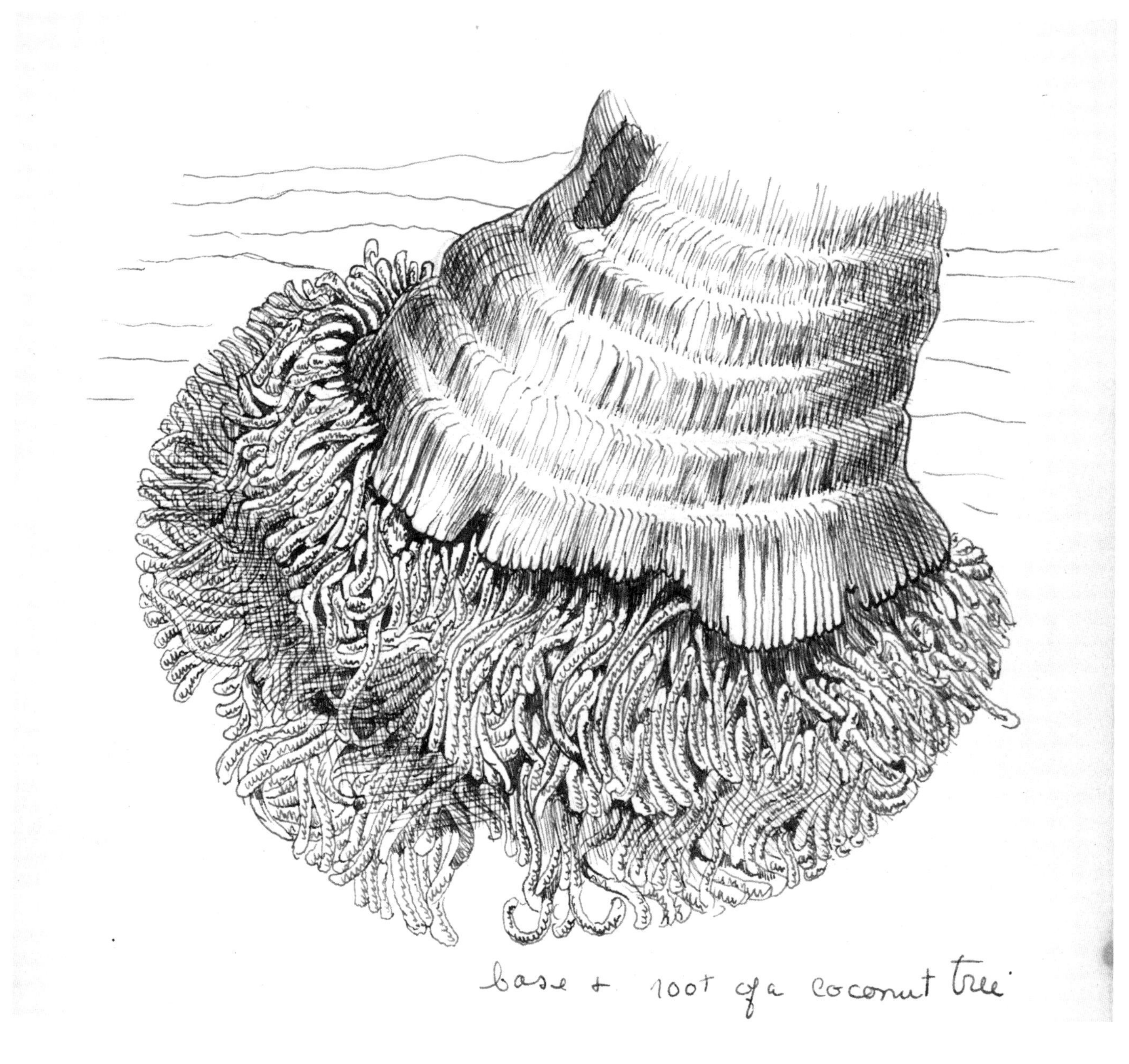

FIVE YEARS LATER

THE SAME APPEARANCE WOULD HAPPEN

A THIRD TIME.

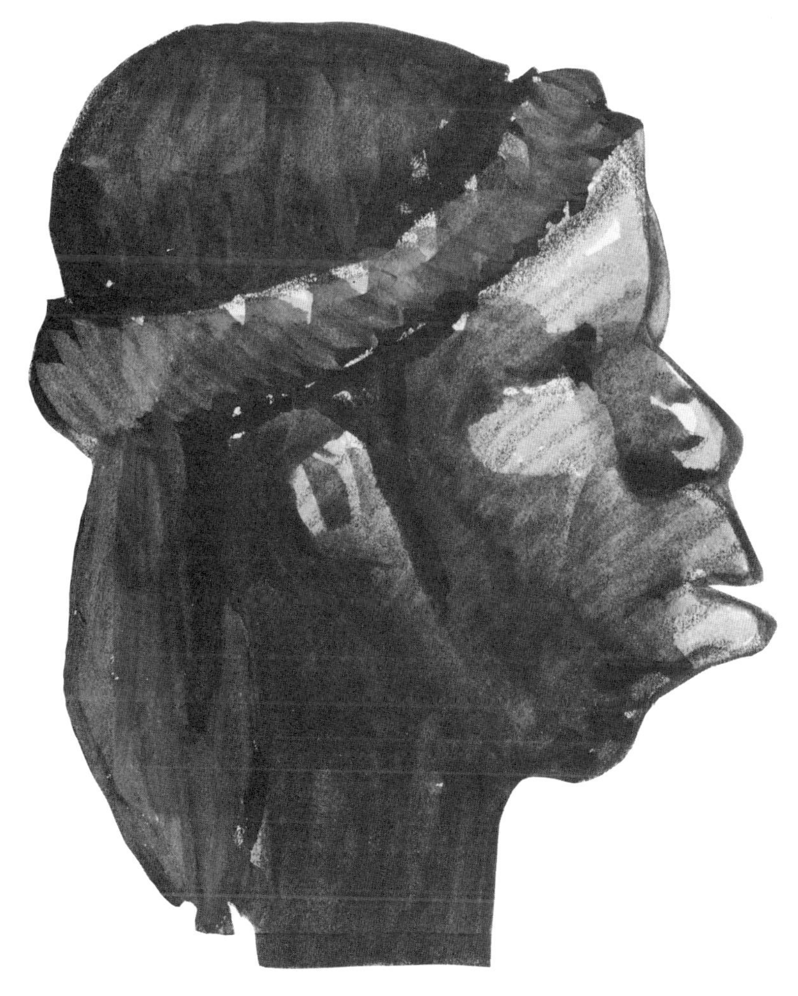

ON THIS THIRD TIME,

HE SAID,

I WOULD FOLLOW HIS ANCESTOR

INTO DEATH.

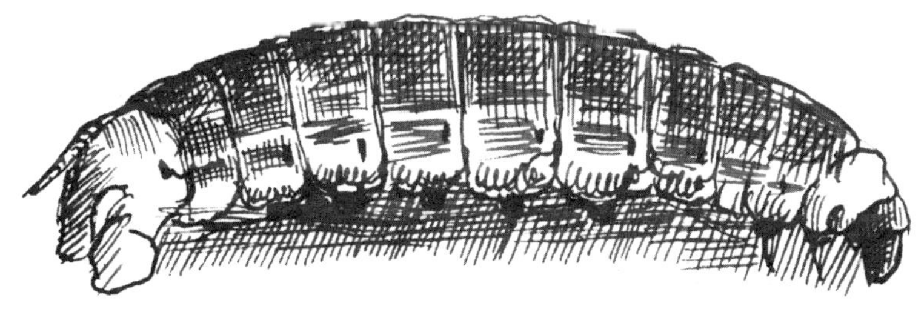

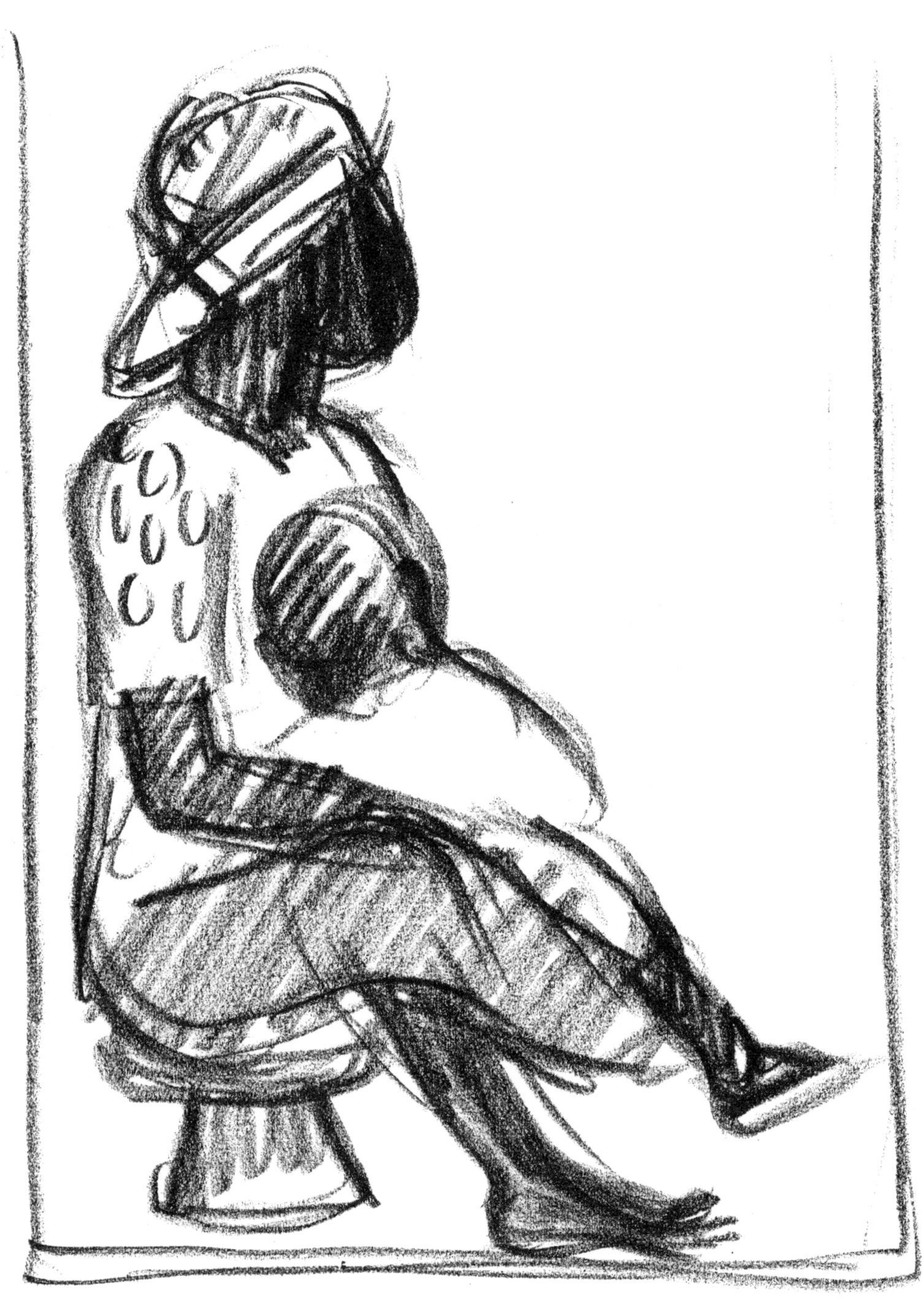

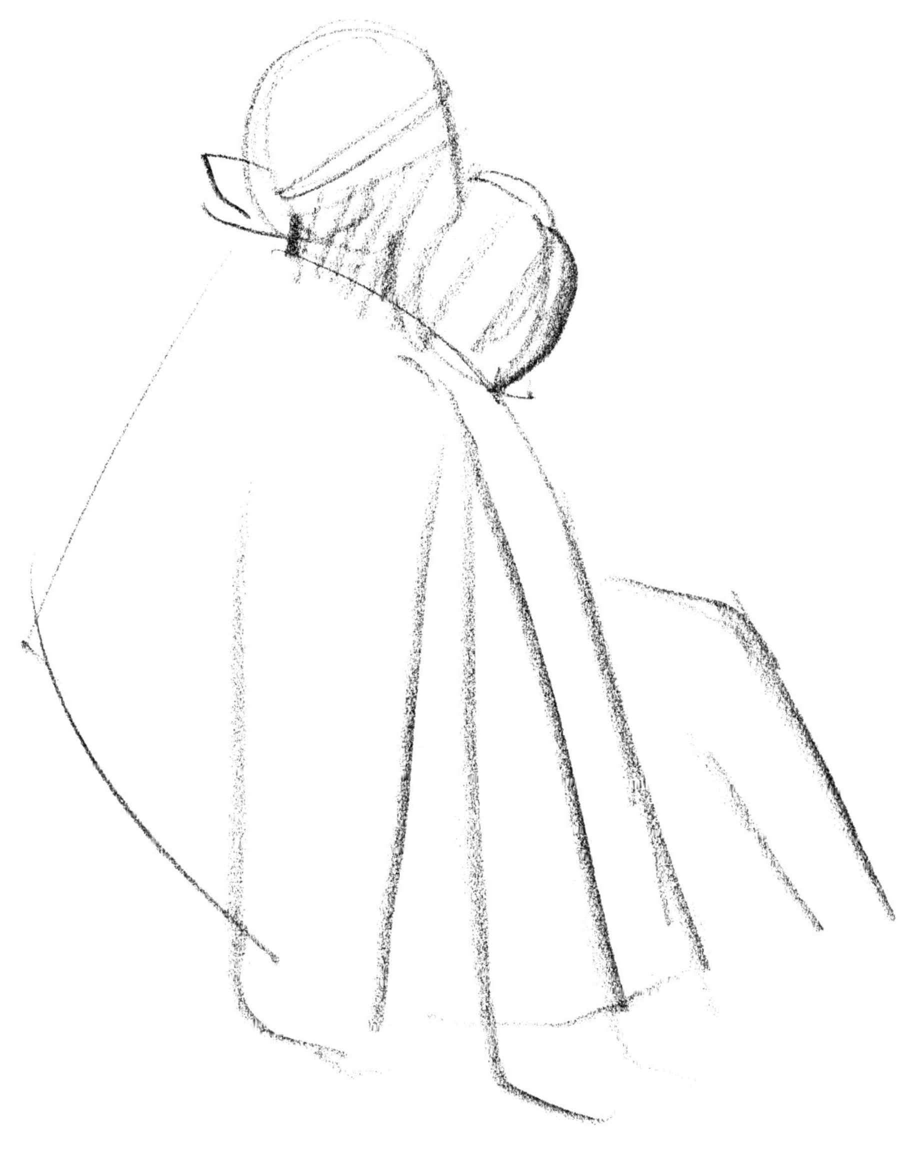

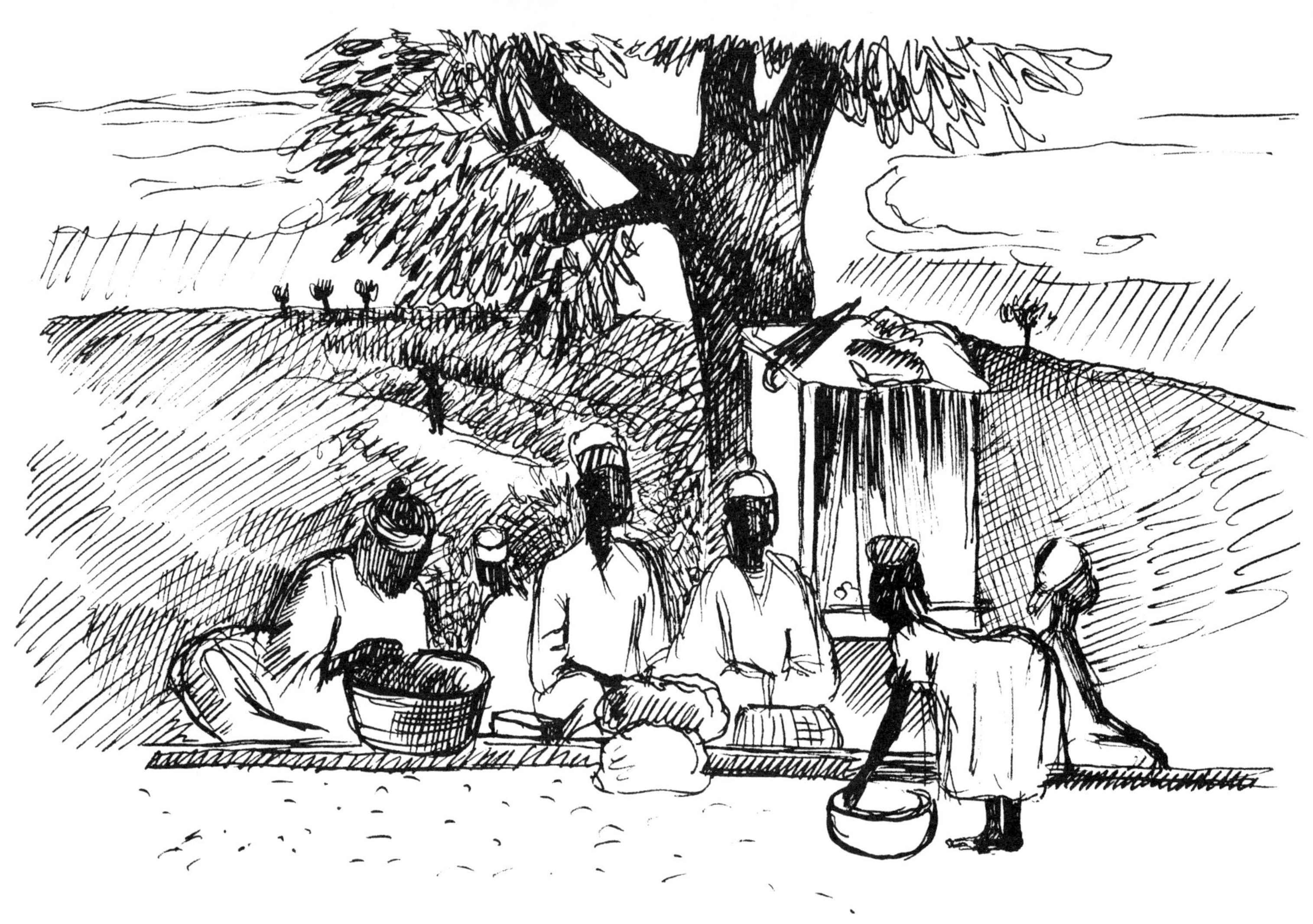

MAY 8

PACKED AND LEFT FOR MAMOU. GOT A HOTEL ROOM
FOR 5 FRANCS A DAY. ON A WALK I WAS CAUGHT IN A
RAIN STORM. WENT IN AN OLD HOUSE. THERE WAS AN
ORGAN IN IT. I PLAYED ALL DURING THE STORM.

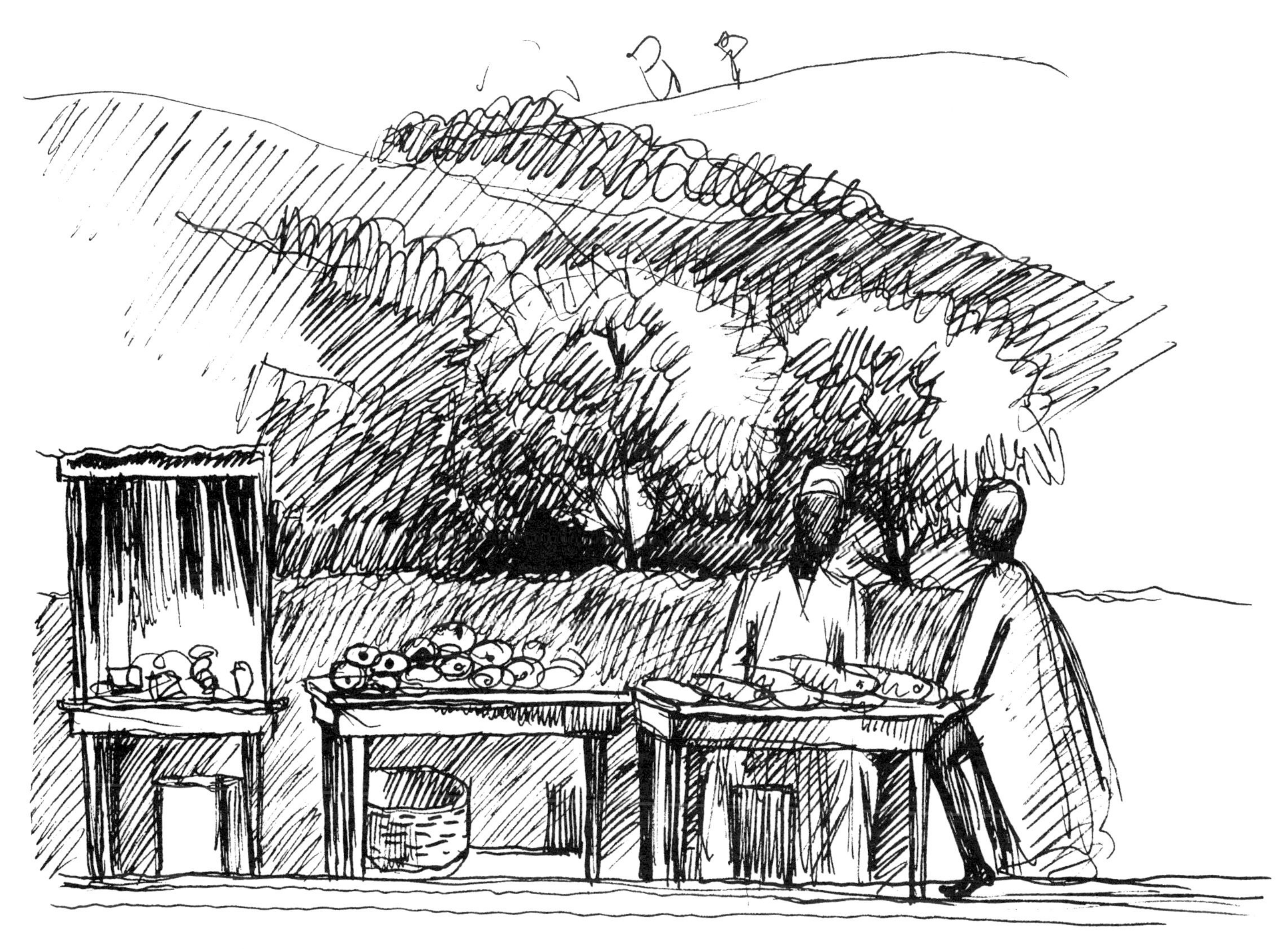

MAMOU

TAUGHT MORE KIDS TO PAINT. HELD CLASSES MORNINGS AND AFTER-
NOONS. I GAVE THEM WATERCOLORS TO DO, SHOWED THEM HOW
TO MIX COLORS, ILLUSTRATED EVERY MOVE ON A HUGE SHEET OF
WATERCOLOR PAPER.

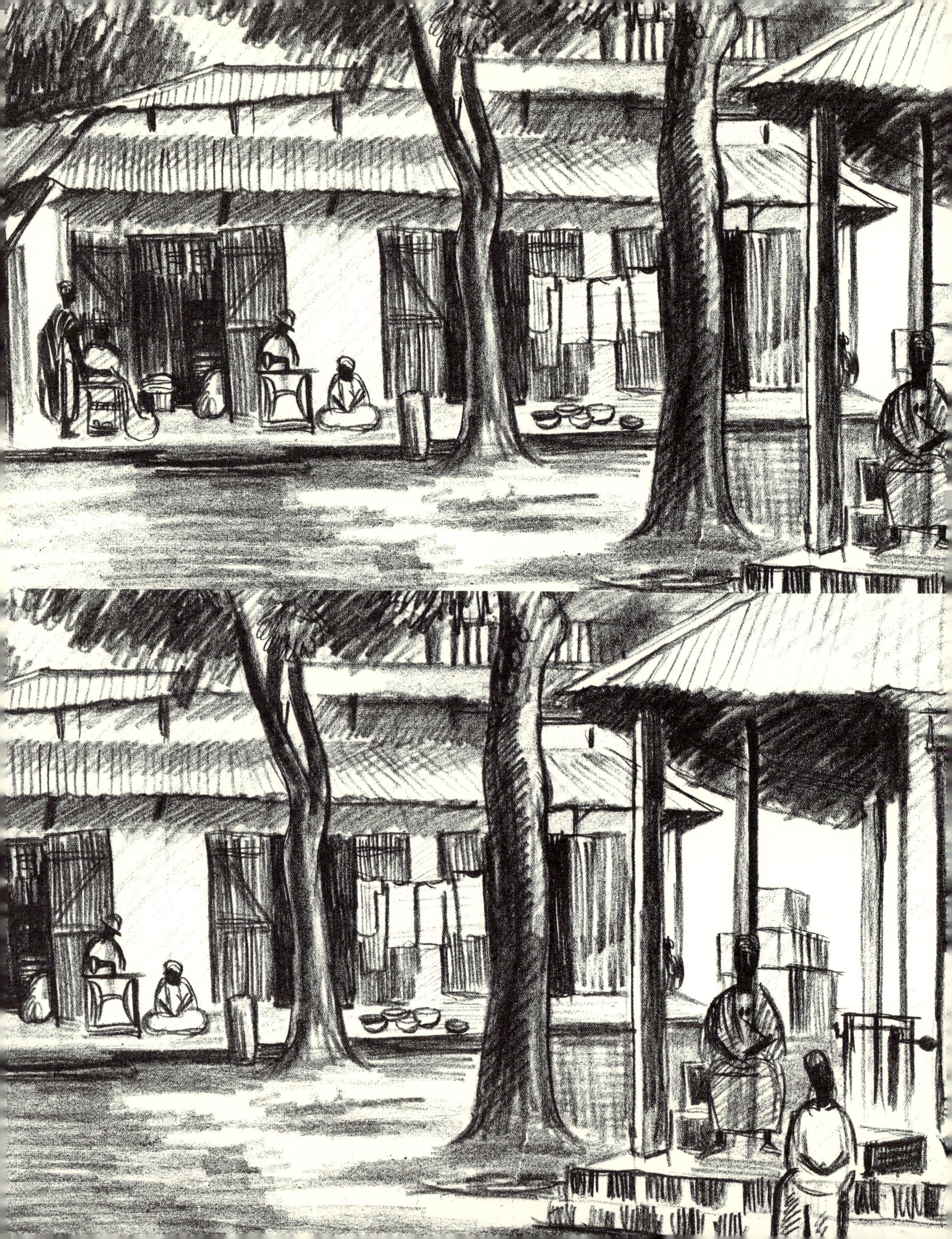

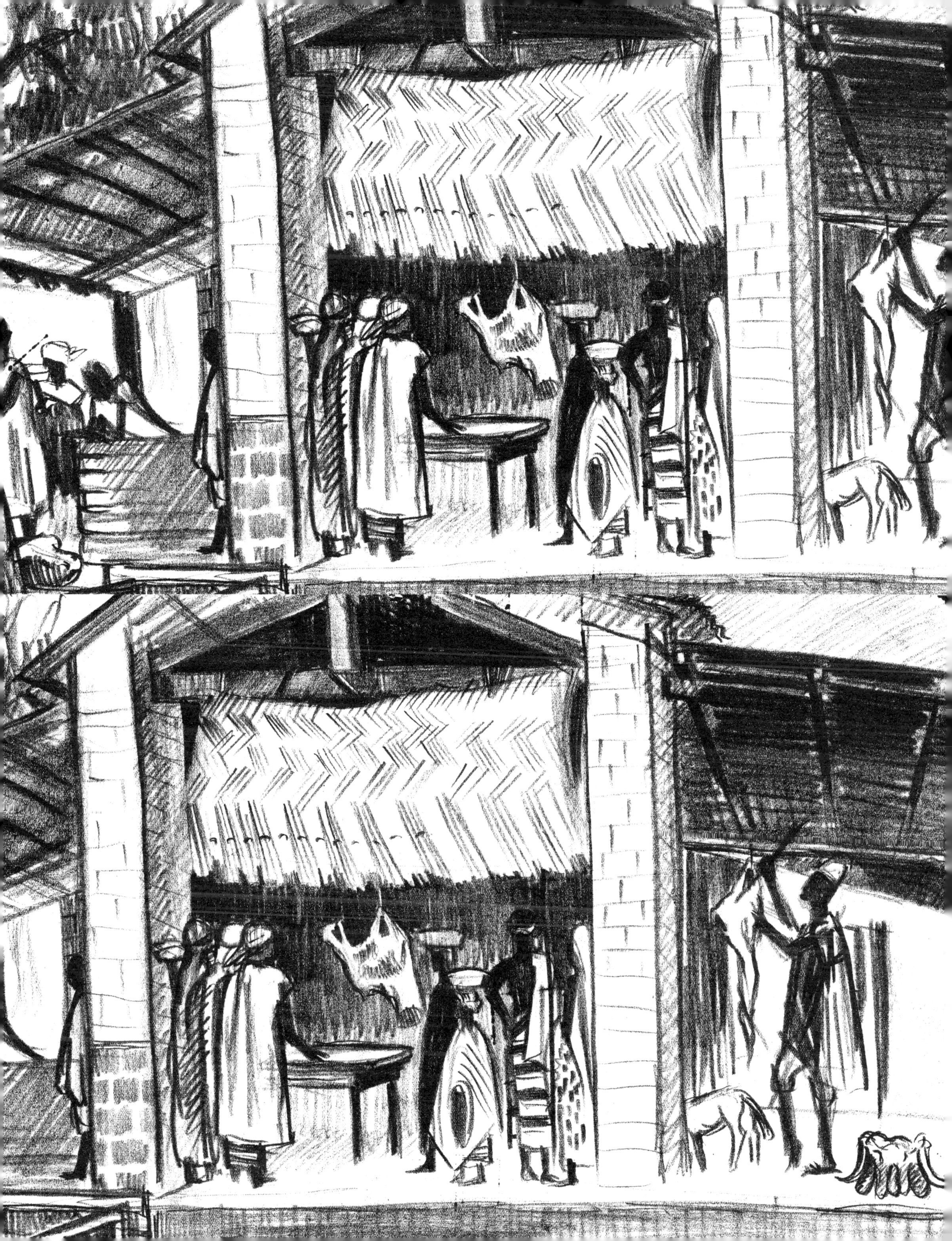

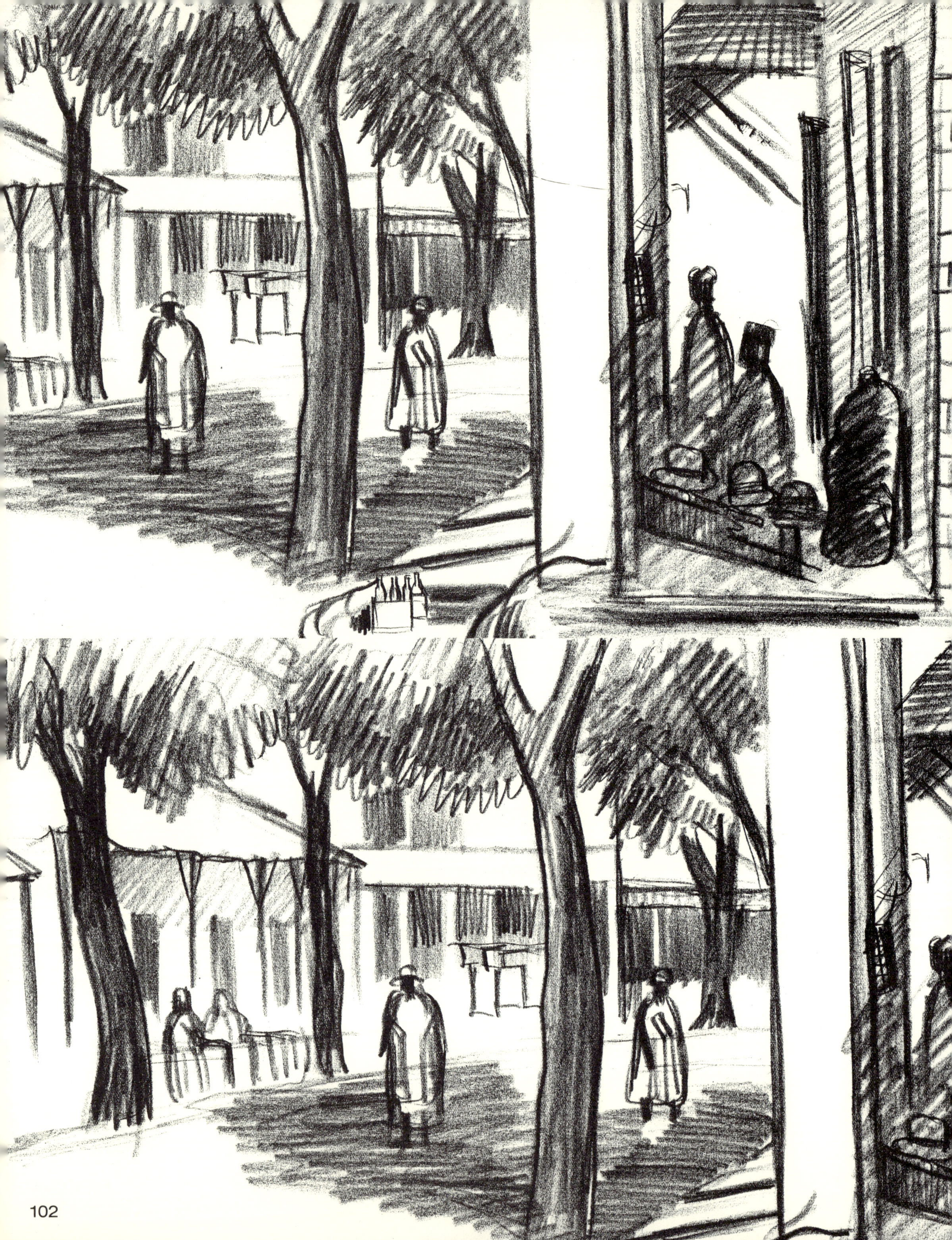

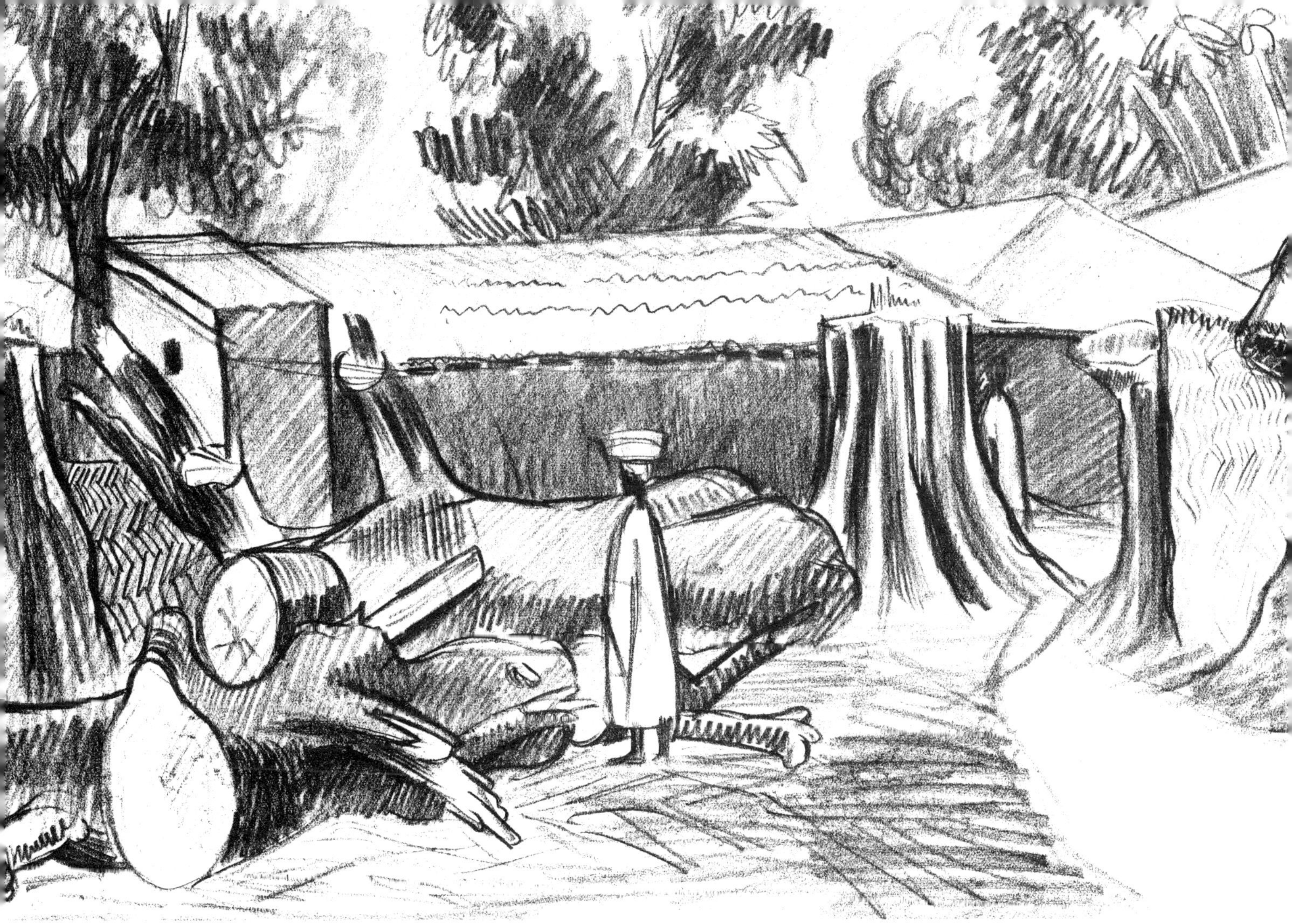

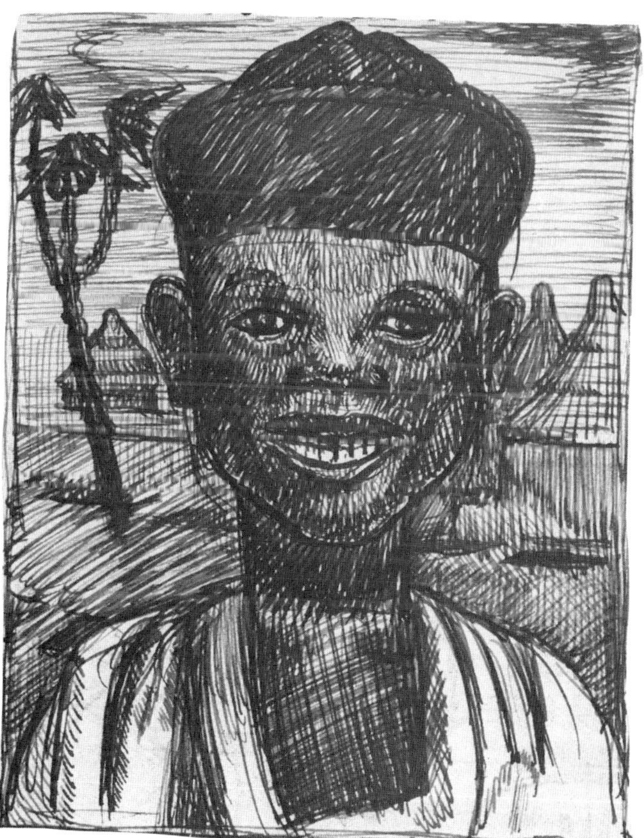

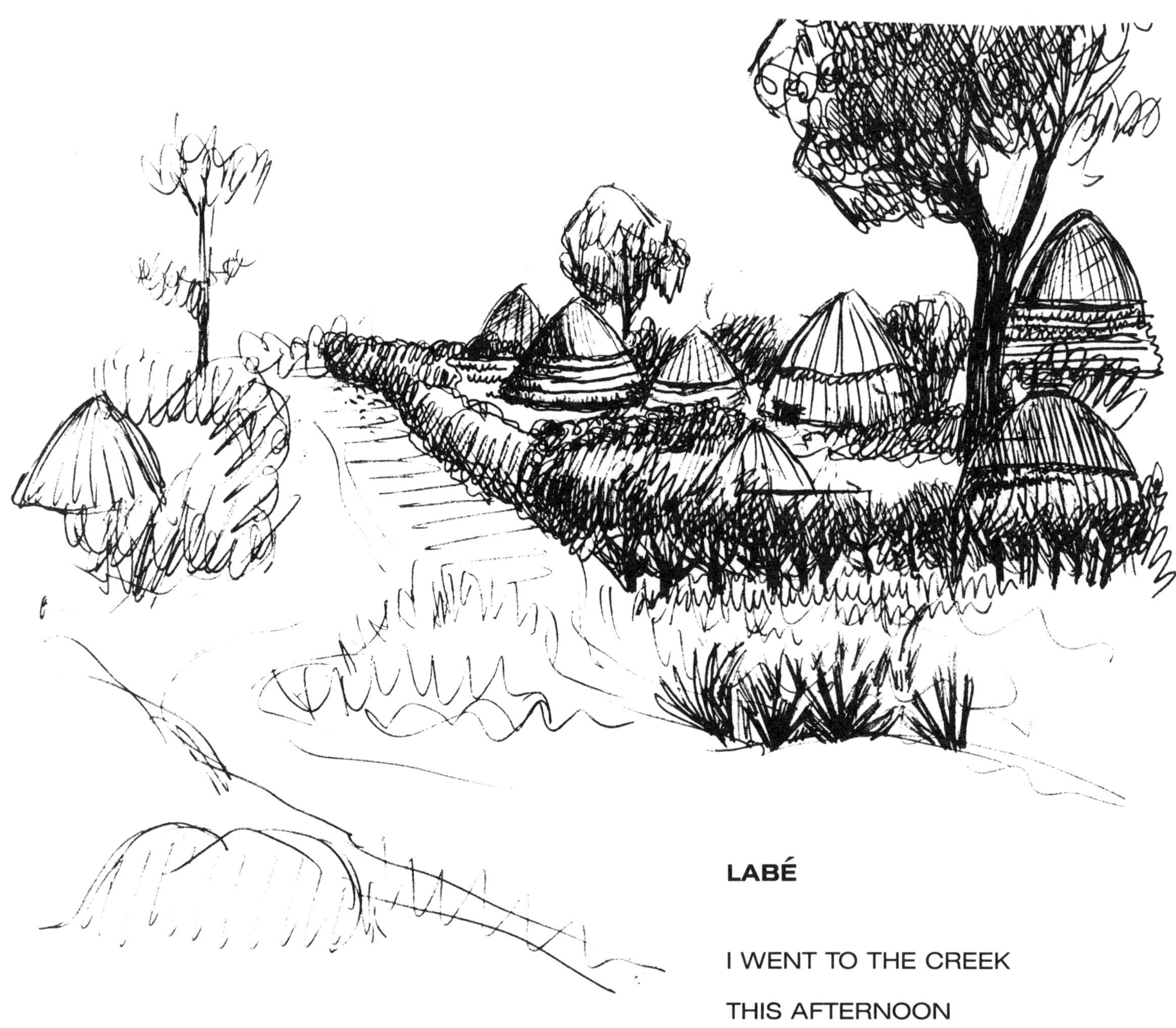

LABÉ

I WENT TO THE CREEK

THIS AFTERNOON

TO LOOK FOR BOAS CONSTRICTORS.

PASSED A GARDEN OF PINEAPPLES, AVOCADOS, GUAVAS, LEMONS, BANANAS, PIMENTOS, MANGOS, AND STRAWBERRIES. I CRAWLED IN A CAVE ON THE WAY BACK AND SAW A HEAD. THE HEAD WAS ABOUT THE SIZE OF A LARGE APPLE. IT SURE WAS HOT. BACK AT MY HUT I FINISHED A PORTRAIT OF BONJIGARA. A WOMAN WHO USED TO BE A PROSTITUTE HAD MEASLES. SHE POSED FOR ME.

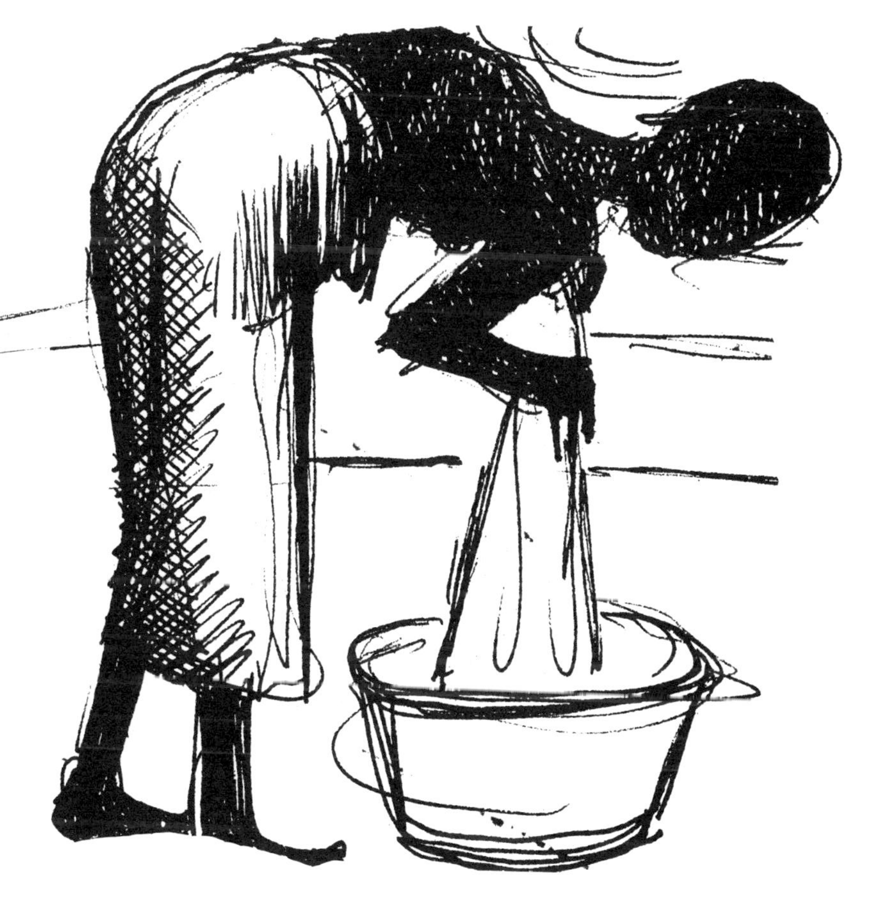

MY WASHERWOMAN HAS A BABY. HERE IN LABÉ THE NATIVES ARE FORCED TO HAVE THEIR BABIES IN A NATIVE HOSPITAL OR GO TO JAIL. I GO TO THE HOSPITAL TO SEE HER. IT'S A BREEDING PLACE OF GERMS AND DISEASE.

THE FILTHY SHEETS WERE SPOTTED WITH BLOOD AND AFTERBIRTH. FLIES WERE IN ABUNDANCE AS NOTHING WAS SCREENED. BLACK WOMEN THINK THEIR BABIES WILL DIE IF THEY'RE NOT FED SOUR MILK THE FIRST WEEK. THEY HAVE THEIR FRIENDS SMUGGLE IT IN TO THEM. ALSO THEY SHAVE DESIGNS ON THE KIDS' HEADS ON THE EIGHTH DAY. IT WAS AWFUL TO SEE THEM WORKING ON A BABY. THE KNIFE LOOKED LIKE IT WAS GOING THROUGH THE HEAD. ALSO THEY CHEW COALA NUTS AND PUT IT ON THE KIDS' SOFT SPOT. IF THE BABY HAS BOOGERS IN ITS NOSE OR PUS IN THE EYE, THE MOTHER LICKS IT OFF WITH HER TONGUE.

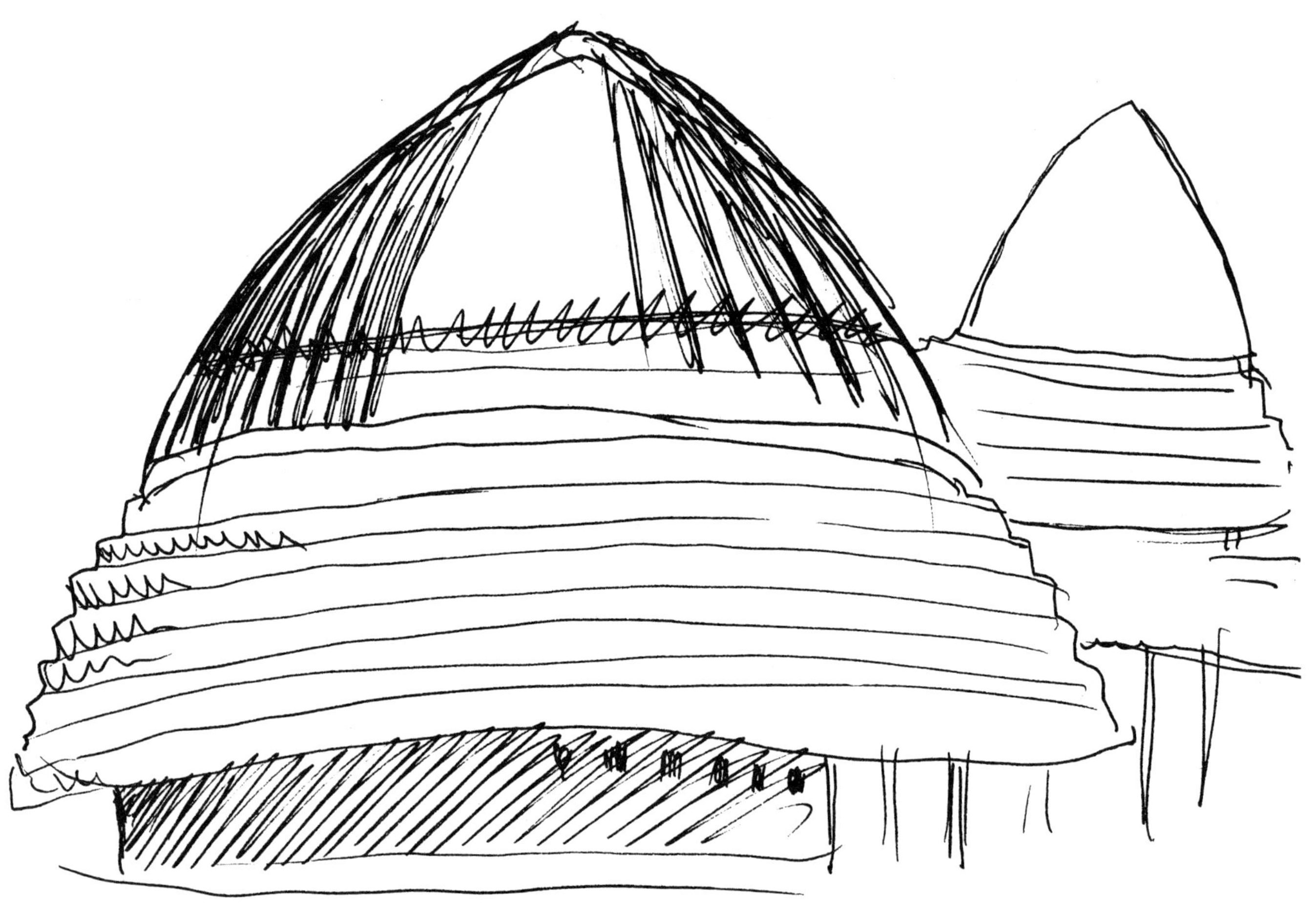

MAY 21

EXPECTED A MISSIONARY TO PICK ME UP AND DRIVE ME TO MAMOU EARLY THIS MORNING. I WAITED FOR THE TRUCK UNTIL 11:00. FINAL-LY WAS PICKED UP BY A NEGRO. I GET IN FRONT WITH HIM. HE STOPPED AT THE MOST UNEXPECTED PLACES. THE ENGINE GOT SO HOT IT MELTED MY SHOES. HE STOPPED AND FLIRTED WITH TWO LADIES. WE WERE SIX HOURS ON THE ROAD AND I NEVER HAD SUCH A RIDE.

MAY 26

WENT TO CONAKRY BY CAR. DRIVING IN AFRICA CAN BE DANGEROUS. HAD ONE HELL OF A TIME. STOPPED TO COOK COFFEE ON THE ROAD. BABOONS, GREAT BIG FELLOWS AS LARGE AS A CHILD ABOUT 12, RAN OUT AT US. IT WAS GOOD FUN.

WENT FOR A WALK ALONG THE OCEAN. THE ROCKS ALONG THE EDGES MUST HAVE BEEN USED AS THE BUSH BECAUSE THE ODOR WAS FOUL. MY CONSCIENCE BOTHERS ME ABOUT THE MISSIONARIES. THEIR MOUTHS TURN DOWN AT THE CORNERS. I DON'T BELIEVE SUCH SELFISH PEOPLE WILL EVER GET TO HEAVEN. I AM PUT OFF BY PEOPLE WHO TREAT NEGROES ROUGHLY. WENT OVER TO GET TICKET. TO SAIL FOR BORDEAUX NEXT MONDAY AT SEVEN IN THE MORNING. MY WHOLE STAY IN AFRICA, TRANSPORTATION INCLUDED, ONLY COST ABOUT $100.00, AND ABOUT $40.00 OF THAT WAS FOR CURIOS.

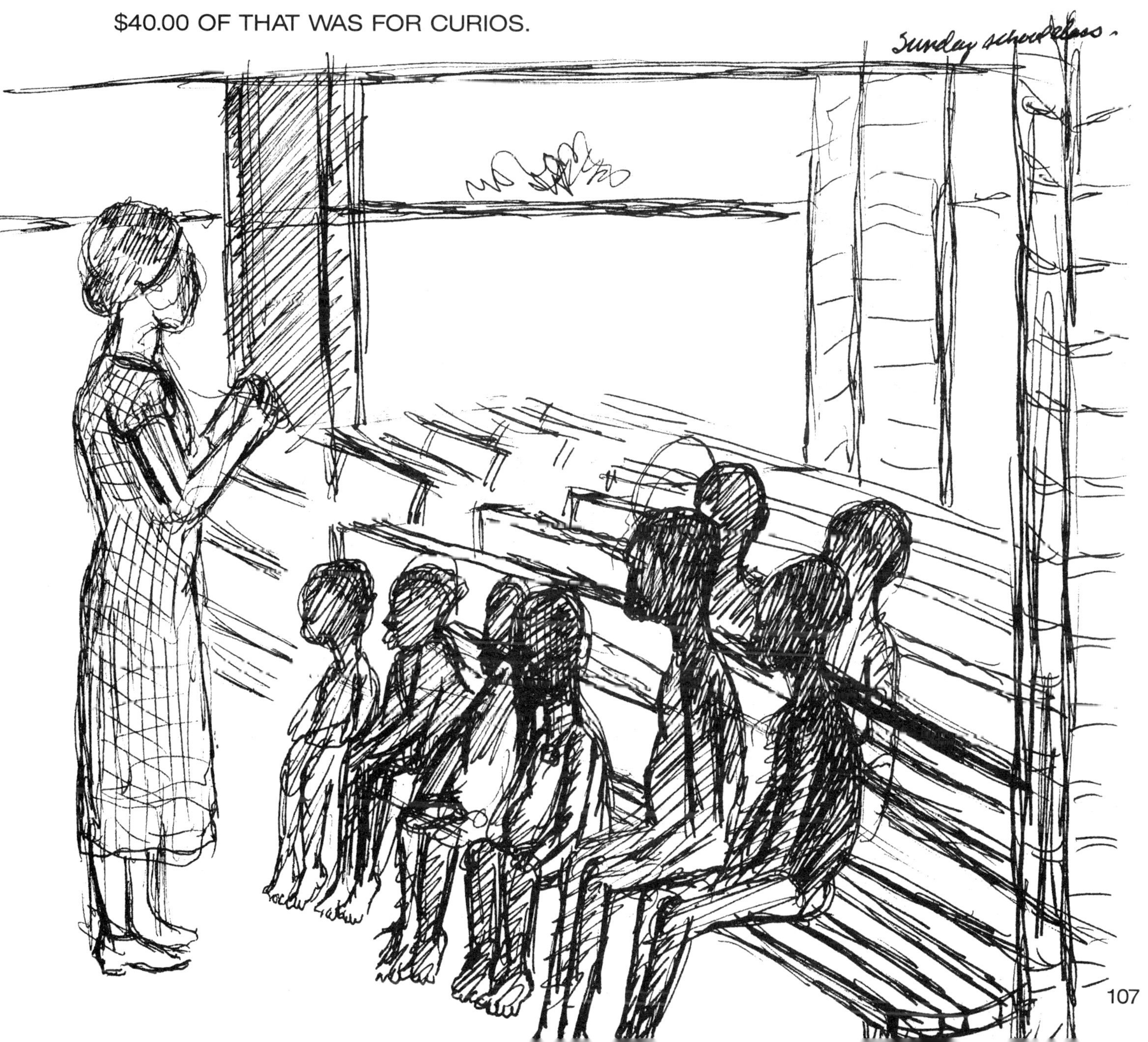

afterword

One autumn night Wanda and a friend, Connie Conarroe, walked along a desolate New Jersey beach. Dusk dimmed to darkness. A mild wind gusted from the ocean. Suddenly a person was seen approaching from afar, moving nearer nearer, finally face to face, eyes meeting eyes. An ancient African, his hand rising, his eyes burning. Wanda searched into the darkening of his face, glimpsed a glimmer of the infinite. As he beckoned Wanda, even the waves went silent, and little by little, the man vaporized, vanished.

Wanda's eyes lighted in strange glow in telling the tale, as though she held a constellation in her hand, "Death's a flight to another glorious life on earth. I'll be a musician, a composer, next time. Dying's not hard."

Her words, "dying," "feeling the fade," shined excitement of life. Acquaintance with death danced wings into her life, songs of spontaneous waves from her lips, and talk of lives around the world, spanning centuries; like life in ancient Egypt, planning and painting calliopes of colors to exterior edifices, transferal to today, clear bright colors that bounced laughter into hearts.

Connie's face flexed in relating the same experience, sole supersensation of her life, smooth white skin furrowing, tainting, as though demons were pushing lead and ash into her cheeks. "A putrid odor—A corpse-like form—It was evil."

Wanda's friends begged her away from ocean shores the next two times prophesized in Africa, death at the third. Later at the Art League in South Jersey, Wanda, noting no African American had exhibited there, invited such an artist to present his portfolio. At appointment, she greeted him, fell to her left. The man stepped quickly, caught her. Sudden unexpected death. Massive stroke.

Later we wondered about the artist of African descent. He disappeared as members of the League gathered round. No name in Wanda's book, no trace of him ever found.

During a memorial service at a little church by the sea, a few, including the officiating clergyman, Wanda's friend, Francis Lyndall of Chicago, and myself, saw luminous colors like an aurora borealis playing over the altar.

Sheila Hollander, a member of the Art League, said, "An angel passed among us, showed us the direction, and departed."

georgiana peacher

afterword

One autumn night Wanda and a friend, Connie Conaroe, walked along a desolate New Jersey beach. Dusk dimmed to darkness. A mild wind gusted from the ocean. Suddenly a person was seen approaching from afar, moving nearer nearer, finally face to face, eyes meeting eyes. An ancient African, his hand rising, his eyes burning. Wanda searched into the darkening of his face, glimpsed a glimmer of the infinite. As he beckoned Wanda, even the waves went silent, and little by little, the man vaporized, vanished.

Wanda's eyes lighted in strange glow in telling the tale, as though she held a constellation in her hand, "Death's a flight to another glorious life on earth. I'll be a musician, a composer, next time. Dying's not hard."

Her words, "dying," "feeling the fade," shined excitement of life. Acquaintance with death danced wings into her life, songs of spontaneous waves from her lips, and talk of lives around the world, spanning centuries; like life in ancient Egypt, planning and painting calliopes of colors to exterior edifices, transferal to today, clear bright colors that bounced laughter into hearts.

Connie's face flexed in relating the same experience, sole supersensation of her life, smooth white skin furrowing, tainting, as though demons were pushing lead and ash into her cheeks. "A putrid odor—A corpse-like form—It was evil."

Wanda's friends begged her away from ocean shores the next two times prophesized in Africa, death at the third. Later at the Art League in South Jersey, Wanda, noting no African American had exhibited there, invited such an artist to present his portfolio. At appointment, she greeted him, fell to her left. The man stepped quickly, caught her. Sudden unexpected death. Massive stroke.

Later we wondered about the artist of African descent. He disappeared as members of the League gathered round. No name in Wanda's book, no trace of him ever found.

During a memorial service at a little church by the sea, a few, including the officiating clergyman, Wanda's friend, Francis Tyndall of Chicago, and myself, saw luminous colors like an aurora borealis playing over the altar.

Sheila Hollander, a member of the Art League, said, "An angel passed among us, showed us the direction, and departed."

georgiana peacher

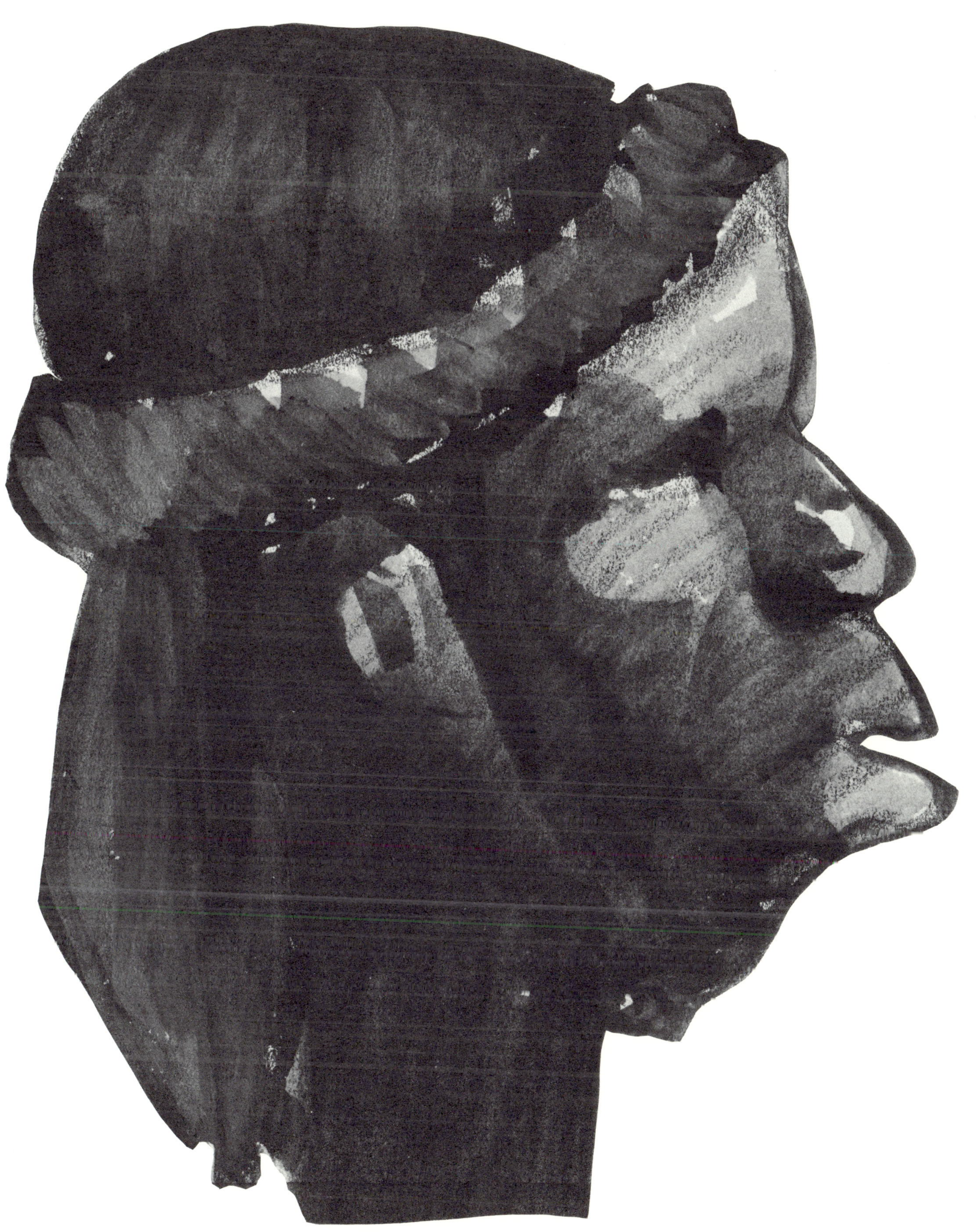

Printed by Penmor Lithographers
Lewiston, Maine

Acid free Mohawk Satin Paper

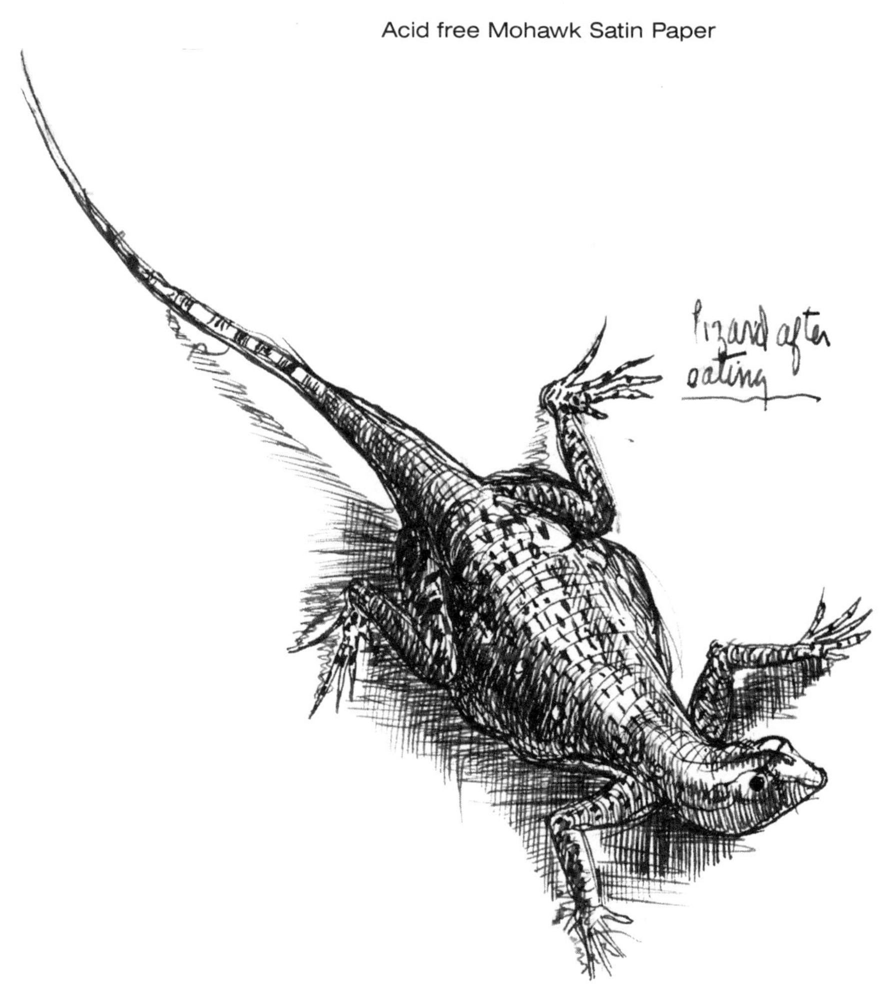